A
PLACE IN TIME

by
Roger Longpre

as told to
Janice Longpre

Illustrations by Delores Barrett and Constance Skerman

Note for Librarians: A cataloguing record for this book is available from Library and Archives
Canada at www.collectionscanada.ca/amicus/index-e.html
ISBN 1-4251-0553-x

Printed on paper with minimum 30% recycled fibre.
Trafford's print shop runs on "green energy" from solar, wind and other environmentally-friendly power sources.

Offices in Canada, USA, Ireland and UK

Book sales for North America and international:
Trafford Publishing, 6E–2333 Government St.,
Victoria, BC V8T 4P4 CANADA
phone 250 383 6864 (toll-free 1 888 232 4444)
fax 250 383 6804; email to orders@trafford.com
Book sales in Europe:
Trafford Publishing (UK) Limited, 9 Park End Street, 2nd Floor
Oxford, UK OX1 1HH UNITED KINGDOM
phone +44 (0)1865 722 113 (local rate 0845 230 9601)
facsimile +44 (0)1865 722 868; info.uk@trafford.com
Order online at:
trafford.com/06-2311

10 9 8 7 6 5 4 3

To

Ann Roush

Whose dedication will always be remembered.

And to

Those who were part of my life on Petty Creek but are not in these pages:

The Hector Deschamp family, Mike Flynn, Pete Strizich, Roy Marceau, Margaret Strizich, Dave Carrierre, Paul Bjerke, and Arlyn Simms, and to the memory of Dr. John Strizich, Wayne Bestwick, Vern Sanderson, Web Bowman, and Honest Tom Bailey.

Introduction

Time hasn't dimmed my memories of our ranch on Petty Creek, and it seems necessary to recount tales of living there. I don't know why, except that the country slides into focus now as a place out of time and worthy of mention in a foreign world that developed around it.

Forty miles southwest of Missoula, Montana is not the end of civilization, but the rugged mountains that grow there made it seem so. The ranch nestled precariously in that corner of the Rocky Mountain Bitterroot Range like the eye of a storm in a raging sea of mountains, so precariously that it was never given a ranch name but was always known simply as Petty Creek. The creek bubbled out of the draws seven miles above the ranch. From there it wound its way through timber and meadows until it spilled into the Clark Fork River on the ranch's southern border. Except for us, it passed no signs of civilization on its seventeen mile course.

To cross over the line into Petty Creek country, one left a comfortably wide ribbon of valley floor through the heavily timbered Bitterroots where great domes of sky sweep down behind the mountains beyond. Thirty miles west of Missoula, the traveler crossed the Clark Fork River Bridge, to be swallowed by the iron jaws of Petty Creek Canyon, whose walls of rim rock jut vertically without warning, towering boldly over a long and rutted wagon road that snaked its way across the creek for ten miles. That gateway to our home could be as treacherous as it was beautiful, and it changed its effect on the traveler as its moods changed with the seasons.

Steel-gray crags rise threateningly in winter, harboring daggers of ice that plunge from their clefts. A shadowed foreboding hovers through the gray stillness of the frozen shaft where an ice-covered creek hides under a silent coverlet of snow. Along the banks, the skeletons of alder trees claw the still air, their nakedness softened by snow.

When winter slowly merges into spring, steel walls soften into shades of blue as the sun's rays struggle to penetrate the roofless towers. Once-solid ice labors downstream in mournful dissipation and creek waters rise gradually from melting snow. Winter's still and silent trail of white transforms into swirling water that soars through the canyon, depositing limbs and uprooted trees along the banks. Beaver dams crumble from the pressure and walls of water gush over broken piles of sticks to threaten the beaver family below. Mule deer and mountain goats stoically trail across canyon walls like sentinels whose mission it is to guard the wildlife below. Timid little white tail deer peek through alder on the creek bottom at passersby. Brown and black bear in search of food lumber through the creek bottom day and night. A quick eye may glimpse a coyote darting from cover to cover.

White clusters of choke cherry and june berry blossoms crowd together as delicate ground cover, replacing winter white with a fragrant promise of spring. A thin and sparkling layer of water bubbles gently over slippery green rocks, filling the canyon with the earthy smell of wet moss. June berry limbs bow to the ground, weighted with tiny circles of dusty blue. Hungry bears anchor limbs down with giant paws to chew the limb clean - twigs, leaves, berries, and all. A storehouse of nature's treasures, our Petty Creek Canyon.

Abruptly the canyon closed the traveler into her mysterious depths, and ten miles later it burst just as suddenly into the openness of our 220 acre hay meadow. Petty Creek wandered then under an open sky through expanding waves of timothy and clover. The wagon road straightened before it bowed into a sweeping turn around a grassy knoll to descend for a hundred yards to our home.

And there, as testimony to an attempted taming of the surrounding seas of wilderness, our tiny log house stood alone with a grassy hillside behind it and Petty Creek bubbling contentedly at its front door. A big log barn stood solidly at the edge of the hay meadow, neatly enclosed in a system of sturdy log corrals. West of the house, eight rising miles of jack pine, alder patches, slide rock and canyons halt at the ranch's western border at the base of Deer Peak. Like a pointed hat the treeless triangle juts into space for 700 feet above the timbered turbulence below, where we were dwarfed into ant creatures crawling through survival in a narrow path of flat land in nature's vast and rugged terrain.

As far as you can see in all directions, wave after wave of ridges and canyons, draws and valleys, and fortresses of rock walls placed among hair-like billows of sparkling greens and distant shades of blue.

And in the middle of it all—one tiny log house, a barn, and a handful of cattle wandering unseen through the timber.

I simply grew into that country, as children do, until I was old enough to remember my life there. That happened when I was five, and it was then that I took up the business of living on Petty Creek.

1

"Hold it there, Jake. Stand still, Queen. We'll be done in a minute," my dad said to his fidgeting team as he deftly removed a folded work harness from the back of his bay mare. He had skidded logs with his work team that morning to replenish our wood supply for winter, and I raced across the meadow to the barn when I saw the big black and the bay plod back onto the road through the timber by Gus Creek. My dad had promised another trip into the West Fork to look for elk tracks when he finished his work for the day, and the morning dragged by until he returned.

It was mid-October of 1943, my fifth year, and at that time of the fall season alder brush along the West Fork of Petty Creek should have blazed in deep gold and crimson. But I remember it had only begun to pale into light yellow and orange which meant that winter would stay away for a while, and the elk we were hunting would still find sufficient feed in the high country. So until deep snow at higher elevations drove the herds to their wintering grounds in the West Fork near home, we could only hope for a straggler or two to replenish our dwindling meat supply.

It was for that reason that my dad and I hiked into the West Fork timber every day to check for tracks at a natural salt lick. If any animals were in the lower country they would stop there before traveling on to the meadows to feed. Grazing animals thrived in the West Fork where a bubbling tributary intersects to widen the banks of Petty Creek at the head of the canyon. Towering columns of Douglas fir, tamarack, and ponderosa pine scatter through needled branches, nourishing the ground into a thick cover of clover and red top. Alder brush confines itself to the creek banks, and on the shaded north slopes, moisture brings a thicker growth of timber, providing good cover for the animals. On the south and west slopes, occasional warm winter winds bare the hillsides of snow, uncovering the ceanothus and elderberry brush for browsing. Through the bottom land, fallen pine cones rest on a flat, grassy bed with pine and tamarack needles sifting between golden blades. Peace pervaded a park-like forest in the West Fork, always one of my favorite areas on the ranch.

On the afternoon in question, we had been searching about two weeks, and I was as eager to get to the West Fork as the horses were impatient for their freedom. When the harnesses were removed, I jerked the horses' halter ropes loose from a slip knot on the manger pole and ran across the road to the grazing meadow, with Queen and Jake trotting in tow. By standing on top of a swinging pole gate, I reached the buckles to remove their heavy leather halters, and then I scrambled under the weight of them back to the barn. My dad was hanging a harness on the wall so I dropped the halters beside him to wing my way back through the short-cropped meadow. Jake and Queen busied themselves by pulling tiny blades of grass through clenched teeth as if they knew a waning fall sun was about to cut off their supply of green feed.

I sped past them, ducked under a barbwire fence onto the road and opened the pole gate at the end of the driveway to be ready when my Dad got there with the pickup. It was better to spend my time swinging on the gate than to loll along beside him at his slow, deliberate pace. Seldom did I walk at my dad's side. Most of the time I only caught glimpses of him as I ran ahead or behind him through timber and meadow. That day I watched from the gate as he strolled slowly across the meadow, stopping along the way in a studied posture to watch his horses graze. When he finally drove through the wide open gate, I ran it to a quick close, hopped on the running board of his old blue pickup and plopped in the seat beside him.

"Think they'll be there today?" I asked.

"Yup. I think today's the day."

We chugged around the sweeping turn to follow the edge of the meadow for a mile before turning west at the head of the canyon onto the cow trail that took us through the big timber of the West Fork. Three miles later my dad stopped the truck and reached for his 30-30 long-barreled Winchester. Like a hungry cow pony on his way home after a long day of chasing cattle, every muscle strained forward while I held back at my dad's pace for the quarter-mile hike to the salt lick. I knew the rules. I was to hunt with a closed mouth and quiet feet, in close proximity to my dad. It was a tolerable assignment. He stalked through the timber on beds of dry tamarack needles like the elk we hunted—quiet, wary, his green eyes darting through the countryside, his short stocky frame turning from side to side at every step we took.

When the patch of dry ground came into view through the trees and no animals were present, I broke loose and ran for the prize. But like every other day before, a trackless salt bed spread dryly at my feet. I started to turn back to my dad with the news when a feeling of something that didn't belong in the woods came over me. I looked across the salt bed to see a grassy hillside where two Indians on horseback sat gazing at me silently. As in a dream I stared back, frozen to my spot when I wanted to run. Nothing moved—not horses nor humans nor a blade of grass. Not a sound was heard.

Two statues resembling horses were motionless under piles of meat. An elk hide hung over each horse with the saddles placed on top of the hide so the cinch pinched the hide into folds under the horses. Boned chunks of meat from fist-size to a flour sack hung from rawhide strings all around the saddles. Fir boughs covered the meat on the horses' backs. From high atop the boughs on one horse, a woman stared at me from the edge of a bright-colored blanket. On the other horse, long braids framed black eyes of a young boy who looked straight at me with icy stillness.

A flood of relief swept over me when I heard soft steps through the tamarack needles behind me. With my eyes still on the hillside, I groped for my dad's leg, then ran around and peeked from behind him. When the woman saw him she kicked her horse in our direction, jerking him to a stop a few feet in front of me.

"*Comments allez vous, Mose*," she said.

"I see the change of seasons brought you luck," my dad answered in French.

"Men kill two elk yesterday. Today boy and I bring 'em back. Tomorrow I make jerky."

"Where did they get them?"

"Three hours back. High on mountain. Lots of feed. Elk still high."

"Is this your first elk?"

"Just deer so far. This first elk. Got two elk on horses. Sometime stop and see us."

She slapped her horse on the rump with a fir bough, kicked him into a squaw trot, and disappeared down the creek bottom with the boy trailing behind. My first meeting with Mrs. Big Sam was over.

I had heard stories of how my grandpa traded with the Indians when he first came to Montana, and I had seen a few Indians ride by the ranch on horseback the year before, but nothing I had seen or heard prepared me for the sight on the hillside. I thought we'd been invaded by foreigners, but in reality the situation was reversed. It was my French Canadian ancestors who had encroached upon the Flathead corner of the Bitterroots after Lewis and Clark opened up the country to Hudson Bay fur traders in the mid-1800s. Petty Creek had been a traditional fall hunting ground for the Flatheads before the white man came. By the time I met them, only a remnant of the tribe trekked back each fall for a winter supply of meat and hides.

From their reservation in the Jocko Valley, thirty miles northeast of Petty Creek, five big Indian families gathered horses and teepees, and crossed the Nine Mile Valley to Petty Creek, driving heavy-laden pack horses in front of them. Except for jeans, a few calico dresses on young girls, and guns to replace bows and arrows, it could have been a scene from a century before. Over a hundred saddle horses splashed through Petty Creek Canyon, carrying babies in board cradles strapped to their mother's backs, or little ones with arms wrapped around their mothers from behind the saddle. Grandmas and children who were old enough to ride had their own horses. Men flanked the pack horses to urge them back and forth across the creek. Folded teepees and sacks of supplies rocked on the pack horses' backs under squaw hitches, the Indian way of packing a horse with a single rope wrapped around the horse's belly, twisted tight with a stick, then tied in a knot on the side of the pack.

Wordlessly they rode together through the red and yellow canyon until they reached the mouth of the West Fork. Then the pack horses belonging to the Grand Joe family were cut from the rest and driven into the timber, with the family members spreading out behind to keep them from turning back. The other families rode on, urging tired pack horses up the road until they reached the ranch house. The procedure was repeated when the Adams family turned onto the hillside behind the house to camp at Ed's Creek. On up the creek the remaining families rode until they were fanned out in camps throughout the lower country.

After the Indians settled into their camps, we knew by the spots of drifting haze that circled through the mountains where the hunts were first successful. The haze meant that smoky fires were burning under strips of elk and deer meat on willow drying racks. It was the irresistible sight of drying meat that first brought me out of the shadows and into friendship with the Flatheads.

The day after my encounter with Mrs. Big Sam, my dad suggested we stop by the Grand Joe camp in the West Fork where Mrs. Big Sam stayed. I agreed, but I refused to leave the pickup while he visited with the Indians. When he returned, he tossed a small object in my lap that resembled a piece of charred wood.

"Here. Want some Indian meat?" he said as he pulled himself into the pickup. "Mrs. Big Sam sent it for you."

I stared incredulously at the oblong piece of bark in my lap and lost my appetite.

"It looks awful. It doesn't look like meat."

"It's how it tastes that matters. Smell it first. Smells just like the fire when we burn brush. Indian kids think it's as good as candy. You have to suck it first, then you can chew it when it's soft."

My dad seemed to think it was something special so I decided to give it a try. I held on to one end and put the other end in my mouth very slowly, ready to jerk it out fast if I had to. It didn't have a bad taste. In fact it didn't have a taste at all.

"It doesn't taste like anything," I said.

"You have to suck it before you get any taste."

So I started sucking, and the taste of alder smoke filled my mouth. It was like nothing I had ever tasted before. I kept sucking and the smoke taste got stronger. As saliva flowed to compensate for the dryness of the meat, my mouth filled with smoky liquid. Gradually the meat softened, and when the taste of liquid smoke left the meat I swallowed, cramming another piece in my mouth. There was something wild-tasting and very satisfying in those little pieces of Indian meat.

"It's good Dad," I said, wondering if the Indians had any other worthwhile tricks I didn't know about.

The following day, when we dropped off salt blocks for our cattle that were pastured in the upper West Fork, my dad made his stop again at the Grand Joe camp.

"Want to come with me and see if there's any more smoked meat?" he asked when he got out of the pickup.

"No. You ask if you can have some more."

My dad laughed as he turned around slowly, sauntering into the timber.

He had been gone longer than I liked to sit in the pickup so I jumped down from the running board with the intention of staying right by the truck. Then I saw the tips of teepee poles through the trees, and my curiosity led me stealthily through the path my Dad had taken into the timber. When I tiptoed to within fifty feet of the nearest teepee, I saw a thicket of alder to hide in and look into camp. I remember lying on my stomach in the brush and parting it with my hands into an opening just big enough to see through.

I could see three teepees in a clearing with the creek running behind them through the trees. Two piles of wood, one of sticks and the other of firewood, were stacked in front of each teepee. The clearing looked clean, almost like a lawn with all the sticks and branches picked up to use for kindling. A horse was tied to a tree on the edge of camp and two more stood in a makeshift corral made from poles that were nailed between three trees, forming an enclosure. Dogs of various colors that all looked like a cross between a wolf and a coyote slinked around under skinned elk quarters that hung on meat poles out of their reach. No Indians were in sight except two older men in jeans and buckskin jackets who talked soberly with my dad near the horses.

The sight held me spellbound until it all disappeared from interest when I saw a lodge-pole meat rack in the middle of the clearing. Four posts were driven in the ground with two poles tied parallel to each other on top to support a woven willow rack. On the rack lay thinly-sliced chunks of elk meat, barely visible through thick clouds of alder smoke that billowed from the fire. I watched and smelled the meat for a long time before I knew that I had to move in that direction.

While my dad continued to talk to the Indians, I waited in hopes that they would move to a spot where they couldn't see the meat racks. But they stood fast so I decided to take my chances. Crouching low, I dashed to the drying rack, holding my breath in the smoke while I crammed my pockets full of meat. Then I tore back down the path and dove into the alder brush. When I whipped around to see if I had been discovered, I saw my dad and the Indians turned in my direction, laughing. Apparently I hadn't learned to be the silent stalker that I thought I was.

It was on the way back from Grand Joe's camp that day that my fear of the Indians melted into acceptance of them as people who were worthy of my concern. We had driven about a mile down the trail when I saw a whole group of Indians standing together in the trees. Their heads were all cast down and some of them were crying.

"Why are the Indians crying, Dad?" I asked.

"A baby who belongs to them has died. Little Joe told me when I was in camp. They feel bad because they're putting it to sleep in the earth."

Sympathy welled inside me for those people who cried. I wanted very much to be able to help them.

After the trip to the Grand Joe camp my fear of Indians was dispelled, but not my shyness in meeting strangers. Other than aunts and uncles who braved the creek crossing to visit us, few people stopped at the ranch. When strangers did appear I looked upon them as intruders in my secluded life, and my social amenities extended as far as the confines of my bedroom where I hid.

But when a haze of smoke drifted past the house, I knew it was from the Adams camp close by the house at Ed's Creek. (Most of the tributaries were named for the boys of the family who homesteaded the ranch before us.) It was time to put my shyness aside and introduce myself to the people that were responsible for smoking meat so close to home. The camp was inaccessible by truck so we hadn't stopped there before. I had only been told where John Adams and his family were camped.

I told my mother that I was going for a ride, and then I hopped bareback on my black horse, Jack. We climbed the bare, grassy hill behind the house, then turned west across the ridge into the timber. Although the canyon was smaller than the West Fork, the country was similar with big timber and a grassy bottom. I guided Jack across the ridge, following the smoke trail for about a mile. Then I saw smoke puffing out from under a smoke rack in a camp that looked exactly like Grand Joe's, complete even with the same kind of dogs. While women in calico and buckskin milled about quietly through camp, a girl about my size in a calico dress carried a bucket to the creek, with a fawn following at her heels. I gave Jack a kick, descending to the timber below.

My courage faltered before I got to camp, so to introduce myself I used the subtle method of trotting my horse around and around the edge of camp. When not one head turned in my direction, I almost gave up my efforts to meet the Adams. I was about to turn back up the hill when I saw the little girl untie a small sorrel horse, jump on bareback, and ride toward me. I pulled Jack up short as her horse approached. Her black braids shone like raven wings in the sunlight, and pink and orange ribbons danced all over them as her horse trotted along.

"What's your name?" she asked, pulling her horse to a stop.

"Roger."

"You live in house by road?"

"Yes. What's your name?"

"Sugar. Your horse is pretty. He's big."

"His name's Jack. Do you want to ride him?"

"You ride my horse."

When we traded bridle lines, I jumped on her horse and took off on a lope through the trees, with Jack and Sugar following right behind. I stayed in the lead for a long ride through the canyon. Neither of us spoke a word until Sugar turned back to camp, and we had tied our horses to a tree near the creek.

"You want to play with my fawn?" she asked.

Sugar's fawn had probably been orphaned, but whatever was his origin with the Adams, he had adopted himself to Sugar, following her everywhere like a pup. We ran through camp with the fawn beside us, and climbed up the hillside to pick tender shoots from juneberry bushes for the fawn to eat. I had found a playmate, the only one I had ever had on Petty Creek, and I galloped home across the ridge that afternoon with my pockets filled with smoked meat and a head filled with stories to tell my mom and dad.

The memories of my seasons in the Adam's camp melt into one as I think about the easy, unassuming ways of those quietly industrious people. And one of them, big John Adams, stands in my memory as the stoic guardian of our country when time was measured by seasons that signaled his return.

I met John when Sugar and I were fishing in the creek outside camp. She produced two willow sticks with fishing line and a hook tied to them. We each dug a worm to put on our hooks, and then we sneaked to a hole along the bank where we could see speckled trout moving back and forth on the creek bottom. As we stared wordlessly into the quiet water, waiting for one to grab our worms, the fish suddenly streaked out of sight at the sound of a crashing thud of horse hooves. I looked up to see a big, white horse rip through the brush on the creek bank, then stumble into the water directly across from us.

It was helpful to have been prepared by the Big Sams for the sight of Flatheads returning from a hunt, but I couldn't believe that the scene across the creek was really happening.

The biggest Indian that I had ever seen rode limply in the saddle, almost hidden by four intact quarters of bull elk. The front quarters were tied on either end of a rope and draped over the saddle horn with legs pointing up and back toward the rider, and the hind quarters hung in the same manner in back of the saddle. The total picture resembled some kind of huge cage that should have been carried by an elephant rather than a horse. When the contraption splashed across the creek, Sugar dropped her pole and ran along at the horse's flank until he stopped in front of a teepee. I caught up with her, staring upward in awe. A giant Indian stared down at us quietly from his forest of elk parts before he spoke in a soft pidgin French.

"You find new friend?" he asked Sugar.

She nodded a yes.

"You Mose Longpre's boy?" he asked, turning his snapping black eyes to me.

I nodded back, spellbound.

"We have Longpres on reservation. They maybe your cousins?"

"I don't know."

"That's nice big horse," he said, nodding toward Jack. "He your horse?"

I nodded again.

"Maybe you stay and eat," he said as he hefted a leg over two front elk quarters. He slid to the ground, handing me the bridle lines.

"You tie horse up to tree, then come and eat," he said.

I pulled the reluctant horse to the tree to tie him up before I ran to the teepee in the magical wake of big John Adams.

Meal times in Indian camps happened whenever anyone was hungry. Every teepee had its own version of a stove inside. John's looked like an old boiler with a chimney attached that carried the smoke about four feet high so the draft through the teepee would draw it up and out of the top. Women in camp gathered roots, wild onions, and berries from hillsides to mix with potatoes and dried meat that they had pounded into flour. A pot of the thick stew bubbled on the stove all the time, and except for boiled meat when an animal was first brought in, it sufficed as the staple of their diet.

John handed me a bowl of stew when I entered the teepee, and then he filled one for himself and sat down on the ground to eat. The smoky taste of dried meat permeated the soup, and I loved it. While we ate, Mrs. Adams fried lumps of dough into hard, flat circles of bread. I could barely swallow the first bite so I dunked it in the soup to soften it. John gulped his soup in silence like it was his first meal in a long time. When he finished, he put the bowl down on the ground and wiped his mouth with the sleeve of his buckskin shirt.

"We take elk off horse now," he said as he walked lightly across the clearing. He lifted the quarters easily from the sagging old horse, hung them on the meat poles, and took the saddle off the horse, tossing it on a pole that was nailed between two trees.

"When you get home you tell Mose he has fine boy," he said as he turned back to the teepee.

Never had I been dismissed so graciously. Never do I remember an instant case of hero worship that engulfed me as it did in the presence of John Adams.

The figure of John was an imposing one. He was a big man among his people— big boned, broad shouldered, and crowned with thick black braids that hung to his waist. Extra weight padded his broad, high cheek bones, hiding his fifty-some years under smooth pockets of deep-bronze flesh. For all his extra pounds he walked lightly through the woods, like a cat. He wore jeans tucked inside moccasins that were laced to his knees. A plain-cut buckskin shirt that was gathered at the neck with a draw-string completed his uniform. That was all that John ever wore. When it was cold outside, he wore two buckskin shirts.

But more impressive than the looks of John was his easy going approach to the task at hand and the people in his presence. He spoke little in camp, but I was at his side whenever I could be, with an incessant barrage of questions interspersed with pleas to be taken on a hunt. He was too patient to show annoyance, too kind to hurt my feelings with a flat "no" for an answer. He would say, "I go too far. Your horse get tired," or "I go all night. You get sleepy." I accepted the tone of finality in his refusals and I didn't ask twice. But one day when I rode onto the hillside above camp I saw him leading two pack horses out of camp with his saddle horse. I galloped down the hill to catch up with him.

"What are you going to do with them?" I asked, pointing to the pack horses.

"I need horses to bring back elk."

I assessed the situation. He would be gone two days to do a lot of hunting, and all he carried with him was a rifle in his scabbard.

"Are you going to stay in the mountains all night?"

"Yuh."

"Where are your blankets?"

"Under saddle. I sleep on saddle blanket."

"Where's your food?"

"I have jerky in my pocket."

"Where's your coat?"

"I wear two shirts"

"Can I go with you?"

"I gone all night. Your mother worry."

I had only hunted in the West Fork with my dad, and we brought the elk home in the back of the pickup. When I saw John ride into the mountains to stay overnight with nothing but a horse and a gun, I became obsessed with being included in the mysterious Indian hunt. Although I had stopped begging to hunt, my desires must have shown because one day shortly after that John looked down at me while he saddled his horse and said,

"Okay. Today we hunt."

I didn't say another word for fear he'd change his mind. As the big white horse plodded by, I turned Jack to follow him up the game trail into the head of Ed's Creek Canyon. I hardly dared breathe for fear I'd make too much noise.

As we climbed, we passed grazing horses in the canyon meadows. In all camps the Indians let the horses graze that they weren't using. They raised their camps at the bottom of the meadow so the horses couldn't get by them and back to the road. Leaving the horses behind, we climbed through thick jack pine and tamarack on the north slopes, through alder brush and slide rock until Deer Peak came into view through the trees. I had never ridden so far from home. As we rode into a clearing below the peak, John stopped his horse and turned to me.

"I saw tracks here before. Elk are maybe on Deer Peak today. Two horses will scare 'em away. You wait here. If I not back soon, you go home. Come to camp tomorrow to see if we got elk."

I sat rigid on my horse for a long time, waiting to hear a shot before I turned back to the ranch. I had hunted with John Adams and my life was complete. He knew my horse would take me safely home.

All of the Indian camps weren't as relaxed as Johns. In the camps of Pinto McClure and Rattlesnake Moss, younger men brought horses with them to break on the hunt. While John plodded out of camp on his old white horse, the McClures and Mosses would thunder down the canyon behind a herd of half-wild horses. They drove them into sturdy camp corrals to catch them and proceeded from there to break them for saddle or pack horses. Indian horse breaking didn't entail a step-by-step procedure like I was used to seeing on my grandpa's ranch. It was more of a "throw the saddle on and head out and he'll be broke when we get back" situation. I hid behind trees while hooves of bucking horses flew through camp, and I watched the same horses come back from the hunt as well-behaved animals.

Horse breaking was the only lively activity in any of the Indian camps. All other tasks were accomplished in such a casual manner, I wondered at first why the Indians bothered to come to Petty Creek at all. But with little conversation and slow, easy movements, women were at the creek soaking hides, scraping them with sticks when the hair loosened, and rubbing in bone marrow and elk brains to soften them. They boned and skinned every animal and cut the meat into thin slices for the meat rack. They kept the fires going all day and cut firewood for the teepees and smoke racks.

When the meat was dry, they pounded most of it into flour and stored it in flour sacks for the trip back to the reservation. Making it into flour was an easy way to transport it, and as in camp, they added ingredients to make a stew as the staple of their diet at home. The rest was left for jerky that seemed to be eaten mostly by children who spent their days wandering through camp with a piece of dried meat in their mouth and a dog at their side. The women spent quiet afternoons with needles in hand, sewing the newly-tanned hides into buckskin shirts and moccasins. When time allowed, they fished at the creek, bringing home trout to fry when the men came home.

A division of labor as in the old days still existed in the camps. The men brought meat home and hung it on meat poles, then rested until the next hunt. After every hunt they refreshed themselves at the creek with sweat baths. Small igloo-shaped huts were made from soft willow sticks and covered with canvas. Fires with rocks in them burned continually outside the huts. At bath time, the Indians used a shovel to scoop out the rocks from the fire into the hut. They then poured cold water over them to make steam. They soaked in the steam for a long time before they opened the flap of the hut to plunge into the icy creek. From my point of observation there was something magical in the sweat baths. John always came back from the creek wearing only his jeans and moccasins. The rest of him glistened like a brand-new copper kettle. His pearl-white teeth gleamed through a sparkling copper face, and his wet and shining black braids plastered themselves to his chest.

Enchantment permeated all aspects of life in the Indian camps. At first I simply thrilled at the wonder of a life so different from my own. But as seasons with the Flatheads passed, a sense of what I can only term "Indianess" developed in my consciousness. With John as the leader, the band of Flatheads who rode through our land instilled in me in those early years an unformed but gnawing awareness that it was they and their natural ways that belonged to our country, not we who had tamed it with barns and fences.

When the last leaves from the alder trees crunched underfoot and clouds gathered in cold stillness above the mountains, the Flatheads brought their horses down from the canyons. A seasons' harvest of meat and hides were piled high on the pack horses, and families and animals gathered at the mouth of the West Fork. As stoic as always, they got into position for the exodus back to the reservation. Pack horses were driven to the front, squaws and children jerked excited saddle horses under control. Small children clung silently to their mothers' waists, dogs barked noisily as they circled through the melee, and Sugar's fawn grazed quietly in the meadow beside the road. As they had ridden up the canyon in the warmth of the first signs of fall, so they descended in the cold of a gathering winter. Those few who chose to live by hunting would go back to the reservation to join with those who chose the comfort of white man ways.

I had ridden to the West Fork to say good bye to my friends. I rode up on a grassy knoll at the mouth of the canyon to stay out of the way. When John came out of the timber with his pack horses, he drove them up front with the rest before riding back to the hill where I stood.

"We come back next time. You be bigger boy then. Maybe we hunt more," he said.

He turned the big white horse around, trotting around the gathering to start the pack horses down the canyon. When the clatter of hooves and barking of excited dogs diminished into faint echoing through the canyon walls, I turned my horse for home … and a hush fell over Petty Creek. Only the quiet flowing of diminished waters broke the stillness of a world held in abeyance, waiting again for the icy claws of winter to penetrate its dimensions.

2

The solitude of winter settled over Petty Creek when the Indians departed from our mountains. The countryside turned pale under a circle of lifeless sun, until a gathering of clouds against a somber gray sky dropped a covering of white that cloistered us into an impenetrable winter seclusion. A ceaseless round of the usual seasonal activities diminished into a slackened pace in winter when our work day consisted mainly of providing the necessities of winter survival—feed for the stock and warmth for the house.

I kept busy in winter by accompanying my dad to the hay meadow, morning and night, when he fed cattle with the team and a sled. I helped load hay on the sled and then I spread it to the waiting cows with my broken-handled pitch fork that was kept in the meadow hay mound. At milking time I filled my lard pail with milk from one side of our Guernsey milk cow while my dad filled his three-gallon pail from the other side.

In the evening we ate our supper by kerosene lantern in the crackling warmth of our kitchen while raw winter winds screamed through the black and frozen desolation outside.

"Extra feed is all that's going to keep the cows warm 'til this breaks up," my dad would say when the bawling of unsettled cattle pierced through stormy nights. "Sure feels good to know we've got enough to give 'em, doesn't it."

Gray winter days turned sunny as my mother's pleasant countenance filled the kitchen like the comforting warmth of her wood cook stove. She spent her winter days preparing pans of frying meat and kettles of steaming vegetables to help insulate us against the winter cold. Loaves of butter-topped bread, light, flaky biscuits, custards, pies, and cobblers poured from the oven in her tiny, simply-appointed kitchen. She caught up on her mending in winter and made our rust-colored soap from lye and tallow. She kept the glass chimneys of our kerosene lamps glistening and brought the old gas-driven wringer washer into the kitchen when it was too cold for her to stand outside to wash our clothes. She had preserved the fruits of her garden through summer and fall. In winter she would dash through the cold outdoors to the cellar where she stored her crocks of corned elk meat, salt pork, crisp dill pickles, and carrots. Shelves in the cellar were lined with the opulence of hundreds of jars of vegetables, fruits, relishes, and preserves in a myriad of colors, textures, and tastes.

The security of home awaited me whenever I returned from the outdoors to the welcoming smell of my mother's cooking that seeped from under the kitchen door. In later years the memory of that appealing bid to rest and refresh would remain with many visitors who would speak of the sparkling little kitchen and the delicate gentleness of the lady in charge. No matter how long and tiring my mother's work day may have been, her black eyes shone through a flawless, pink complexion that was framed by scalp-hugging waves of dark brown hair. "It's good to see you. We're so glad you could make it. Why didn't you come sooner that this?" rang sincerely from her lips as she graciously welcomed everyone as if they were the most important person to ever walk through her door.

But in my early years it was mainly my relatives that flocked into our kitchen at winter's end to enjoy my mother's untiring hospitality. As I splashed through puddles of melting snow in the warming rays of a springtime sun, I looked forward to the event that signaled the real beginning of the new season on Petty Creek—the arrival of my aunts and uncles. It was a happy time when the family united around our round, oak table after their winter isolation, filling the kitchen with more aunts and uncles than there were chairs to accommodate them. I enjoyed their company when they arrived singly or in groups, but my favorite time with them occurred when the visit included the patriarch of that close-knit family, Absolom Longpre.

"Tell me a story, *Papere*," I shouted when Grandpa entered the kitchen that spring of my fifth year. My memories of the fall season with John hadn't dimmed, and I looked forward to comparing notes with Grandpa when he told me stories about the Indians that he had known when he first came to Montana.

"Already you want to hear a story?" Grandpa asked, smiling down at me through his thick, white, walrus-style mustache. He was so tall and lean, so straight and strong, so dignified even in the striped, bib overalls and flat-bottomed shoes that he always wore. His eyes twinkled beneath a thick mass of white hair, his manner of speaking was soft and kind, and he spoke French when he was with his family.

"I will say hello to your mamma and papa. Then we'll have a story."

Seated on top of the pine wood box next to the cook stove, I waited impatiently for Grandpa as the din in the kitchen rose to a deafening roar amid the refilling of mugs from the coffee pot that steamed on the stove. Finally, Grandpa rose from his chair and motioned to me to follow him as he walked through the kitchen door onto the porch. He sat down on the wooden bench and pulled me onto his lap when I sat down beside him.

"Ah, this is a fine, sunny spring day. Just look at the buds on the cottonwood trees," he said. "Soon you will have shade for your house. It's going to be a mild spring. We'll have lots of time to help your papa build a bunk house."

"Will you tell me a story now?"

"I see you haven't changed your mind about a story. Which one do you want to hear?"

"Tell me about the Indian killer horse."

"Wouldn't you like to hear a story you haven't heard so many times?"

"No! Tell me about the Indian horse."

"All right, we'll talk about the Indian horse. And don't you forget to tell me if I leave out something."

I settled into the stiffness of Grandpa's overalls to hear again the story that I believe best typifies the kind of life Grandpa led.

"It was shortly after I homesteaded near the Flathead Indian Reservation, about 150 miles from here, when I met your favorite Indian horse," Grandpa began. "Most of the Indians who lived near there weren't really my friends. They were wary of me because they didn't trust the white man. I traded with them often—value given for value received every time - and I gave them things like salt and tobacco whenever they stopped by my place. But I was a white man living on their land, and to many of them that meant that I was an intruder. Because of one young buck's feeling for the white man, he tried to get the best of me once, and he had a very clever way of doing it. I can't blame him, really. But if it hadn't been for the chief of the tribe who was the best friend I had among the Indians, I might not be here telling you a story about it.

"The Flatheads were always on the move, going to other parts of the reservation to hunt and trade and get together for powwows. They passed right by my place most of the time, bringing along extra horses that they used for trading stock. I noticed that one young buck had a fine, thoroughbred-looking horse that he always led, never rode. Oh he was a fine looking animal—long, sleek, and shiny, and full of life. So I went to the buck and told him I had a good, well-broke horse that I'd like to trade for his horse. When we made the trade, I brought my new horse home and put him in the corral. I was busy with a lot of things at the time so I didn't start working with him right away. A few days later, the chief came by and went straight to the corral. I went out to see what he had on his mind.

"When I walked up to him he looked at me with a frown on his face and said,
'Don't ride horse. He bucks. Stomps you. Killed three Indians.'

"The chief hadn't told me anything wrong yet, so I believed him. I knew I had a problem on my hands because Indians were very good riders. If they couldn't break the horse, I'd better find a new way to work on him.

"I thought for a long time about how I'd break that horse. Finally an idea came to me. I was a good swimmer, and Flathead Lake was nearby—maybe I could break him in the water. The next morning I led him to the lake with my saddle horse. When we reached the lake I tied my saddle horse to a tree and waded into the water, pulling the Indian horse along behind me with his halter rope. I swam out with him swimming along behind until the water was about thirty feet deep. Then I swam around beside him and slipped on his back.

"The chief had been right. The horse went to bucking. Headed straight for the bottom and came up blowing water all over the lake. It was a hard ride for both of us.

"I got off and swam to shore, leading the horse behind me again. I led him up on the bank so we could both rest. Then we went back in and the same thing happened again. When we got back on the bank that time, I didn't let him rest very long. I knew that the only way I'd ever get the upper hand was for him to be tired. We went out in the lake for the third time, and when I slipped on him in the water, this time he stayed right on top. He threw a little fit, but he was tired of having his ears filled with water. So I swam him around the lake for a while. When he was good and tired we swam back to shore.

"I was sitting tight when he walked onto solid ground, waiting for him to start bucking, but he didn't. He was tired and he thought if he bucked he'd be under water again. I got off and led him back home with my saddle horse. He had earned a good feed of grain when I put him back in the corral.

"The next day I started working him with a bridle. He was a gentle horse. Somewhere along the way somebody had treated him wrong to turn him into a killer. I kept a tight rein on him all the time those first few days. I wouldn't let him buck. I had a big advantage, of course, with him thinking he'd drown if he started bucking. I spent a long time in the corral with him before I took him out in the field. Once we got out in the open I found out what kind of horse I had. He was the fastest, most powerful horse I had every ridden. He'd go until he dropped in his tracks if you didn't make him stop. He'd turn on a dime, too, with just a touch of the reins. I never opened a gate with him after he was broke. He cleared fences as high as seven feet. I was proud of my work and proud of my horse.

"One day I thought I'd sashay on over to the Indian camp to let them see how their killer horse and I were getting along. I rode in there, trying to look brave, but I wasn't. I had no way of knowing what the horse would do when he got back there among the people he'd killed in the past. I slipped my feet out of the stirrups. If he started bucking, I'd jump off. I didn't stop and talk to anybody. I just rode back and forth around the camp while the Indians stood spellbound, without saying a word. A few of them slipped into teepees to tell the others, and more Indians came out to watch. Before long the whole camp was watching the horse, including the man who traded him to me, and all of a sudden they broke into hollers and hurrahs! I had my moment of triumph, setting that young buck back a peg or two.

"That horse became well known in the valley where I lived, and people borrowed him when they needed to get somewhere in a hurry. A neighbor of mine asked me if he could use him one day for a trip to town. I told him that would be fine, but I warned him that he was a hot-blooded horse who would run himself to death if you didn't keep a tight rein on him. My neighbor said he'd take good care of him. I always treated people the way I like to be treated so I took my neighbor at his word. A few hours later the man came back, riding home on a dead run. The horse was lathered from one end to the other, completely exhausted and wind broke. Whether he got out of control or my neighbor allowed him to run, I don't know. But he was a sick horse and he stayed that way until he died a few days later. I've had every kind of horse there is, Roger, but I never found one again to match my Indian killer horse."

Grandpa couldn't find a horse to match his Indian killer horse, and I have never found a horseman who could match the skill of my grandpa. He was a natural handler of horses and mules. They sensed it and acquiesced.

Grandpa migrated to the United States from Montreal, Canada in the 1890s to set himself up in a freighting business. So as Grass Valley, an area half way between Petty Creek and Missoula, was populated with French Canadians that were enticed to the country by the followers of the original handful of Hudson's Bay trappers who settled there in the 1860s, Grandpa was busy traversing the United States, moving people across the country from east to west with wagons and teams of horses and mules. On a trip through western Montana he saw good ranching potential in the thick, wild-grass meadows that covered the valleys near Flathead Lake and he homesteaded on 160 acres there. By that time the Flathead Indians had peacefully given up their summer camps in Grass Valley and their winter home in the Bitterroots to settle on the reservation. Grandpa set up a house for himself and brought cattle in on shares. For wintering the cattle, the rancher gave him a share of the spring calf crop which was the beginning of his herd.

Grandpa had been in the Flathead Valley for only a few years when several of his relatives settled in Grass Valley to farm, and he decided to join them there. By then, at the turn of the century, Grass Valley was known as Frenchtown Valley, named for the little town in its center half way between Missoula and Petty Creek, where a mercantile and St. John the Baptist Catholic Church filled the needs of the valley's cluster of French Canadian immigrants. Grandpa was in his mid-thirties when he bought a piece of ground in the valley, and apparently he was ready to settle into a family life. He married Sarah Ledieux, the first white child born in Missoula, and they increased the population of Frenchtown with eight children, with my dad fourth in line.

Survival among these pioneering families demanded hard work from all the family members. Their roots took hold in their new country because they loved the land and their animals and they desired to establish themselves as respected citizens who took pride in their homes and ranches. Through the channels of hard work and good management, Grandpa acquired more and more land until he was able to buy his ranch at Nine Mile, twenty miles northeast of Petty Creek.

The ranch covered the entire, fertile Nine Mile Valley where gentle, rolling hills protect the bottom land, and timbered mountains that rise above them circle the valley to enclose it into peaceful quietude. Cattle and horses grazed through the grassy bottom, drinking from Nine Mile Creek that runs the valley's length. For me, visiting Nine Mile was like stepping into another world. Electricity lit the house and barns and an oiled road ran from the frontage road to the ranch. Towering poplar trees lined the gravel road to the white, frame ranch house, standing straight and tall like Grandpa did then. From the blacksmith shop to the poultry houses, every outbuilding and corral stood in solid perfection. A saddle shed was lined with a huge array of saddles, bridles and work harnesses, all in a state of immaculate repair. The bunk house gleamed as a miniature of the ranch house in sparkling white with forest-green trim.

Giant work horse stallions stood in extra strong corrals, and a vicious mammoth jack, used for breeding mules, ran the length of his pen, pawing and braying all day long. Turkeys mingled through a tidy pen, and milk cows chewed contentedly in white-washed stanchions. When my aunts and uncles left the order of Nine Mile for a visit to the primitive world at Petty Creek, I believe they enjoyed the atmosphere that was inherent in their pioneering heritage. There was a challenge for them to help establish order in the relatively untouched wilderness in which my dad had chosen to settle. Although Petty Creek would always be the central gathering place, in those early years there was a definite purpose for my relatives' frequent appearances at the ranch. It had been a mandate from my grandpa that they assist my dad in the building of his livelihood.

A few years after my dad finished high school, he had left Montana to seek adventure in Alaska, and he had stopped in Juneau to work in a smelter for a while. While he greased a piece of equipment at a spot where racks of sludge from the ore were raised onto a conveyor belt that carried the debris out into the bay, the shirt sleeve on his right arm caught in a pulley. His arm was sucked into the machinery while his body was pulled up with the rising racks, and he was thrown onto the conveyor belt. His arm had been severed just below the shoulder. Someone saw his limp body riding on the belt, and pulled him to safety. He was in the hospital for a year before he returned to Montana to work on the ranch at Nine Mile.

Shortly after my dad came home, Grandpa decided to divide the ranch among his boys, with the stipulation that he remain there and work with his stock as long as he was able. The youngest boy, Sonny, had been killed in a horse accident several years before, so there were four remaining sons to inherit Nine Mile. At a family meeting, Grandpa told three of his boys, Dan, Dick, and Bill, which portions he had decided to give them. Then he turned to my dad and said,

"And Mose, you aren't capable of managing a ranch now. You can stay and work for Dan if you wish. Whatever you decide to do, your brothers will take care of you."

"Ha!" my dad said in recounting the incident to me years later. "Can you imagine him saying that? I guess I showed them who needed help. Who stayed on the home ranch where everything was all set up, and who moved out here?"

I can visualize the "I'll show them" gleam that must have sparked through my dad's eyes in his resolve to establish his own life. Shortly thereafter, he bought 500 acres on Petty Creek, married my mother, and together they moved into a lean-to shack on the ranch. (The ranch house had burned and the shack had been constructed as a temporary shelter.) When I was born two years later, we moved into our completed log house that my dad had built with help from his family.

In my early years I accepted my dad's handicap as a natural part of him and I enjoyed my duties as his helper. It was exciting to provide my shoulder as a resting place for his gun barrel when we hunted. I had fun holding the end of boards when he sawed a piece of lumber, and I was proud to hold the horse's head still with a halter rope when he put on the bridle. It wasn't until many years later that I understood the struggle that was an integral part of everything that he did. From falling trees with a cross cut saw to driving a team of spirited horses, each task in his work day harbored danger for his incomplete, inflexible body.

It wasn't only the missing arm, but the misshapen contours of his upper body that made his work difficult. His neck vertebrae were crushed when he was thrown onto the conveyor belt, and with time they fused together, so that his upper body was rigid. He couldn't rotate his neck so he pivoted from side to side to see around him. Constant use of his left arm strained his shoulder muscles, and his left side sagged out of line with his right. His chin tilted back as if frozen on top of his shoulder. He pulled his hat brim low onto his forehead to keep it from falling off. You could see the piercing depth of his green eyes only when he was in the house with his hat removed.

For my dad to receive help from his family was not an act of accepting charity. Helping each other was a way of life among ranching people, and my dad reciprocated by helping at Nine Mile whenever he was needed. As I look back on that time span in my life, I see him as a contented man. His pride had been wounded from his disinheritance of Nine Mile, but he was compensated by a satisfaction in having dared to venture into a wilderness life despite his physical limitations. He was thirty six years old when I was born, and he was ready to enjoy the benefits of a domestic life. He was proud of his ranch, proud of his beautiful, capable wife, and very happy to have a young son at his side to whom he could teach his knowledge of outdoor life. And I was happy, too, to travel through our mountains with this slow-moving dad of mine "who knew so many things."

So we were pleased to have our family visit that spring to help us erect a much needed log bunk house on the ranch. Grandpa Hebert, my mother's father, was also there to offer his services. He didn't frequent the ranch as often as the Longpre side of the family. With his own scattered family of thirteen children to visit, his spare time was divided among his many offspring.

Grandpa and Grandma Hebert had migrated from French Quebec in the early 1900s to the state of Maine where Grandpa worked as a logger. After they had two babies, they left their home and traveled west by train, settling in Sawmill Gulch, two ridges west of Petty Creek. Eleven more children were born to them on their little farm there where they lived the rest of their lives. Grandpa worked as an axe man for the sawmill that gave the area its name. He gained a skill in his trade that earned him a reputation as one of the finest axe men in the region, and he was called for building projects of many sorts in the Missoula-Frenchtown area.

A family gathering was never complete without the presence of our hired man, Louie Albert. Dark skinned, small, and wiry, with prominent features in his angular, lined face, Louie seemed to be always old and always a natural part of the ranch. He had grown up with my dad, but he never married, and like many bachelors who were raised in Frenchtown Valley, he stayed in the area to work for the people he had known all his life. He lived in his own log cabin at the mouth of the West Fork, but most of the time he ate meals with us.

Louie was somewhat of an incongruity in my mother's immaculate kitchen. He washed his hands and face before every meal when he was at our house, but that was about the extent of his washing, of himself or of his clothes.

"Now, if you go down to see Louie, I don't think you should eat anything there," my mother would say when I rode my horse in that direction.

Louie didn't work on the ranch every day. He was called upon only when there were specific jobs to do such as building fences, falling timber, or putting up buildings. The rest of the time he kept busy hunting, cutting wood for his cabin, and drinking whisky. He would disappear for days at a time and come back with red eyes, a drooping unsteadiness when he walked, and an even older appearance than before he left. But when he was asked to work he worked steadily and hard, and for that my dad saw that all his needs were met for the twenty years that he lived on the ranch.

So our little kitchen buzzed with the commotion of my French-speaking family for two weeks while the bunk house was built. Both English and French were spoken in our home, but French came naturally to me. I understood a few words of English, but I spoke only French, so it was especially comforting to be with my family who used only the French language when they were together. Just before meal time every day, I sat on top of the wood box to watch my mother and my aunts scurry from the stove to the counters to the table while they talked about recipes and gardening, and what to put in which serving dish. From the other end of the kitchen, the stronger voices of the men rose above the feminine chatter to discuss the projected price for cattle in the fall, plans for spring planting, and news of who was doing what on ranches in the valley. Then a hush would fall over the kitchen as platters of meat, plates of biscuits, saucers of jam, bowls of creamed vegetables, and mounds of home-churned butter were spread across the table.

"Ah, Stella, you outdid yourself again," would be heard from one side of the table.

"I don't know how I'll manage it, but this time I'm going to make sure I leave room for some of that cream pie," another uncle would chime in.

"You know, I'd stay here and build things the rest of my life if I would get fed like this every day," could be heard above the clatter of spoons and forks as mountains of nourishment were heaped on the plates.

"It's just plain old food, but thank you for the compliment," my mother would answer. "With the way you're all working you need lots to eat, so help yourselves to all you want."

My dad would beam with pride, his eyes twinkling through his ruddy face as he responded to the accolades.

"Well, if the rest of you were as good looking as I am, maybe you'd have cooks like mine."

Hearty laughter would resound through the kitchen, and then only the tinkling of forks against plates would be heard as a crew of hungry men fell into silent enjoyment of a satisfying meal.

When work resumed on the bunk house I was out there watching—always watching- so that some day I would be able to match the skills that my family members possessed. Jake and Queen stepped high and fast, pulling a big, pine log down the trail with my straight and agile grandpa marching behind them, snapping them into rapt attention with the lines. Chips of wood flew like dust in a whirlwind at the building site as Grandpa Hebert notched the logs with the precision of a machine. A staccato rapping of hammers rang through the air as my uncles laid sturdy pine boards over pole floor rafters. Two weeks after they started, the composition roof was tacked into place, and the basic structure was complete.

I was proud of the new, freshly-peeled log building that glistened yellow in the sun, and proud of the workmen who built it. I looked forward to haying season when the crew that came to help would have a bunkhouse. And I would enjoy my association with the first residents of the new building for a season. Then the bunkhouse would dim in memory as I was thrust into a world away from Petty Creek where my thoughts would turn only to survival.

3

Missoula. That far away depository for concrete and traffic may have held promise of intrigue for some, but for me trips to the city were only tiresome necessities. Fortunately, they were infrequent. When the cows were sold in the fall, my mother bought sugar, flour, spices, beans, and coffee to last for the year, so trips in between were mainly for feed, machinery parts when they were needed, and fuel. My dad carried two, fifty-gallon barrels to town in the pickup to be filled with gasoline, and we siphoned from them for pickup fuel on the ranch.

Usually my mother and dad went to town separately, in which case I could stay home, but on occasion they rode in together, which meant that we would visit my mother's sister, Aunt Yvonne, and Uncle Roy. Those relatives who were a natural part of my life at home appeared almost as strangers in town where there was nothing to do at their house but watch people and cars go by. I couldn't imagine what prompted them to live in such awkward surroundings.

I realize now that for its population of 30,000, the town of Missoula was actually a pretty western town, nestled at the mouth of Hellgate Canyon under the protective cover of the bunch grass slopes of Mt. Sentinel and Mt. Jumbo. Its main business district ran for eight city blocks on Higgins Avenue from the brick railroad depot south to the Clark Fork River. It was crowded with rows of banks, shops, and cars, but mostly with throngs of people. There was no skipping through the streets in Missoula. I clung to my mom and dad for fear of being swept away with the swirling mass of humanity.

In spite of my feelings about our trips to town, my mother told me one morning in early September of my sixth year that we needed feed and pickup fuel and we'd be going to town that day.

"I can't go," I protested. "The Indians might come today."

"Oh, they're not coming today."

"They might, and John said we'd go hunting."

I had felt the first gentle bites of frost in the morning air and I knew it was almost time for the Indians to return. My dad had told me that the first full moon in September is the time of a killing frost, and it is then that the bull elk bugle their mating call through the canyons to establish their territory. Just before the elk started bugling, the Indians would come to Petty Creek to be ready to hunt when the sound of the bugles would lead them to the bulls. I knew that the moon would soon be full, so it was under protest that I was scrubbed, polished, and directed to the pickup.

My dad, in his customary manner, kept the truck at a crawling pace down the canyon road. It amazes me now that we ever made it through the creek at such slow speed. Only a handful of bridges helped us cross the creek, and it was often a sink or swim situation through swift current in spring or up a slippery bank of snow and ice in winter. But he shifted into low gear at the bank, and somehow the old pickup chugged through, up, and over the creek. It was an hour after we started from home that we clattered over the railroad tracks before crossing the old wooden bridge at the Clark Fork River. We turned west then onto a gravel road to pass Fred Thompson's pasture along the river. Trains steamed by on the opposite bank, blowing their whistles at the canyon crossing.

One mile later we crossed the tracks again at the entrance to Alberton where the Milwaukee freight depot gave the town its reason for existence. Directly across the street from the poplar-shaded depot was the rest of the town—the Alberton Mercantile, two saloons, a service station, Bestwick's Meat Market, and the post office.

We stopped to pick up our mail from among the rows of brass boxes that lined the walls of the small, square room. A fire snapped and popped from the pot bellied stove behind the barred window where Mrs. Flanders, the friendly postmistress, sold stamps and received packages. She chatted with my folks for awhile, and then we were ready for an uninterrupted trip to Missoula.

The road east of Alberton wound through the timbered foothills of Petty Mountain for a few miles, where dense lodge pole pine obscured the view beyond ten feet of the road. And then, as if the hands of nature gently parted the hills, the country opened into the wide expanse of Frenchtown Valley. Cattle grazed through stubble fields of harvested wheat, Holstein cows fed in fields close to dairy barns, and two-story frame houses poked here and there through the protection of surrounding Canadian poplars. Midway between the ranch and Missoula, Frenchtown settlement lay peacefully in the bottom of a gentle dip in the valley floor, where a collection of houses and a general store clustered around the wooden spire of St. Anne's Catholic Church. A big sky arched above the Petty Mountain range to the south, and the Jocko range to the north, until the mountains closed in the valley around the rocky crags of Hellgate Canyon and the town of Missoula that spread from its mouth.

Our first stop in Missoula was at the one place that held my interest—the Montana Feed and Flour Mill on the western edge of town. It was a big, tin building with a silo along side of it for storing grain and a loading platform that ran its length. Inside, the hollow structure was filled with stacks of flour sacks, ground grain, and blocks of salt. Flour dust settled over everything. As men carried feed sacks to waiting trucks, they left footprints in the cement.

After my dad backed his pickup to the loading platform, we climbed wooden stairs that led to a small office. Inside the door, a knotty- pine counter divided the waiting area from the office space. Clerks stood at the counter to write out the orders, telephones rang, and ladies sat at typewriters with their fingers flying busily over the keys. From behind a closed door, roaring mill presses filled the room with the earthy smell of freshly-ground grain and molasses.

"Where are we going now, Dad?" I asked when a warehouse worker threw the last bundle onto a fat pile of feed sacks in the pickup bed.

"I think your mother wants to visit someone for a while."

"Can't she visit next time?"

"I don't know. You'll have to ask her."

I climbed into the pickup and asked my mother if we were going to visit Aunt Yvonne.

"No, not today."

"Don't we have to visit anybody?"

"Yes, but just for a while."

"Who?"

"Some people you haven't met. We'll be there soon."

We began a slow crawl east along the edge of town. My dad wasn't used to driving through city streets, and his handicap increased his caution, so we usually crept down Higgins Avenue like a hearse, with a whole procession of cars behind us. But that day he stayed on the edge of town until we turned into a residential area and stopped in front of a massive, three-story brick building. Dormers ran along its roof, ropes of ivy climbed its surface, and a long walkway led to a high, cement porch.

"Why are we stopping here?" I asked.

"This is where the people live that I want you to meet."

"I don't want to meet anybody. I want to go home and see if the Indians are there."

"This will only take a minute."

She descended from the pickup and took my hand. I turned to my dad as I slid across the seat.

"Are you coming to see the people?"

"No. I have to fill the barrels. I'll be back a little later."

After a long climb up a set of cement stairs, my mother and I stopped in front of a pair of gaping doors, one of which held a circle of iron that was attached to a metal plate. By then I wasn't asking questions. An ominous feeling of hostility from the other side of the doors overpowered me.

When my mother tapped the iron ring on the metal, a loud, heavy sound reverberated around the porch. The wide doors swung open and a pale, expressionless woman looked down at us through folds of black that hung, draped, and billowed from the top of her head to the tips of her pointed shoes. My mother spoke to her in English. From time to time the woman nodded without expression, and then she looked down at me and thrust out her arm. I recoiled, scrambling behind my mother.

"There's no need to be afraid. This lady wants to talk to me for a while longer. Let's step inside for just a moment."

On the other side of the doors the sound of my feet on a hard, tile floor echoed through the emptiness of a cold, cavernous interior. The ceiling was as high as our barn roof, and long, narrow windows stared grimly from white-washed cement walls. In the center of the room was a big writing desk, the only piece of furniture.

The stark, black figure that had answered the door sat down behind the desk. When she beckoned me to come to her I clutched my mother's hand. Then my mother took my other hand in hers as she knelt down in front of me.

"We brought you here, Roger, because it's time for you to start school. You can't go to school in Alberton because the bus can't come up the road to our house. Instead, you'll be able to stay here at the Catholic school. You'll live in this house, and go to school in another building that isn't very far away. School starts tomorrow. You'll make lots of new friends. You'll have your own bed to sleep in and good things to eat. Dad and I will come and get you so you can come home for vacations. The lady who is sitting at the desk is called a sister. She'll teach you to speak English better, so be a good boy and I'll be back to see you soon."

She held me tight for a moment before she rose, vanishing through the front door. While I stood in dumb horror, staring at the closed doors in front of me, a clicking noise came at me from behind. I whirled around and saw the lady in black charging toward me. Blindly, I bolted for the doors, but her strong fingers dug into my shoulder. I burst into terrified sobs as she pulled me down a long dark hall. When we reached the end of it, I was jerked into a small room where another lady in black sat behind a desk. The lady with her fingers in my shoulder pushed me down into a wooden chair. She spoke briefly with the figure behind the desk before she whisked out of the room with a scowl. I buried my head in my hands, anticipating another attack.

And then a voice that I will never forget broke through my sobs.

"*Bonjour, Roger. Je peus avoir tu amis.*" (I want to be your friend.)

I lifted my head slowly to see a lady with a kind face, soft brown eyes, a beautiful smile, and a hand outstretched to take mine. She walked around the desk and knelt down by my chair. She put her arm around me, holding my head on her shoulder as she spoke again in French.

"My name is Sister Louie. You cry if it makes you feel better. Then I want to learn all about you."

My tears subsided as she chatted reassuringly with me about the academy, and soon I was trotting at her side on a tour through the dormitory building. Although each room was gloomy and austere, my terror diminished into a general acceptance of a temporary stay at the academy with Sister Louie in charge.

As we walked through rows of iron beds in the dormitory, she pronounced the English word for various objects, coaxing me to repeat them.

"Good, Roger, good," she would say, clapping her hands in approval. "You're learning fast."

We spent the rest of the afternoon in that manner. At supper time she sat beside me in the cafeteria. Like a bewildered puppy in a new home, I blanked out the harshness of my unfamiliar surroundings in the soothing presence of Sister Louie. I can't imagine the outcome of that day had I not been touched by her gentle hand.

But when she tucked me in bed that night, a disturbing presence in the form of another lady in black whisked down the rows of beds, speaking sharply. It wasn't yet dark, but she pulled the heavy curtains across the dormer window before strutting out the door.

"What did that lady say?" I asked.

"She said that everyone must go right to sleep because you will get up early in the morning to get ready for school."

"Is it hard to go to school?"

"No. You will like it very much. And when you're finished with school for the day, we'll speak English again. Good night. I look forward to seeing you tomorrow."

Sister Louie walked quietly from the room as I fell into an exhausted sleep.

It was still dark when the lady who had pulled the curtains sailed back into the dormitory with a shout. She flipped on the light switch and disappeared. All of the boys jumped out of bed and began to dress. Following their lead, I took my short gray pants and blue sweater from a drawer in the night stand beside my bed. Then the lady reappeared, speaking sharply as the room full of little boys lined up at the doorway. I stood by my bed to wait for Sister Louie. I assumed that she would be with me wherever we were going. But the lady grabbed my arm, pulling me to the back of the line.

The boys moved forward, and I with them, through a long, dark hall until our feet clipped across the tile floor in the room with the double doors. Another lady waited there to lead us into a cold, gray morning where the first streaks of daylight were arranging themselves in the sky. We walked down the porch stairs to cross the lawn where several more ladies in black stood guard around a statue that was barely visible in the morning light. Then everyone bent down on their knees, lowering their heads as if they were going to cry.

Fear of the unknown overwhelmed me. I turned to run back to the building to find Sister Louie, but swirling black skirts raced toward me with a bucket dangling somewhere in the middle of them. A mound of gravel from the bucket was poured onto the ground in front of me, while another lady in black slapped her hand on top of my head, pushing me down on my knees into the gravel. Over and over she twisted my head while tiny pieces of gravel ground into my bare knees. I shut my eyes tight and screamed in terror. (I would learn later that the children were offering prayers to the Virgin Mary. Kneeling in gravel was punishment for not conforming.)

When everyone stood up again, the gravel lady pushed me into another line. I stumbled along into a building close to the statue. My knees bled and tears ran down my cheeks when we filed into another dismal, high-ceilinged room where we sat on hard benches to hear a man in black chanting in a strange language. When the talking ended, a another lady in black was there to lead me to the cafeteria where she left me standing by myself.

Following the others, I picked up a tin tray from a stack and filled it with lumpy oatmeal and prunes. I found a seat at a table away from everyone else, watching them as they ate, talked, and laughed together. My breakfast hadn't been touched when a whistle blew that emptied the cafeteria.

I had still talked to no one because I couldn't communicate in the English language, so when everyone gathered in pairs or groups to walk down the street to the school building, I followed along by myself. In my confusion I trailed off on my own. Hot tears stung my cheeks again as I wandered down a street into town. Cars honked on the streets and people dashed by without seeing me. I started to run, just run, because I didn't know what else to do.

But soon the strong arm of a lady in black reached at me from behind, grabbing my wrist. She marched down the sidewalk with such a brisk stride that my feet barely touched the pavement as I bounced along beside her.

I had been reported missing from the first grade room, and the pale-faced lady came to look for me. When we entered the school building, she pulled open a door to push me inside. She spoke briefly with a lady who stood by a desk, then disappeared, leaving me standing alone in front of a classroom of staring first graders. The lay teacher did her best to welcome me, but I cringed in terror at her touch.

The rest of the day is hazy in my memory until I was summoned into the office of Sister Louie. She explained to me that because of her other duties, she couldn't be with me all the time, but we would meet each afternoon until I learned to speak English well. It was almost enough to make me stop trying to learn, but I wanted to please her and I knew that my welfare at the institution depended on my ability to understand the spoken language. That concept was further enforced that evening at bed time.

I was in the dormitory, preparing for bed, when the sister with the pale face appeared in the doorway, calling my name along with some of the other boys. When everyone lined up at the door, I followed along. We were led down the stairs until we stopped abruptly in front of one of the closed doors. At a command from the nun, everyone began to disrobe, until a line of sober little boys stood naked on the cold floor, shivering in the dampness of the dungeon-like surroundings. Then the door opened and the first boy in line disappeared into the room. An instant later his screams echoed through the hall. When I cried out for Sister Louie my mouth was slapped shut. I believe that I went into a state of shock as each boy disappeared into the room. I don't remember the beating that I received that first night, but subsequent sessions stand out vividly.

After each child was beaten on his naked body with a long switch, he stood on the other side of the doorway until the punishments were complete. Then we all picked up our clothes from the floor, dressed, and walked in a line back to the dormitory with an order to go immediately to bed.

When I got into bed I curled into a knot under the covers, sobbing myself to sleep. My first bewildering day at the academy had ended as it began—with physical punishment—and I had no idea why. I would learn that it was because I tried to run away from school that morning.

The academy system couldn't have been as misdirected as it seemed to me or it wouldn't have stayed in existence. Parts of it were definitely amiss, but for those who were already established in church principles and could understand what they were told, the adjustment would have been easier. Such was the case for my cousin, Billy, who lived at home in Missoula and attended classes at the school.

I had little in common with any of my cousins throughout our childhood, including Billy, who was three years older and much bigger than I. None of them could keep up with my style of living, and when they visited Petty Creek they were at my mercy as I led them through adventures in the mountains. So when I met Billy in his territory he devised an ingenious plan for revenge.

We seldom spoke when we ran into each other at school, but he approached me one day with a plan that almost made me start to like him.

In our game room in the dormitory building, where tables were set up for puzzles, checkers, and other pastimes that held no interest for me, a chart for recognition for the things that we did right was displayed on the wall, which also didn't interest me. If we kept our drawers neat or made our beds without wrinkles, we received a gold star in a column next to our name. When ten gold stars appeared on the chart a red star was placed in the column. I didn't understand the significance of the chart so I ignored it until Billy approached me one day in the school cafeteria.

"Hi, Roger. Do you want to get some gold stars?" he asked.

"No."

"Do you know what you get for ten gold stars?"

"No."

"You get a red star."

"I don't want a red star."

"If you get one, you get to go to the store to buy some candy."

There was merit in further inquiry.

"How do I get a star?"

"There's lots of ways, but the best one is if you do penance."

"What's that?"

"That's when you give away something you want to make up for when you've been bad. If you give me your dessert, I'll tell the sister and she'll give you a star."

My cousin had learned how to beat the system. I passed him my dessert. The explanation of penance was irritating because I didn't think that I had been bad and therefore giving up dessert was a useless gesture. But since everything we did at the academy fell into that category, I simply weighed the merits of trading watery pudding for candy from the store, and the candy won.

Every day I ran to the game room to check my chart and every day another gold star shined down next to my name. I finally had one bright moment each day other than my time with Sister Louie. When the big red star appeared beside my name, I took my place in line with those who would receive a nickel to spend at the store. The coins were passed out, and the red star group paraded together across the street.

It took me a long time that day to pick out my five pieces of penny candy from the trays of bright-colored balls and wrappers behind the glass case. The store owner waited patiently for our decisions as he filled our sacks, one by one. When we all clutched a brown paper bag in our hands, we filed back to the lawn in front of the dormitory, and then we were on our own. I had already decided to ration the candy to myself, one piece each day, so I hurried to the dorm to hide my sack before anyone saw it.

My cousin must have known what I would do. When I got to the top of the stairs, he was leaning against the wall outside my room.

"Hey, Roger. Do you want some more gold stars?"

"Sure."

"Okay, give me your candy. I'll tell the sister you did penance again, and she'll give you some more gold stars."

"I want to eat my candy."

"Go ahead. But I'll tell the sister you were bad, and she won't ever give you any stars."

I knew I'd be beaten for whatever my cousin might tell her. I threw my sack of candy at him, ran to my bed, and buried my face in my pillow for another bout with tears. I also kept Billy supplied with candy for the remainder of my academy career.

After the candy episode, I had only one happy event to anticipate—my trips back to Petty Creek. Every third weekend my dad picked me up after school on Friday to take me home. I would dash to John's camp for smoked meat and a quick check on numbers of elk brought in before I raced back home to see what might be happening at the ranch. Each time I hoped that they would let me stay. There was never enough time in two short days to cover familiar ground before my stomach gnarled at the thought of returning to school. But the most difficult time to accept my situation was when I learned of a family event during the first weekend in November.

When my dad met me at school on Friday, he told me that he had a surprise for me at Aunt Yvonne's.

"Then are we going home?" I asked.

"No. We'll stay at Aunt Yvonne's this week end."

My heart sank.

"Is John still in camp?"

"Yes. He wants to get two more elk before they leave."

"I don't want a surprise, Dad. Can't we go home?"

"You wait until you see this one. Maybe you'll change your mind."

My mother was wearing her bathrobe when we arrived at Aunt Yvonne's, so I thought she wasn't feeling well. After our happy reunion ended, she told me to come with her into the bedroom to see my surprise. I followed her to a basket that was sitting on a chest in the corner of the room. She stepped aside, telling me to look inside. A tiny baby lay sleeping under a fuzzy new blanket.

"Why is there a baby here?" I asked.

"We brought him home from the hospital this morning."

"Is that my surprise?"

"Yes. That's your new brother."

"Is he going to live with us?"

"Yes. We'll take him home in a few days."

"He sure is little. Why is he asleep in the day?"

"He sleeps most of the time because that will help him grow so that he'll be big enough to play with you. His name is Robert Pierre."

So Robert Pierre was added to the family, and in the two days that I stayed with him I got used to the idea. I held him, tried to share a banana with him, and I looked forward to playing with him when he got bigger. After meeting him I dreaded the return to school more than ever.

The week after my introduction to my new brother had taken place, the first winter snowfall blanketed western Montana. We stayed mostly in the dismal game room during our free time while I grew more despondent than ever. I thought about my dad and Louie feeding the cows with the sled and the team. I wanted to climb up the hill behind the house and speed back down on my sled where a kettle of hot chocolate would be simmering on back of the stove. I missed the smell of wood smoke and baking bread. It became harder rather than easier to accept my situation, and I believed I was there because no one wanted me at home. I had no friends at school because I didn't want any. I withdrew into a world of my own, alone and confused. At night I shivered in the dampness of my dormitory bedroom, crying myself to sleep. One night I felt particularly threatened. I don't remember why because I spent so much of my time in fear, but I do remember crawling under the bed to hide. Wearing only my pajamas, I curled into a ball on the cold, cement floor to keep from shaking. I don't remember another thing until I saw black shoes and skirts beside my bed and heard voices talking about my disappearance. I remained silent. I knew that I would be beaten if they found me. I slipped into unconsciousness, and when I woke again I was in a hospital room with my mother and dad standing beside my bed. I had developed a severe case of pneumonia.

My parents knew that a mistake had been made in sending me to the academy, but at the time they used their best judgment in their concern for my education. They had both been raised in the Catholic faith, but they didn't attend church because the closest parish was in Frenchtown. For them it was inaccessible in gas mileage and time away from the ranch.

Possibly I had received instruction from them in some aspects of Catholic teaching, but I don't remember it. They had tried to prepare me for the concept of school in general, but it didn't penetrate. I couldn't imagine any cause serious enough to take me away from the ranch. So they evidently decided to leave my indoctrination into school and church in the hands of the academy staff. They didn't realize the severity of the institution's discipline policies or how it would affect me.

But a case of pneumonia gave me a permanent reprieve from the school. While I was still in the hospital, I was told that arrangements had been made for me to live with Grandpa Longpre, where the bus would pick me up for school in Alberton. Since the main ingredient in any healing process is the desire to get well, the days of my convalescence passed happily by. The Missoula experience was behind me, and I would soon be free to roam with Grandpa through my second favorite place in the world—Nine Mile.

4

I had sailed through the wonders of Nine Mile for only two weeks before it was time for Christmas vacation. Winter at Nine Mile was a quiet time in the absence of the spring and summer cycles of roundups, horse breaking, and harvest. It was especially quiet that year because of the hard and early winter. Four feet of frozen snow had been piled on the ground, and little could be accomplished in the outdoors.

So after the cattle were fed each day, Grandpa worked in his tack shop beside a sputtering pot bellied stove. A single light bulb hung above his work table in the center of the square, wooden building. Draping work harnesses, bridles, riding saddles, head stalls, bits, and sheets of unused leather hung in order on almost every inch of wall space. Each piece of equipment shone with a protective coating of bear fat and paraffin, filling the shed with that pleasing smell of leather grease and horse sweat.

In one corner of the room, rough plank shelves held equipment that was in need of repair. Riding saddles that needed work were stacked on the floor. Next to the shelves, a wall space was filled with broken pieces of equipment that had been used all through his years on the ranch. When Grandpa assessed the need for repair, he searched through the old assortment until he found the appropriate part. He chose a tool from an array of leather tools and needles, and with the skill of a master craftsman he sewed, cut, and spliced until his broken piece of tack looked like new. When Grandpa wasn't working with his tack, he was busy in the blacksmith shop. Sparks flew from the forge as he sharpened plough shears and molded pieces of iron into horse shoes. While he worked, he told me stories from his colorful past.

"Tell me in English," I would say when he started a story in French. Wounds from the academy hadn't healed. Only in unguarded moments did I speak French again for many years. Grandpa understood and did his best to remember to speak English when I was with him.

But for all the love and activity that surrounded me at Nine Mile, it wasn't enough to squelch my yearning to be home. Aunt Ruby, one of my dad's sisters, had been widowed shortly before my grandma died, so she had moved back home to keep house for Grandpa. A large, buxom woman, she possessed a genuine concern for the welfare of her fellow man that was extended to an interest in the quality in which I was being reared at Nine Mile. I appreciate her interest in my development now, but at the time I thought that since I wasn't home, I shouldn't have to follow binding rules and regulations.

I was still terrified of a classroom situation, and school remained a threat to my peace of mind. So much had happened in a short time that I don't remember well those first weeks of adjustment to my new school in Alberton except that I waited impatiently to return to Petty Creek for Christmas vacation.

When my mother picked me up from school it seemed that the pickup barely crawled through the deep snow of a winter canyon. A three-day warm wind had turned the snow into heavy slush, and the tire chains ground on rocks when she gunned the motor to force the truck up soggy creek banks.

"I wish we could go faster," I said impatiently when we were half way up the road.

"So do I because there's someone at home that's waiting to see you."

"Who?"

"Bill Lapel."

"Really? Did he stop to visit with us?"

"No. He's living with us now. He's going to help Louie with his work."

I was stunned with the news. I had been intrigued with the man from the first moment that I saw him. I never dreamed that he would be living on the ranch.

It was the summer before I left for the academy that 400 acres, six miles north of the ranch, had been purchased and a cabin erected on the property. The people who bought the land had hoped to make their living raising cattle, and they brought Bill with them as their ranch hand. I don't remember the owners ever stopping by the house, but I'll never forget those first visits from Bill.

We didn't see Bill often. He only stopped to pay a visit when there was a need for it. Barging through the door without knocking, he would holler, "Get the coffee pot on!"

Then he would plop himself on the wood box next to the stove, leaning forward with his elbows resting on his bent knees, looking like he was all legs and bones. He was in his early thirties, six feet tall, lean and rawboned, with a pointed chin. A shock of curly brown hair covered his forehead, and his deep blue eyes squinted through the smoke of a Camel cigarette that dangled continually from his lips.

Unnecessary dialogue was not a part of Bill's makeup. When someone asked him a question he answered politely, though loudly, but his conversation was limited mainly to his reason for stopping.

"I need a saddle horse in the mornin'. I'll bring a sack of grain for usin' him. See ya after daylight."

And with that he would gulp down his coffee, vanishing as fast as he entered.

I would sit at the kitchen table like a mouse when Bill paid a visit, wondering if he even knew that I was in the room. He never looked at anyone or anything. His eyes swept around the kitchen like flames on a dry pine branch. His intensity fascinated me. It was as if an underlying current would blaze at any moment. It wasn't until he left that I received recognition.

When Bill reached the door on his way out, he would suddenly stop, whirl around and look right at me.

"Been ridin' your black horse lately?" he would shout through his cloud of cigarette smoke. Not waiting for an answer, he would say, "Watch ya don't kill yourself."

It was attention such as that from the rough, tough, ready-for-anything neighbor of ours that left me wishing for more. And now, on my way back home, I learned that he would be part of our family.

When the pickup stopped in front of the house I bounded through the yard, scattering paper Christmas ornaments that I had made at school. When I ran into the kitchen, Bill was perched on the wood box, dressed for the outdoors in a plaid mackinaw and knee high rubber boots. A cigarette hung from the corner of his mouth.

"Hi, kid. I'm gonna feed cattle. If ya want to come hurry up cuz I'm not gonna wait for ya."

He slid off the wood box, picked up his shot gun from a corner by the stove, and bolted out the door.

I plowed across the grazing meadow through the heavy snow, trying to keep up with his long, fast stride. When we reached the barn, he propped his gun in a corner by the horse stalls, led Jake and Queen into the barnyard, and harnessed them with quick, heavy movements. Not a word had been spoken since we left the house. I stood silently in a corner by the barn door to watch him. When he hitched the team to the bobsled, I ran behind the barn to open the gate.

Bill jumped on the sled, laying the shotgun at his feet. He urged the horses ahead as the creaking sled labored through the gate.

"Sit down in back and be quiet," Bill ordered. "We might see some ducks out there today."

With a flick of the lines we moved slowly over the meadow to the haystack, a half mile away.

At almost any time of day, a few wild ducks could be seen feeding through the haystack for grain. But with heavy snow on the ground, about two hundred of them surrounded the bottom of the haystack that day, filling their crops in a haven for winter-hungry ducks. They were used to the horses coming by so they would peck away until we passed through the barbwire fence that kept the cattle away from the haystack. Bill stopped the sled within shooting distance of the ducks.

"I never seen that many birds here before," he said. "I think we'd better have us a duck supper tonight."

He bent down to pick up his gun.

"You get up here and hold these lines tight 'cuz when I start shootin' the horses are gonna jump and wanna run."

I had driven the team on a limited basis, but never when there was shooting beside them. Since I knew the potential danger in that situation, my heart pounded as I crept up from the back of the sled. The two horses in front of me suddenly took on elephant proportions as I grabbed the lines, stepping back until they were taut. Bill crawled to the back of the sled, cocking his gun on the way. I stood stiff as a poker, braced and ready, staring straight ahead into the rear end of 3,400 pounds of horse flesh.

Then the first shot crashed through the stillness. The horses' tails arched and their heads flew up. A second and third shot followed. With a jump of their front feet they took off, paying no attention to the forty pounds of pull behind them. With each succeeding shot that echoed through the meadow, they ran faster until they were in a dead run around the fence. I stretched back at a 40-degree angle, pulling on the outside line to keep them from running into the fence. That maneuver made them run in a wide arc around the posts, making the circle of flying ducks a perfect target for Bill.

Cattle had tramped the snow around the fence into ice. A warm wind had melted the top layer so the sled runners reached the manure level, churning up chunks that flew in my face. I couldn't see or breathe. I stood stiff, pulling until my hands were cramped and numb.

Finally the shooting stopped, but the horses didn't. Bill ran for the front, grabbing the lines from me. I crawled across the rumbling sled and lay down on my back, supporting myself by digging my fingers in the slivers of the planks. Four feet of slush didn't stop the team when Bill drove them in the deep snow. They were in a frenzy then, racing in a zigzag pattern through the meadow with blobs of salty foam flying from their lathered hides. I lay rigid on the sled, licking the flying salt and snow from my mouth.

Finally the rumbling and the motion quieted and then stopped. I lay motionless in the silence that follows a spell of terror, listening to the heaving gasps of two exhausted horses.

"You better git up!" Bill's voice echoed through the quiet. "We got a lot of ducks to pick up back there."

I sat up and looked toward the haystack—four miles away. When I staggered up front, Bill turned around to look at me.

"Take your sleeve and wipe your face. Your mother'll think you've been eatin' with the hogs," he advised.

When the horses eventually recovered, Bill started them back toward the haystack. As we came upon the first duck that was lying in the snow, I jumped off the creaking sled and tossed it onto the platform. About 40 ducks lay around the haystack and out in the deep snow for 300 yards. I ran along behind the sled, throwing ducks onto it until every one was picked up.

Then Bill drove the horses beside the haystack and tied their halter ropes to a fence post. When he climbed to the top of the stack, I grabbed my broken-handled pitchfork from the bottom of the hay. By then I had forgotten all about the run away. I put everything I had into pitching hay so Bill would see how fast I could work.

When the hay reached to a nine-foot mound Bill hollered that we had enough. I threw my pitch fork back in the haystack and scrambled up beside him.

"Do ya think ya learned somethin' about drivin' horses?" he asked.

"Yes."

"Okay, drive 'em around the stack while I feed the cows, and drive slow!"

I swelled with pride to know that Bill was willing to put the horses back into my hands. Of course they were too tired to do anything but plod through their job, knowing it would soon be time to go to the barn, but I didn't know that then. We circled the stack while Bill threw hay to the waiting cows. When it was all scattered he shouted,

"Okay, head for the barn!"

I guided the team away from the haystack, straight in line with the barnyard gate.

We were part way through the meadow when I saw my dad standing at the fence. Assuming that he was there to praise me for my driving ability, I slapped the horses with the lines to urge them on faster. I turned around to see Bill stretched out on the sled beside his pile of ducks, taking a cigarette break.

"Dad's waiting for us, Bill," I said proudly.

"Yeah. I see that."

By then we were within shouting distance of the barn, and a bellow shot across the meadow like a cannon.

"What in the hell were you doing with my team?"

I had forgotten about the runaway and I had to think fast.

"Look what we got! A whole bunch of ducks for supper," I said when we were close enough for him to see the birds.

"Forget about those ducks! Just get the horses in here. NOW!"

I pulled the team to a stop as soon as we passed through the gate. My dad stomped over to the sled, flaring at Bill.

"What were you trying to pull out there, giving the team to a kid to let 'em run away for the sake of more damn ducks than we can eat in a year????"

Bill picked himself up slowly, stepping off the sled.

"Aw, the kid had a good time, and the horses aren't hurt," he said casually.

My dad looked from Bill to me to the ducks. It was a long time before he spoke.

"Well, put the horses away and put blankets on so they don't chill. Then you two duck hunters better get busy. You have a lot of birds to clean."

Bill looked at me and winked as he walked away to unhitch the team. I stared after him, feeling as tall as Bill himself. I knew then that I had a partner for adventures yet to come, but I had no idea how soon the next one would take place.

When Bill left the little ranch above us, Fred Baldwin, a dark, slender middle-age man, took over his old job. Fred had worked with horses all his life, and he stopped by the house often to talk ranching and horses with my dad.

It was the morning after the duck-shooting incident that Fred stopped in while we were eating breakfast. He poured himself a cup of coffee as he leaned against the side of the stove to warm up from a bitter cold that had moved in the night before.

"It's too cold to be outside if you don't have to be, but I need meat. Would you have time to hunt with me this morning, Bill?"

"Yup. Soon as I finish eatin'."

Then he looked across the table at me.

"How about it, kid. Are you tough enough to give us a hand?"

I looked pleadingly at my mother.

"If your breakfast is finished when they're ready to leave, you can go."

I bolted down my breakfast while my mother left her half-finished meal to bundle me in my snowsuit and mittens. When the horses pulled the sled out of the barnyard, I was waiting for them at the road gate. Fred drove the team that morning, and Bill leaned against the hay rack with his rifle in his hand. When they stopped to pick me up, Bill pointed to a block of wood in the middle of the sled.

"That's for you. If you sit still and keep your eyes open maybe you'll find the game. Remember, eyes open and mouth shut. Ya hear?"

As we climbed the road behind the house to Ed's Creek, snow began to fall. I squinted through the flakes, never taking my eyes from the hills. We traveled many empty miles through the silent, timbered canyon while I sat on my block of wood like a little eagle, swiveling in 360-degree turns. I don't remember ever wanting anything more than to spot a deer for Bill.

Finally, on a rocky hillside above, I saw the shadowed outline of a feeding mule deer buck. I sprang off my seat and pulled on Bill's arm, pointing to the deer. Bill motioned to Fred to stop the horses. He jumped off the sled and leaned his rifle against a tree. Fred pulled back hard on the lines. I sat motionless on my block of wood while Bill sighted in the buck with his rifle. Then a clear shot cracked through the canyon, and the buck was down.

A steep climb lay ahead to retrieve the deer. Before he started up the hill Bill turned around and said,

"Your mother won't like it if ya get hurt so stay where ya are. Turn the horses around, Fred. I'll be back in a minute."

Fred drove the team up the canyon until he found a turning spot. When we returned, Bill was dragging the deer downhill. Fred gave the lines to me and climbed up the hill to help him.

"Nice buck," Bill said as he and Fred lifted it onto the sled. "I'm glad ya found him for us."

I ran at Bill's side through the rest of my vacation, knowing that I was contributing to the responsibilities of a man's world. The academy experience had destroyed my feeling of self-worth, but my confidence was restored when I assisted my friends and heroes, doing the things that men were supposed to do.

Bill had come into my life when I needed him. I would rely on the assurance he gave me through the difficult times ahead.

5

It was 1944 when the sale of timber on Petty Creek gave my dad the opportunity to expand the ranch borders. It wasn't a dramatic turning point in his little operation because there never were any fences between his land and that immediately surrounding it. Neither were there any restrictions to keep him from using it, so he had always grazed his cattle across the boundary lines.

The surrounding acreage on the south and west sides was owned by Anaconda Copper Mining Company. When the corporation made a decision to log their Petty Creek land, they offered my dad the logged-over acreage in trade for existing timber from his land. The estimate of timber on the ranch didn't meet the value of the Anaconda ground, so an agreement was reached for my dad to pay the balance on terms. With the signing of the contract our ranch grew to 4,000 acres, and Petty Creek took on a new face.

Before any trees were fell, a road to accommodate the logging trucks was built through the canyon. Construction began in the fall while I was at the academy. When I came home on weekends it was fun to see the progress of the project. The new road didn't traverse the creek like the old wagon road. Instead, it followed its crooked path through the canyon. Each time I came home we'd ride a little father through a wide path of fresh-smelling earth. Construction projects didn't happen every day on Petty Creek, and I was fascinated with the might of the noisy yellow caterpillars with big silver blades that had the power to alter the order of the canyon. Limbs, roots, and dirt rolled high in front of the cat as the big blade cut through the canyon floor. Then another machine followed to smooth the soil into an even surface of brown.

The work continued on through spring as the cats crawled their way past the ranch. By early summer the roar of the engines faded in the distance to be replaced by the faint sound of saws and hammers skipping across the hay meadow where, at the mouth of Horse Creek, a mile across the field from the house, a logging camp was under construction.

It was an exciting time that summer on Petty Creek, not only because of the new construction but mainly because I was home for the season with Bill. My summer was so filled with long days at Bill's side that I hardly paid attention to the growth of the logging town at Horse Creek. We had our own logging operation at the end of the grazing meadow. With Bill and Louie on either end of a crosscut saw, timber fell to be used for a machine shed that would be built near the bunkhouse. When all of the trees were down, Jake and Queen were brought in to skid the logs to the building site.

Two miles of new fence was put up above Printers Creek that summer. I brought my pole to fish in the stream while Bill dug post holes. When the posts were in place he strung wire for the fence, and I stayed at his side to hold a can of staples for him. When Sundays came Bill stopped his work and we were off to the mountains to fish.

My mother would pack a big lunch which Bill carried in a knapsack on his back. We'd sling our creels over our shoulders, following game trails as we hiked up the mountains, climbing our way up through pine trees, scrambling through slide rock and alder bushes. Bill never slowed down a step for me and we never stopped until we reached the highest ridge above our trail. Hot summer air hung in breathless stillness over waves of timber that surrounded us. The smell of hot pine needles stung our nostrils as we stretched out on dry grass to eat our lunch while we watched the stream roll by.

Bill wasn't given to poetic interpretations of the beauty of our mountains, but taking his temperament into consideration, he came close to it once during our rest time in the high country. I remember the statement because it was so out of character for him.

"Never leave your mountains, Roger. You'll never find a better way to live."

Then he jumped to his feet, saying, "We're not gon'na get any fish if we sit here talkin' all day."

And with that we were off, fishing downstream all the way to the ranch, finishing in our meadow stream with as many trout as our creels could hold. As soon as we reached the meadow I would run across the field to show the catch to my mother.

By summer's end the canyon road had been graveled all the way to the West Fork. The sawing and hammering sounds from Horse Creek diminished in number as the camp building reached the finishing stages. The only foreign sound on Petty Creek then was near the house, a scraping of rock against metal as pebbles ran down the length of a raised truck bed to fall to the road.

Fall was in the air when the gravel trucks passed the ranch house. The Flatheads would be back for their fall hunt, the school bus from Alberton would drive up the new canyon road to pick me up, the logging operation would soon be in full swing, and I was home to stay.

6

As the gravel trucks worked their way past the house, I noticed a few men traveling up the road now and then. Some of them walked alone with pack sacks on their backs, others rode up in a big car that sped back and forth by the house. It looked as if the logging operation was about to start, so I jumped on Jack one afternoon, taking off on a lope for my first trip to the Horse Creek Camp.

I don't know what I was expecting, but I was amazed when I rode into the little town.

In its symmetry and newness it looked too systematized to grow out of the middle of Petty Creek. Eight rows of bunk houses fanned out at the bottom of a draw on the hay meadow's edge. Across the creek was another group of buildings, similar to the bunk houses, but constructed in an L shape. A rectangular shed, 24 by 200 feet, stood to the side of the complex. Like every other building, it was painted a buff color with green trim.

While I sat on my horse on the edge of camp, I was startled to see a girl who was my own age come out of one of the houses. She was a wiry, small-boned little girl with fine features, blue eyes, and blonde hair. She walked toward me, calling out,

"I'm afraid of horses. Why don't you tie him up and come see me!"

It wasn't a very strong beginning for a lasting friendship, but I was curious to find out why she was in camp.

Her name was Patsy Bailey. She told me that she would be living in camp with her parents while her dad drove a logging truck. He wasn't working then because there weren't enough logs to haul yet. Mr. Harper, the owner of the company, would bring in more timber fallers, and then her dad would go to work. She also asked me, while pointing to a building across the creek, if I wanted to meet Percy and May, the camp cooks who gave her cookies. I followed her as she walked over the wooden foot bridge to the cookhouse.

When loggers move into a logging camp the center of its vitality must be ready and waiting, and so it was at Horse Creek with Percy and May Simmons in charge in the cook house. Only a handful of men had started work that morning, but the cook house hummed with activity.

The T-shaped building had been built in front of the bunkhouses. The stem of the T housed the kitchen where huge kettles hissed and steamed on a wood cook stove that measured eight feet long. A butcher block stood in the middle of the room for working space, and shelves were nailed to the walls for counter tops. Under the counters, large wooden storage bins rotated outward for easy accessibility. A doorway in back of the kitchen led into the dining room which was the cross part of the T. Paned windows all around the oblong room allowed a view of the timber, mountains, and meadows around the camp. Homemade wooden tables and benches, enough to seat eighty men, were lined up in rows of shiny white. The entire interior of the cook house glistened with white paint.

True to Patsy's word, Percy and May were very nice people. They were both in their early fifties, and they were slim and energetic. They owned a little farm in the Bitterroot Valley which they leased out while they worked for Harpers. They were at the logging camp to supplement their income for retirement. On that first day they gave me a tour all around the cook house, including a peek inside their big walk-in cooler whose generator was so loud that I could hear it hum at night clear across the meadow. The tour was concluded with the offer of a cookie. I was to find out that a cookie from Percy and May was not just a treat; it was more like a Thanksgiving feast.

Some of the rotating bins under the counters contained flour and sugar, but the rest were filled with an unbelievable array of logger-size cookies. One bin was filled with peanut butter cookies the size of saucers, from another came mounds of chocolate chips and nuts. Some bins glittered with big circles that were sprinkled with colored sugar, and round nuggets of shiny chocolate filled another. It was the cookies, I believe, that were the secret of Percy and May's success in earning our respect through the years. We knew they were busy with their work, and if we didn't take advantage of their hospitality, a treat would be waiting when they had time to visit with us.

A few men walked down from the draw behind camp while Patsy and I ate our cookies. I could tell that they were tired by the way they shuffled down the hill with saws on their shoulders. When Bill spent a day falling timber he always said that he needed a little shut eye, and he went to the bunk house early, and Louie was so irritable that I stayed as far from him as I could. So when I saw that the loggers' work day had ended, it was time for me to go home.

After turning Jack into the grazing meadow at the house, I ran into the kitchen to tell my mother about the logging camp. Bill was stretched out in a chair rather than in his usual spot on the wood box, and he wore suspenders which he had never done before. Something out of the ordinary was going on, and I needed to know what it was.

"Why are you wearing suspenders, Bill?" I asked.

"I need 'em when I work."

"What are you doing?"

"Falling timber."

"For the machine shed?"

"No. For Harper."

I couldn't believe it. My partner was part of the operation.

"Can I go with you?" I asked breathlessly.

"Nope. You have to go to school"

"Will you be working when I'm not in school?"

"Sometimes."

"Can I go then?"

"Nope. There's too many falling trees. No kids allowed."

By the end of the conversation I knew that it was only a matter of time before I would be watching trees fall on the mountain in back of Harpers camp.

It was the Saturday after my first week in school that I decided to visit the logging site. I told my mother that I was going to play with Patsy, then I saddled Jack and left. When I reached Printers Creek, I crossed the flat, turning up the mountain in the direction of the wood cutters' sounds. When I was almost near enough to be seen, I tied Jack to a tree, proceeding on foot.

Two men were working with a saw that was imbedded in a massive pine tree. While gripping the wooden handle on either end of the blade, they rocked back and forth with a rhythm and speed that made the saw sing as it bit deep into the trunk. I had watched my dad, Louie, and Bill work crosscut saws, but I had never seen such speed and synchronization. Suddenly the saws stopped and the men stepped back. The tree slowly gave up its creaking hold on the stump and fell to the ground with a high, reverberating bounce.

The men wiped sweat from their faces with their shirt sleeves before they picked up their axes and walked to the fallen tree. Pine limbs rolled off the trunk while wood chips flew in a continual stream. As I watched them work I thought that it must have been like that in Grandpa Hebert's logging camp. When he had told me about the years that he worked in the woods, I was amazed at his working conditions. Now I gained an even greater respect for his abilities.

Grandpa Hebert had migrated from French Quebec in Maine when he was a young man. It was there that he started logging with the rugged pioneer breed that cut their way through the forest with an axe and little else. Like so many pockets of immigrants in our country, he and my grandma homesteaded on a few acres, raised a cow or two, some chickens and pigs, and planted a few acres of grain. To supplement their meager incomes, the homesteaders worked in winter at whatever industry was available. In their part of Maine the industry was logging.

Winter was logging time then because it was expedient to skid logs through the snow. Grandpa left his family, walking to the logging camp that was 20 miles from home. There was only one bunkhouse in camp for the 50 or so men on the crew, a long building with several wood stoves in it. Straw covered the floor for a mattress with blankets laid on top. The men stretched out in one long row to sleep while their hanging, wet work clothes steamed from the stove heat. Grandpa never mentioned the fact, but I have been in enough camps to know that unless someone got up at night to stoke the fires in those below-zero Maine winters, the men woke up to freezing temperatures, and their clothes were stiff with cold.

Loggers have always been fed well, but in Grandpa's day the cook house menu was limited to large quantities of staples such as meat, beans, and bread. Since there were no provisions for getting beef into camp, the company paid a team of men to hunt moose because they were plentiful and easy to hunt. In that area wild peas grew on thick vines that climbed into trees. The peas ripened in the fall, then dried on the vine, and the moose stood in deep snow to eat all the peas from one tree before moving on to the next. As a result they grew so fat and lazy they could be easily overtaken.

The hunters wore snow shoes which allowed them to run faster over the snow than the moose. When they overtook the animals, they hit them in the head, dressed and skinned them, boned the meat, and divided it among themselves to carry it back to camp in packsacks. All winter long they fell timber in deep snow, piling the logs at the edge of a river with teams of horses and cross hauls. When spring thaw came, the winter log decks were rolled in the river that raged with high water. The men drove the logs down river to the saw mill, steering them toward home with long pike poles. Most of them wore caulk boots as they balanced their way downstream. Grandpa, however, was adept at working with his hands, and he spent his spare time in camp making moccasins. He took pride in the fact that he wore them on the log drives, hanging onto the slimy bark with his feet.

When the drive ended at the sawmill, the men picked up their winter paycheck, and with their packsacks on their backs they started back for their little farms. The cycle continued as they scratched out a living until the first snowfall of the next season drove them back to camp.

Grandpa and Grandma heard of greener pastures in the west when they crossed the continent to a new home, and I assume that the same attitude lured the two men in Montana that were falling timber on Horse Creek. They were stocky and blonde, two of scores of men of Nordic extraction that logged through the years on Petty Creek. Some of them were immigrants, some of them were second generation Swedes, Norwegians and Finlanders who had either lived by logging in the old country or learned the trade from their fathers. For most of them, the dream of greener pastures would never be realized. They would stay in camp for weeks accumulating paychecks. Then I would see them walking down the canyon road on their way to Alberton, alone or in pairs. They wouldn't be seen again for a week or two until they trudged back up the road, broke, disheveled, and red-eyed. I would hear them talk of their escapades.

"Ya, vell I sure did tie vun on dat time. I'll be vorkin' for a long time if dis keep up."

By winter, Harper Logging Company was operating at full capacity with a working crew of 80 men. An L-shaped building housed a combination office and commissary in the camp complex, and a bunkhouse was used for a saw shop. A husky man with dark hair and glasses sat on a high wooden stool at a work bench in the shop, sharpening saws all day long. Racks of saws hung from the ceiling, and shelves of files, sets, and gages lined the walls.

Logging trucks filled the big shed during non-working hours, and in another large shop the cats, trucks, and heavy-equipment motors waited to be repaired. My friend Keith, short, thin, and wearing glasses, was the only mechanic for the entire operation. All day long he darted through the big equipment like a cat after a mouse. Besides his responsibility for all the shop work, he drove to the woods to repair loading jammers and equipment that couldn't be brought out. Keith talked as fast as he worked, and he was very friendly, but I spent little time at the machine shop because then, as now, I detested anything mechanical.

Usually when I felt like catching up on logging news I visited Vic McKinnon in the office. Vic ran the commissary, served as the company bookkeeper, and made a trip to Alberton for the mail twice each week. Husky, red-headed, and 30-years-old, he was a pleasant, accommodating person, and attentive to his work. I enjoyed browsing through Vic's commissary shelves. Black work pants and blue denim shirts were neatly piled beside rows of black wool underwear, caulk boots, and suspenders, all new smelling and clean. To supply the loggers with the remainder of their needs, a counter in the middle of the room contained smoking tobacco, chewing tobacco, and cigarettes. Vic was usually busy at his desk in the other parts of the building. A counter in front of the office separated him from the public, but it was taller than I so he always invited me in for a chat.

A pleasant surprise connected with Harpers awaited me one morning when the school bus stopped at Horse Creek to pick up Patsy. Two red-haired, freckle-faced boys climbed the steps behind her, two peas in a pod who were close in age to each other and to me. Their names were Charlie and Johnny Nichols. Their dad made his living as a pack sack logger, traveling from camp to camp to work as a cat skinner. Charlie owned a fast-traveling Welch pony, and Johnny used an accommodating donkey for transportation. An immediate friendship was formed. We were equipped to explore Petty Creek together.

By then the Flatheads had returned and settled into their camps, so I rode to Ed's Creek to ask John if I could bring Charlie and Johnny to meet him. When I left home I wasn't thinking so much of participating again in Indian life. I was more excited about showing their camp to my new friends. But when I rode across the ridge into the quiet of Ed's Creek country, the excitement I had felt around the operation of saws and dump trucks slowly fell behind. Even at the young age of seven, I experienced the calming peace that pervades the deep wilderness as I sat on top the ridge to watch the Indians move slowly through their tasks. They had only been there for a day or two, and several squaws were busy setting up smoke racks. Suddenly the logging camp seemed far, far away.

As I watched, John came out of his teepee. I kicked Jack into a gallop down the hill. John stood still with a rifle in his hand, watching me. When I reached him I pulled the horse up short, and vaulted to the ground.

"Hullo, Roger. I see you still have Jack," John said.

"Yes. Did you see the logging camp?"

"Yuh."

"I have some friends that live there. Can I bring them here so they can have smoked meat?"

"We don't have meat. You bring 'em anyway. We maybe not have meat for a long time."

"Why?"

"Too many roads now. Elk go far away. They put in more roads, too. Then people come in cars to hunt."

"Can my friends and I hunt with you?"

"That's too many people. We scare game away."

"Do you want to come to the logging camp? Percy and May will give you cookies."

"I stay here. I get ready to hunt now. You bring friends to camp."

I realized as I rode back up the hill that things weren't the same, but I was very young, and my thoughts focused on bringing Charlie and Johnny to John's camp. The three of us visited the Adam's camp several times, but we were usually more interested in what the surrounding country offered us than in the Indians.

Sugar joined us for rides through Ed's Creek, and we fished together near camp. I led Charlie and Johnny on horseback to my favorite fishing holes as we rode through the countryside and up the new logging roads. We romped through the timber from morning until night. The end of play time found us at the cook house for another cookie from Percy and May.

I enjoyed showing my country to our visitors, and I felt important when I excused myself from play to say that Bill needed my help on his days off. I had grown adept at moving cattle through the timber, so for Charlie and Johnny's sake, the animals were sent on several unnecessary trips to another range. I always had to sneak out and return them before my dad realized they were missing.

For five years the ranch teemed with the activity of the loggers and their equipment. When the timber was harvested, 50 miles of logging roads webbed through every creek drainage on Petty Creek. To a casual observer our country hadn't changed. A few dirt roads that led into the timber were hardly a drastic interference in the wilderness setting of our home, and the same mountains sheltered our log house and barn. Only choice trees had been cut for lumber so their absence was barely noticeable through still-standing timber. The same stillness permeated the mountains, and the same pungent smell of pine refreshed the clean air. But the roads were there, and friends, acquaintances, and outdoorsmen found a hospitable atmosphere awaiting them in the now accessible quietude of our country.

"I don't like the idea of all the hunters we're going to have up here when all these roads get put in," my dad said when the logging first started, "but I won't be putting up any no trespassing signs on my land."

My dad's philosophy, noble as it was, had taken away from that small band of Flatheads a last vestige of their ancient traditions.

My mother felt the effects of accessibility, too. Acquaintances became friends as visitors streamed to the house almost on a daily basis. It was not uncommon to have ten to fifteen people at the supper table several times a week. My dad enjoyed the company of his new visitors. Most men that stopped by would spend time helping him, enjoying the satisfaction from physical exertion in the outdoors. The environment of freedom from complexity was extended for them at meal time with the wholesome simplicity of my mother's cooking.

Convivial evenings at the supper table belied the growing tension in our family. Annual land payments had to be met now. The herd was increasing, and land had to be cleared and planted for hay, which required the purchase of more equipment. Loans were taken out while my dad struggled to meet his obligations, feeling an ever increasing burden in his limited physical capacity. His patience grew short with me. As the process of growing up increased my work load, I couldn't please him no matter how hard I tried.

I realized that my playmates would soon be leaving to go back to a world that I knew nothing about. My school days at the academy had served as a catalyst for an increasing disinterest in school. A fear of the classroom remained when I transferred to Alberton. I wanted to learn, but I fell behind so I retreated into a survival mode. If I did nothing, at least it wouldn't be wrong.

My babyhood days were ending while the ways of the world encroached through the canyon's gravel road to cast a subtle but lingering shadow over the serenity of Petty Creek.

7

Something's wrong with the cows," my dad said when he slumped into his chair at the kitchen table. "They're losing too many calves. It's more than just coincidence. I'm going to Alberton to call Doc Stall."

It was November of my tenth year, and I was home from school on a weekend. Bill had left the ranch to take a mining job in Idaho, and our new hired man, Harry Felix, and my dad had just come in from feeding cattle. It was the third time that they had found remains of aborted calves in the meadow. Cows were losing their calves months before they were due.

My dad made his trip to Alberton to use the pay phone, and Doc Stall came out the next day. Doc's parents had owned a ranch just a few miles from my dad's boyhood ranch in Grass Valley, and the families had known each other from the time Doc was an infant. He had been our vet from the beginning of his practice, ten years before.

When Doc arrived the next day, his usual cheery smile was replaced by a somber look.

"I sure hope it isn't what I think it is, Mose," he said when he sat down for a cup of coffee.

"You think it's bangs, don't you."

"I'm afraid so. I guess you know it's sweeping the country."

"Yup. Well, let's go out and see. I have one of the cows in the corral."

When we reached the corral the less-than-gentle range cow ran to the other side to jump the fence. My dad told Harry to stand at the pole gate by the barn. When I scared the cow into the corner of the barn, Harry would swing back the gate against the barn wall, trapping the cow. When we maneuvered the cow into position, Doc Stall took a syringe from his black bag. He quickly plunged the needle into her neck, extracting a vial of blood. He took a numbered tag from his bag, and clamped it on the cow's ear.

"We'll know by Monday afternoon if number four, here, is infected," he said as he wrote the number on a strip of adhesive, attaching it to the vial. "If you can go to Alberton then, call me. If it's positive we'll make an appointment to test the rest of the herd."

Bangs, or brucellosis, was new to our country at that time. I'm not clear about its history in western Montana, but it was new enough then so that cattle weren't vaccinated for it. The virus doesn't contaminate the meat, but it causes cows to abort their calves and it contaminates the milk for human consumption by producing undulant fever. There is no cure for the disease; it can only be prevented by vaccination. Our ranch was so far from any other my dad apparently didn't think it was necessary to vaccinate. Once the disease is contracted, all infected animals must be sold for slaughter.

On Monday afternoon my dad came back from his phone call to Doc Stall with the bad news.

"The cows haven't been close enough to any other cattle to pick up the bug," he said. "It had to come from those bulls I bought at the sale. I guess they didn't test 'em. Doc'll be out on Saturday to test the rest."

On Saturday morning, my dad, Harry, and I saddled our horses right after daylight and separated at the barn gate to ride to the far corners of the meadow. Even with the gloom that had settled over our household, I looked forward to the morning because it was always fun to ride for cattle with Harry. He was a full-blood Flathead, but much different in temperament than the other Indians I knew. Ranching absorbed his interest more than hunting.

Harry was about 25 years old then, tall, lean, and craggy boned with a carefree zest for life. He never talked about his parents, and he would stay with an elderly couple when he went home to the reservation. He mostly performed menial ranch chores, and he was always a willing worker, but when he got on a horse he was in his element. He lived the role of the wild-west cowboy, whooping and hollering, waving his hat in the air, pushing the cows as hard as if we had a time limit on a long drive.

Within an hour or so after daylight, our 150 cows were in the corral. Doc Stall arrived with a metal squeeze chute on a trailer that he pulled with his pickup. The cows were driven in separately to be tested and tagged.

Brucellosis test results are sent through the mail from the state. Two weeks after the testing my dad returned from the post office with the envelope in his hand.

"Positive—every one but the two milk cows. They're the only ones that weren't bred by those bulls," he said.

He poured a cup of coffee and sat down at the table. My mother and I both knew when silence was the best policy in dealing with my dad so we left him alone to think through his problem. It was a few days later that he told us his decision.

"The state allows what they call a reasonable length of time to get rid of the cattle," he said. "Practically every cow in the state's getting sold so the market will be flooded. If we sell now it won't be worth the trip to Missoula. So! I've decided to lease a sugar beet field in the Bitterroot next fall. We'll take what calves we get next spring and sell 'em in the fall. I won't put up any hay this year. The cows can graze in the meadow for the summer. We'll sell in the fall after they've put on weight from the beet tops. By then the price should be up a little, too.

Sugar beets were a big industry in the Bitterroot Valley. A sugar refining plant had been built in Missoula so marketing costs were minimal. The beets were shipped to the refining plant, but the tops were left in the fields. Because the plants had such high carbohydrate content they made an excellent weight-gaining feed for cattle. Sugar beet farmers leased their fields by the acre to cattle ranchers when the harvest was over.

One third of our cows produced calves that spring. They were weaned in late September and sold. During the first week in October the cows were shipped to a 200-acre beet field that my dad had reserved with a cash payment. He estimated that the feed would last for two months.

The cows had been in the Bitterroot for one week when winter hit—hard. Sunny autumn skies turned gray without warning. Temperatures plunged to below freezing, and within a week snow was piled across the entire state. The cows nosed through the snow to reach the beet tops for a few days until the temperature plummeted to an intolerable 40 degrees below zero where it remained for two months. The country constricted into a frozen knot.

Assuming that the cold snap would soon break, my dad bought hay to last for a while from a rancher whose land was near the beet field. To feed the cows he started from home each morning by hitching Jake and Queen to the pickup to get it started. Our water pipes froze, so for water we hitched the team to a stone boat, driving it to Ed's Creek where we chopped ice to melt at home for household use. It was my job also after school every day to drive a few cows that we still had at home to the West Fork where they drank from a warm spring. It took all my strength to pitch frozen hay from the barn when we returned.

By the middle of November, when there was no hay to be found in the Bitterroot, the cattle were shipped from their grim winter range to Grandpa's ranch at Nine Mile. We bought hay from him for the rest of the winter. In spring we would bring the cows home to graze in the ranch meadow. We hoped that by supplementing their feed with protein pellets their weight would be high enough to salvage something from our dwindling cash crop.

My dad spent much of his time at Nine Mile that winter to help with feeding and to keep account of the health of his animals. Veterinarian bills accumulated at ten times their normal rate as weakened cows succumbed to the physical strain of aborting their calves for the second straight year. However, by spring only a dozen cows had died, and twenty five healthy calves romped through the Nine Mile pastures. It was time then to bring the herd home.

Bringing the animals from Nine Mile necessitated traveling for seven miles on the state highway. It was far from a congested roadway, but we couldn't tie up traffic while cows and riders scrambled back and forth across the road and through the countryside. So to eliminate the problem Harry conceived the idea of carrying the calves home in the hay wagon. The cows would then follow along behind. He gathered several twelve-inch boards and two-by-fours from a stock pile in the machine shed to enclose the wagon sides with a four-foot-high railing.

We would need saddle horses to drive the cows home, so the next morning when he hitched Jake and Queen to the wagon we tied two saddle horses to the back of it, and we left for Nine Mile.

Because of the unusually heavy winter snow pack, roaring white water ripped through the length of the canyon, spilling at least 50 feet over the banks. We were thankful for the gravel road as we traveled along. Even trusty Jake and Queen would have balked at pulling a wagon through the swirling waters. At times the water was almost obscured by the floating beds of limbs and uprooted trees.

When we reached the end of the canyon, and the team clopped across the planks of the Clark Fork Bridge, I wondered if the old wooden structure would hold if the water rose over its top. Huge uprooted fir trees and tamaracks with spiny limbs barely cleared the bridge when they cracked and rolled down the wide span of river. I never felt secure on the rickety bridge. It was even more formidable that day.

We made it safely across, however, and the creaking wagon rolled over a little hill to take us onto the highway that twisted through stands of jack pine for six miles. We turned north then through the Nine Mile Valley until we reached Grandpa's house.

After a supper served by Aunt Ruby, Harry and I saddled the horses to drive our cows and calves into the corrals. Then we settled around the living room fireplace for a history lesson in western Montana Indian lore as taught by Grandpa.

Evenings with Harry were always pleasant times for Grandpa. Harry spoke French, allowing Grandpa to spin his yarns in his native language as he talked about Harry's ancestors that he had known when he settled among them sixty years before. He held Harry in rapt attention for long evening story sessions whenever we visited Nine Mile.

The next morning my mom and dad drove up in the pickup. Grandpa told my dad that he would help him get the cows back to the ranch if he needed him. We didn't really need another hand, but Grandpa was eight-five-years old then, and an easy drive like this one would be enjoyable for him. So my mother stayed to visit with Aunt Ruby for a while before taking the pickup home, and Dad, Grandpa, and I saddled our horses while Harry harnessed the team. He hitched them to the wagon, and then he drove it to the corral gate.

One by one we roped the young calves. With each of us on an end we easily lifted them onto the wagon. Harry took his place at the lines as his young cargo bleated for their mothers while the mothers bawled back from the corral. When we mounted our horses the wagon started rolling, and I reached down to open the corral gate. The mother cows stampeded from the pen until they reached the wagon and settled into a nervous walk behind it. The rest of the herd trailed calmly behind. Grandpa and I flanked the cows while my dad trailed through an uneventful four-hour trip through Nine Mile Valley and down the highway.

We were within a mile of the Clark Fork Bridge when my dad suddenly loped past the herd, then slowed into a walk at Harry's side. In a few minutes he rode back to Grandpa and me.

"The bridge has a three-ton limit so we'll only take 15 head over at a time," he said. "Harry will go over with the wagon. You hold the herd back, Dad. When Harry's on the other side, let 15 head go, and hold the rest 'til that bunch gets across. Roger, you go with Harry and watch for trains. You can see far enough down the tracks to get back in time to warn us if a train is coming. If any cows are on the bridge they might not have time to get over the tracks before it gets here so turn 'em back."

When we reached the bridge, Jake and Queen pulled the wagon over the pliant, rumbling planks. I followed along until I was stationed on the other side of the tracks. Then I hollered to send them over.

The first bunch of cows, composed mainly of mothers of the calves, ran in a lope across the bridge, bawling for their young. When they reached the end, another bunch thundered over, including the last of the mother cows. By this time the remaining cows were excited by the running and bawling, and they crossed the bridge in a frenzy. On they came and on they ran to catch up with the herd at the wagon. Then, when approximately 50 cows were left, I heard above the roar of the wild river, a whooping and hollering and a wild beating of hooves. I slapped my horse with the lines, tearing across the tracks.

What I saw at the bridge I re-live now in terror. Grandpa was a third of the way onto the bridge, wildly slapping his horse from side to side with the lines while the terrified horse, with his eyes ablaze, struggled to run above the treacherous water. Fifty cows surrounded them, pushing and crowding each other into the bridge spans. Iron cables clashed in an ominous rattle as floor planks undulated over the mid-river pier. The whole bridge swayed slowly from side to side.

All of this I absorbed in an instant before I kicked my horse into a flying leap over a six-foot bank at the end of the bridge. From there I could hear nothing but the river's roar as I saw the wild eyes of animals and rider surge on. In an almost solid mass of red the herd bounded forward onto the road with Grandpa in the middle of them, ashen-faced and trembling, but safe.

When the bridge was still again, my dad crossed it to meet us. We rode together to the meadow where Harry was stationed. By then the herd was grazing through the tall grass. When Harry started the wagon rolling they moved quietly up the canyon road.

That summer the cows did well. They grazed in the hay meadow, crowding by the fence each evening as they waited for the pickup to turn into the meadow with their pellets. When we fed the supplement from the back of the pickup they lumbered behind the truck like lethargic marchers in a field parade. As I dropped the feed from burlap sacks into small piles, the cow nearest the truck dropped her head to eat while the rest moved on behind us. When the sacks were empty, a long line of contented red cows chewed impassively in the calm of a gathering dusk.

My dad sat in the pickup by himself for a long time every evening, surveying his herd. He was fond of every one of his cows, and he always had a story or two to tell about those that he considered his pets. But that summer he spoke little about them.

The long, hard winter had ended, and the herd that it had taken ten years to build would soon be gone.

When the cattle trucks arrived the next fall to take the cows to the sale yard, my dad helped the drivers load them. As the last animal walked up the chute, he stood back with his sweat-stained hat in his hand. The driver closed the tailgate and climbed in his truck. He waved from the window as the truck moved slowly down the road. My dad's stump raised in response. He wiped his forehead with his shirt sleeve, put his hat back on, and turned toward the house.

"All we can do now is wait and see how much money they bring," he said as we walked through the grazing meadow. "Then we'll have to fill those mountains with something, won't we."

8

"Well, Roger, what do you think of herding a band of sheep around the ranch?" my cousin, Wally Longpre, asked when he and my dad reached agreement on their partnership in a sheep business.

I was an adolescent at the time, the period of life when most ideas that come from adults are either unreasonable or uninteresting. But the idea of herding sheep through the mountains caught my attention. My only association with the animals had been with three lost ewes that wandered onto the ranch two years before. We kept them as pets, and I enjoyed their delicate, mild-mannered company. We hadn't bred them so I thought that it might be fun to have a crop of lambs romping through the meadows the next spring.

The sheep undertaking also carried with it a hopeful side effect, that of encouraging my dad out of a lethargy that crept into his life after he lost his cows. With only a minimal calf crop to see us through for the last two seasons, coupled with the burden of wintering the cows in the Bitterroot, he was forced to take out more loans to meet his obligations. The income from the diseased cows that he had sold in the fall barely covered the loan payments so there was little capital left for investment in a future on our 4,000 acres. It had been a somber year on Petty Creek, living in the shadow of my dad's morose outlook on life, but he seemed to regain a new zest for living when he started discussing our country's intrinsic value for pasturing sheep.

Our serviceberry, gooseberry, alder, and willow brush would provide perfect browse for sheep. Grass grew abundantly through much of the terrain, and the mountains provided natural shelter from the elements. The only thing that my dad lacked to pursue the venture was capital. So for that he would need a partner. Given the nature and location of the business, that could have been a problem had Wally not stopped by the ranch at just the right time.

Wally was only nineteen years old then, and he was about to be married. The solitude of Petty Creek might have been oppressive to some young men who had been raised in town, as Wally had, but he had the ability to fit comfortably into any situation. His large, expressive brown eyes mirrored a quiet joy that he found in simply being alive. He was tall and dark with a loose-jointed bearing that made him bounce happily through the day. At the same time, he carried a serious concern for his financial future. He had always enjoyed Petty Creek, and working with animals was a pleasure to him, so he accepted my dad's offer.

They started the venture with a band of only 500 sheep. To cut costs further, they bought older ewes that would bear only one or two more lambs in their natural life span. It was the fall of my twelfth year when the sheep were shipped by train to the station at our canyon crossing. From there we would walk them to the ranch.

The unloading of our sheep was to be the train's last stop at that station. The little depot had been built in the early part of the century to accommodate a saw mill and the small town of Lothrop that grew around it. As timber supplies dwindled, the mill eventually closed down, so people either left their homes or moved them on barges to the other side of the river into Alberton. When I was born, all that remained of Lothrop was a grain depot and fragments of a saw mill.

For the past several years the station had been rarely used, and its loading pens had been neglected. With boards and nails in hand we arrived at the station early to tack back together fallen segments of the pens. We stopped our work when they were just sound enough to hold the sheep until they were all unloaded.

The old steam locomotive descended upon us with a roar before chugging to a hissing crawl past the station. The engineer braked to a jolting stop when the three-tiered cattle car reached the holding pens. Steam puffed in clouds from the engine boilers, and 500 bleating animals scrambled to regain their feet. We lifted a heavy wooden loading ramp to a height that was even with the first tier, watching frightened little heads peek through wooden slats. Wally walked up the ramp to raise a sliding door, but none of the sheep ventured out. When he walked inside they scrambled out of his way, pressing into the sides of the car. He took hold of a few to guide them through the door. Natural herders that they are, the rest followed one by one, stepping warily onto the ramp. When they had all descended carefully into the enclosure, he opened the door of the second tier and then the third until the pens were filled with 500 milling, mixed-breed sheep, twenty rams among them. The whistle engine blew and the train lurched forward down the tracks. We waited until its deafening jangle diminished into a murmuring rumble before we opened the gates.

With quick, little steps the sheep scurried out of the pen. To start them moving in the right direction, my dad stayed behind with the pickup while Wally and I flanked them. When we crossed the tracks onto the gravel road they settled into a slow, contented walk, looking from the back like a mass of popcorn balls that bobbed up and down between the canyon walls. Crisp leaves crunched under their feet all the way up the road. At the ranch they were herded into the barn corrals for hay and grain before we turned them into the meadows to bed down for the night.

Through the fall and early winter, Wally and my dad built a 300-foot-long loafing shed adjacent to the barn with plank feeders inside that ran the length of the corrals. The sheep were fed hay in the meadows in the morning. In the evening they were brought into the shed to eat grain before bedding down on straw and wood shavings. In the middle of the corals we built a lambing shed, 24 by 40 feet, with a wood stove in its center and portable pens lining the walls. We were ready then for the new crop of lambs that would begin to arrive in February.

I was in school for most of lambing season, but at night I took my turn as sheep tender. In the loafing shed we watched the ewes around the clock, making hourly rounds with a lantern. If it was too cold for a lamb to dry properly, he and his mother were placed in a pen close to the fire in the lambing shed. If a mother died, the lamb was brought into the shed and grafted onto another ewe. If the lamb was too weak after birth to suck, it and the ewe were put in a pen where we held the lamb close to its mother's teats to encourage it to swallow that important first milk. It was not without protest from the mothers that the newborns were carried into the shed. They stomped their feet while we worked with the lambs, then they followed along to the shed, butting us from behind.

As soon as the lambs were born we dipped their navels in an iodine solution to prevent infection. We branded both the lamb and its mother by dipping metal numbers into paint, then pressing them into the fleece on the animal's side. The paint lasted until shearing time which was as long as it was necessary to know which lambs belonged to which ewes. The purpose of the branding was to reunite lost pairs, and to know which mothers had rejected their lambs.

For me it was a busy, exhilarating time on the ranch, assisting in the births of the kinky-haired offspring of our gentle, dependant flock. By the first of April, when the birth process was complete, 800 lively lambs frolicked through the meadow under a sunny spring sky, so clean and white that they looked as if they had been made from the melting snow beneath their tiny feet.

"Not bad for a bunch of beginners, is it," Wally said one evening when the ewes lined up at the feeders for their grain while the lambs capered around them. It was a good beginning for a new start in the ranch business, and we looked hopefully to a bright future with our sheep.

Except for feeding time, the sheep sustained themselves without our assistance through the rest of the month of April. Then it was time to shear.

Uncles Dan and Bill arrived to help on the first weekend in May along with two Basque shearers, a man of 45 and his twenty-year-old son, both of whom looked just as you would expect—dark, husky, weathered, brimming with the vigorous bloom of an uncomplicated, outdoor life. They were French Basques who had been in this country for only a few years. They traveled from ranch to ranch at shearing time, carrying with them a generator for their electric clippers.

To meet railroad shipping requirements, four-hundred pounds of wool had to be packed into burlap bags that were ten-feet-long and two-feet-wide. That was the unpleasant aspect of shearing, and since I was the youngest member of the shearing team, I got the job.

As the bag was being filled it needed to stand in an upright position so we built a high platform near the lambing shed. Before the bag was raised, a hoop with an attached chain was fitted to the open end. The chain was then fastened to a pulley on the platform. When the chain was pulled by someone that stood on the platform, the bag unfolded until it stood straight up with the bottom of it resting on the ground. The wool from three sheep would be rolled into a 40-pound bundle that was dropped into the bag. It would have to be pressed hard by stomping on it to make room for the ten bundles that were needed for each bag to meet shipping requirements.

While the shearers set up their clipping apparatus in the lambing shed, we herded the sheep from the meadows into the corral. Wally and Uncle Bill were in charge of moving the sheep in and out of the shed. When the first ewes were ushered in, the shearers each grabbed one, flinging it to the ground in a sitting position with the sheep's back leaning into the men's legs. In a stooping position they held the sheep with one hand while the buzzing clippers in their other hand peeled off strips of thick wool that crumpled to the ground. With his holding hand the shearer rotated the sheep so that the clippers continued to work until the animal was shorn. The wool was tossed aside as the bleating, disrobed ewe trotted out the door. Another ready animal was caught and the process was repeated.

I watched the shearing for only a few minutes that first morning before the young Basque rolled the wool into a bundle and tossed it onto the platform outside.

"We're ready for you now!" Uncle Dan called.

I left the shed to see Uncle Dan standing on the platform. On the ground beneath him lay the fleece bag.

"Okay, Roger. Crawl inside the bag. Holler when you're ready at the bottom and I'll raise it up," he said.

I crawled on my hands and knees through the hoop to the bottom of the bag, pushing folds of burlap out of my path. I could hardly breathe through the tightly-woven fabric. When I reached the bottom I called to Uncle Dan, and the sack walls rose slowly around me. When it straightened to its full ten feet I was trapped in a dark, airless turret as if I had fallen to the bottom of a well.

"Stand to one side and I'll try to throw this bundle so it doesn't hit you on the head," Uncle Dan said as he looked down into the bag, blocking the narrow shaft of light that beamed from the top. "When it hits the ground, start jumping on it. You'll have to pack it hard if we're going to get 400 pounds in there. Keep jumping 'til I send the next one down."

I pressed myself into one side of the bag while the bundle dropped directly on my head before it bounced off, stopping when it was blocked by my mid-section. I raised my arms, sucked in my breath, and felt it fall to the ground. Then I started jumping. I had to hold my arms to my sides in the narrow cylinder while I bounced like a ball. Bits of oily wool stuck to me, dust and debris from the fleece filled my nostrils, and sheep ticks crawled up my legs, biting like stinging bees. In the ten minutes that it took to shear the next three sheep I rested periodically, mainly to clear the dust from the air. But most of the time I jumped until Uncle Dan hollered that the next bundle was coming.

Forty five minutes or so later the bag was half full. When I was on the up side of a jump my nose stuck out above the hoop, and I was able to breathe fresh air through the wool that was plastered to my face and nose. In another hour the wool reached the top of the bag, and I crawled out onto the platform, covered with fleece and welts from tick bites. Below me in the corral, baby lambs frisked around their shorn mothers. No longer were they the appealing new life that I had helped to bring into the world. I saw them only as bundles of wool that would have to be tramped into wool bags the following year. By the end of shearing I was sorry that we had ever brought them to the ranch.

When school was out in early June the sheep were turned into the hills. With the help of the dogs, we herded the flock into the West Fork. Buttons, a blue and white Australian Shepherd that belonged to Wally, along with Brownie, an English Shepherd-Collie cross who was loaned to us by my cousin, and Bud, a year-old English Shepherd that we raised from a pup, were ready for action when the sheep were let out of the corral. Stodgy, old ewes fell easily into formation as excited dogs circled around them. Capering lambs scurried to their mother's sides as a flock of 1,300 sheep pattered steadily down the road. Wally would stay with the sheep at night and I during the day. The first day, though, we remained together to learn their habits. It didn't take long to establish a routine with them. Sheep are confirmed creatures of habit.

Each morning just before daylight the flock sprang up together as if by an alarm clock. They were ready to eat so they were herded to meadows where they grazed for the morning. By 10:00 a.m. they were thirsty, and they were driven to the nearest stream. When they drank their fill, they lay down to chew their cuds until 3:00 p.m. It was time then to graze again until dark, then they were brought to camp for their feed of salt before bedding down for the night.

Memories of the wool bag faded as I rode into the West Fork each morning at daylight to tend the flock. Wally gave the dogs the responsibility of keeping the sheep together until I arrived. They fidgeted and nervously bleated while the dogs wheeled around them. Wally took his portable bedroom back to the ranch, a canvas-covered wooden stock rack that he built on his pickup, and I signaled to the dogs to move the sheep.

Up the brushy draws they fled like an ascending cloud while I rode along beside them on the rim. At the top I turned them around to graze their way down. Individual sheep scampered to their favorite bushes, little bunches scattered to the top to find meadow grass and sunflowers. The dogs dashed after them, circled, and turned them back down while excited barking mingled with frantic blats. The draw was filled then with the crunching sound of 1,300 mouths that chewed through the bushes like fast-driven lawn mowers.

In the beginning I watched the simple creatures for hours, learning to recognize individuals, seeing twin lambs graze side by side. One couldn't nurse without the other jumping to his own side of the mother. I enjoyed watching them strut when they walked like little soldiers. A thick cape of wool on their chests led them forward, their necks stretched and bobbed in rhythm with their tiny determined steps. Their continual bleating was a gentle, harmonious sound. Their long afternoon rest gave me time to myself.

While the sheep lay down to chew their cuds, I hunted with my .22 rifle through the draws where grouse came down to water. When I had enough for a meal I skinned the birds at the creek, put them in a flour sack, tied a knot on the open end, and anchored them under the frigid water for the day. At night when I brought them home, the meat was cool, firm, and ready to cook. On alternate days I fished the West Fork Creek to bring home trout for supper.

But the days grew long as the novelty of sheep watching wore thin, so I moved up my hunting and fishing trips to morning grazing time, and called a dog or two for companions for me. While I was gone, clusters of unwatched sheep would find their way to the oat crop in the hay meadow. When I saw my dad's pickup in the West Fork, I knew that I had stayed too long in the draws or at the creek.

As summer days passed and the sheep became a permanent fixture in the West Fork, Wally would tell about night time bear invasions. Sometimes a hungry bear would steal a sheep or two, but usually it was the unseen damage that caused the real problems. By the time Wally was awakened by bleating sheep and barking dogs, a bear, natural harasser that he is, would have romped through part of the flock to slap them around and watch them scatter. Scratches under a thick coat of wool go unseen for a week or so until a large wet spot appears on the wool. That means that the skin is crawling with maggots, and the wool must be pulled away to run coal oil into the infected flesh. Even with the treatment, eighty per cent of maggot-infected sheep will die.

Since the bears raided only at night I had no encounters with them that first year, but I saw the damage that they could inflict. When the draws on both sides of the West Fork were grazed we moved the sheep to Gus Creek. During the day I herded them to the ranch, leaving them in the barnyard corrals for the night. The next morning we found sixteen dead sheep and twenty four that had been crippled. The bear had eaten nothing but the bags from three of the ewes. It was such incidents, plus the lonely, monotonous hours of every summer day, that instilled in me a gradual distaste for taking care of sheep. But like it or not, I would be solely in charge the next year.

At summers' end the Missoula division of the Northern Pacific Railroad advertised for help for their train service. Wally saw a more financially stable future with the railroad so he applied for a job and was hired. When I returned to school, my dad kept the sheep on the flats near the ranch during the day, and put them in the corrals at night. When grazing season ended in the middle of November, they were kept in the meadows for the winter and fed hay.

The following spring was even busier than before with 400 lambs from the year before having babies of their own. They were added to the shearing statistics and I was in the wool bag almost twice as long as the previous season. As relieved as I was when lambing and shearing ended, I anticipated with dread the long summer that lay ahead. No longer would the West Fork suffice as grazing ground for a band of 2,500 sheep. They would be turned onto Petty Mountain for the summer, and my twelve-hour sheep watching shift would turn into an isolated 24-hour vigil.

I had never been up the mountain trail that my dad wanted to use for moving the sheep so when school was out for the summer I packed two horses with a tent, grocery staples, salt for the sheep, and other supplies, and my dad and I rode to Petty Mountain. We led the horses down the canyon road for a mile, then we turned east up a rocky knoll onto a grassy bench where we back tracked toward the mountain. Petty Creek gushed through the canyon as spring runoff swelled its banks. The sound of surging water accompanied us as we climbed through stands of pine adjacent to the road. Then the trail wandered eastward, leaving behind the sound and sights of the flatland as it ascended sharply through thickets of new-growth fir. Suddenly we reached the tree boundary to be enclosed by towering swells of grass. So mammoth was the rising field above and beside us, it seemed that the entire world above the canyon was only a sprawling pasture.

As the trail continued upward, stiff breezes from the west assailed us. The horses leaned into the hillside when the trail followed the mountain's natural curve. Thousands of mountain acres caught the sunlight as the grass rippled downward in shades of silver green. The trail circled on and up through undulating pastures until the ground gradually leveled. Spotted timber appeared here and there among rock outcroppings that covered sections of grass. Soon the trail was overtaken by beds of solid rock on the crest of Petty Mountain.

Grassy parks stretched out at our feet for 300 square miles. A network of finger ridges descended in every direction, topping the timbered canyons that plunged precipitously at their sides. Tree-covered hillsides rose and fell until they joined the high ridges at the rugged Idaho border. There the blue sky domes as if the world ended at the foothills of the Petty Mountain range. The country was to my liking. Morbid thoughts of loneliness disappeared as I contemplated the hours that I would have to myself to explore the mountain terrain.

As we continued on over the rocky mountain crest we passed old sheep corrals, a dilapidated set of pens that a sheep herder from the past had used to sort his animals. We descended down a ridge for two miles through a large grassy meadow that ended in a brushy draw with a spring at the bottom. With water for me and the sheep, and enough grass for a few days' grazing, we decided that it would be a good place to set up my first camp. When the tent was up and the supplies were stacked inside, we rode down the mountain for home.

As we trailed our way the following morning to the heights of Petty Mountain, throngs of bleating sheep poured through the tall pasture grass like cream colored dandelion fluff blowing in the wind. Barking dogs wheeled joyfully around them, dipping up and down the mountainside. Far below, where the pasture slopes meet the roadside timberline, the world of our valley home seemed confining.

By early afternoon tiny feet pattered impatiently over the stony mountaintop. The pace quickened as we dropped down along the ridge. When we reached the sloping meadow, the running stopped as little heads were immediately buried in abundant, luxurious feed. Knowing that they would graze contentedly until dark, I called back the dogs and returned to my tent.

The pattern of living on Petty Mountain didn't vary from the West Fork schedule, but a new routine was incorporated into my way of life. In place of the West Fork browse, the sheep fed mainly on meadow grass so camp was moved from ridge to ridge as they depleted their feeding grounds. The country was so big and open that I couldn't leave them at grazing time as I did in the West Fork. When they woke at daylight I called the dogs to keep them together until my breakfast was finished, then I stayed at their side until they took their mid-day, cud-chewing siesta. It was then that I was free to travel the mountains.

I rode all through the surrounding country, not far from the sheep at any time, but covering many miles as the bed ground moved. I fished and hunted rabbits and grouse which supplied me with sufficient meat for all my meals. I didn't hunt elk or deer because I couldn't keep that much meat from spoiling, but I took pleasure in following the elk that roamed through the mountain. At daybreak, from high on the ridges, I watched the big herds slip into the timber after feeding all night in open parks. I found their day time bedding grounds—elk size patches of flattened grass that bordered the timber. I knew where they crossed canyons at what time of day and the streams from which they drank. It was only a pastime then. I didn't know that the information that I stored would be utilized as a part of my future.

But the life of isolation soon closed in on me. My dad relieved me for one day of every ten so that I could return to the ranch for supplies, but the rest of the time I was alone. I was 13 years old, and the bleating sheep didn't fill my need for companionship. I tired of their constant rapping cry, their adherence to routine, their lack of reasoning ability. The longer I was with them the more it was obvious that their docile nature resulted from the fact that they lacked the brain power to be anything else. If they tired of living for any reason they would lie down and die. If one animal fled in fright, real or imagined, the whole flock was right behind her. Such incidents occurred often, but the most disastrous stampede occurred one night when I was helpless to turn them back.

It was in the middle of the night that the dogs barked viciously outside the tent. I grabbed my rifle as I ran into the dark. An animal of some kind was stalking the periphery of the bed ground. I could hear the rustling clear across the way. I had shot around the sheep many times with no reaction from them whatsoever, so I decided to shoot in the air to frighten away the intruding animal. The sheep were quiet, apparently oblivious to the danger from whatever was ready to eat them. But when the rifle fired they jumped to their feet as one, scattering through the timber. The dogs and I brought back as many that night as were close to the bed ground. But it took us three days of searching to round up the rest, and we didn't find them all. You never do in a stampede situation. Straggling through the brush unprotected, they're easy prey for bears and coyotes. The original invader must have enjoyed his fill of sheep from that episode.

Bears continued their night time prowl. I carried coal oil with me from camp to camp to treat maggot infection. I set traps every night, and killed many bear, but there were always more to replace them. No matter how closely I watched the flock, ten per cent were lost by one means or another. Those are the statistics. You chalk it up to profit and loss when you pasture sheep in brushy, steep terrain, even if you're a more dedicated herder than I.

As hard as it was to think of myself as a shepherd, I did my best to keep the flock intact, but I lived each day for the hours that I could leave the sheep behind. Without that time away I don't think that I could have coped with the monotony of my isolated existence. But in the middle of the summer, even break time was taken up with sheep when a new flock was added to the band.

Uncle Bill apparently had so much fun at shearing time that he decided to go into the sheep business for himself. He brought a flock of 40 Hampshires, a black-face, farm-flock sheep that he had raised on his own land. He was concerned about the welfare of their leader, an older, stiff-legged ewe who limped from an injury that she had sustained years before.

"Watch that ewe for a few days," he said when I was ready to take them up the mountain. "I don't know if she'll be able to hobble through those steep canyons. If she's having trouble, bring her down on your next trip, and I'll take her home."

When I drove the Hamps up the mountain, the crippled ewe hobbled slowly but nervously up the trail with 39 equally jittery sheep behind her. Accustomed as they were to flat-land pasture, they weren't enjoying their trip into the highlands one bit. When we reached the mountain flock they huddled together on the fringes of the grazing ground, eyeing expectantly the country beyond, turning down the mountain at every opportunity. The dogs were kept busier keeping the little flock bunched than they had been with all of ours.

The following morning the Hamps' behavior hadn't changed, and I knew that I would have to keep an eye on them even during their morning rest, so I decided to spend the time fishing a stream close to the sheep just below the meadow. When the hook was baited I thought that I had better check on them before fishing my way downstream. As I crawled to the top of the draw, all hope vanished for a supper's catch. In the five minutes that I was at the stream, the crippled ewe had turned for home, heading pell mell down the mountain with 39 black faces right behind her. Uncle Bill needn't have worried about his ewe. For the next five days she and her flock were on the run at least three times a day. That made fifteen chases through the brush to retrieve them, five of them during my leisure time. On the sixteenth trip I found a solution to the problem. I rounded them up and shot their leader.

With five days of sheep chasing behind me my meat supply was gone so when I left for the stream I also took my rifle. Fish, grouse, or stray rabbit, it didn't matter which came first. This time I was dead serious about taking meat back to camp. To be on the safe side I would check on the Hamps although I was sure that I had solved the problem. I climbed up the draw, and like a mirage the Hamps were on the move again. The mountain rumbled as 48 sheep hurtled down behind a barren ewe named Boxcar. I didn't waste any time on that round. As soon as they were gathered together, Boxcar joined her leader in the Promised Land, and the rest of the flock settled into an acceptance of mountain life.

In July, I started thinking that the shepherd life was causing me to lose my desire to even live. When my dad relieved me for one of my trips to the ranch, I asked him if we could have someone stay with the sheep at least part of the time. His ensuing tongue lashing made me crawl back into the mountains in bitterness that bordered on despair. My dad was feeling the effects of another economic crunch that he would explain to me later, and I guess that I was the target for his frustration.

At the time I thought that my future was forever restricted to the boundaries of Petty Mountain in the company of a growing band of sheep. Two days of rain showers didn't help my mood. I lay on the wet ground in a growing state of dejection until I realized I wasn't just upset, I was sick as well. Thinking it would pass, I stayed with the flock. In a day or two I knew that I needed help, but I was afraid that my dad would think I had just found an excuse to come home. In another twenty-four hours I no longer cared what he thought. I was burning with fever and almost too weak to stand. I put the dogs on the sheep before I rode down the mountain.

My mother looked me over when I got home, and found a wood tick on my neck, which meant that I might have contracted Rocky Mountain spotted fever. Only a few woodland ticks carry the fever, but if they do their bite can be very serious if not deadly. I was taken to the hospital where the fever was confirmed along with another case of pneumonia. With a lowered resistance from that combination, mumps were added to the list. For two weeks I was again in the hospital, barely alive for the first few days. But youth bounces back quickly, and a week after my release I was back on the mountain chasing bears from the flock, no happier about the situation than before.

It was in August that I received the news of our financial condition. Like all farm commodities, wool and mutton markets fluctuate from year to year, and our second year as sheep ranchers was during one of the down times. Without any reserve capital to see him through the year my dad couldn't afford to go farther in debt. He told me when he rode up the mountain that he had decided to sell them all, and that when school started I would be relieved of my duties. I felt bad for him—or at least I tried to show him that I did. In reality, I don't remember every feeling so elated. We'd make it somehow. We always did. And I knew that we'd manage better without the sheep.

9

When the sheep experience was over, thoughts of the fleecy creatures tripping over Petty Mountain haunted me like a white plague. It was only the thought of the sheep that evoked that response though. The memory of camping on the mountain was a pleasant one, and the next summer I wanted to go back, just for fun. An opportunity to do that presented itself after Bill's old ranch was sold to the Casper family who had a 15-year-old son, Jim, who was just my age.

Shortly after the Caspers settled on Petty Creek, my dad decided to sell Christmas trees from our land, and Jim and I were hired as cutters. We spent little time apart after we leveled the country of small pine and fir. Jim was 6 feet, 2 inches tall, a lanky adolescent. He had a mop head of curly black hair and an outgoing personality. It didn't take us long to discover our common outdoor interests, especially in the area of horse breaking. We both had tackled just a few at that time, and we were ready and eager for more. It was that attitude that led to our decision to save our tree-cutting money until spring when we would each buy an unbroken horse to work them together. When school was out for the summer, Jim and I kept busy in our spare time with Eagle, a big, gray gelding that Jim bought from my Uncle Bill, and Annie, a 1,100 pound chestnut mare that I had recently acquired with my tree-cutting money. After the horses were well started, I suggested to Jim that a trip through Petty Mountain country might be good for them. A long, consistent ride through varied terrain is a good way to break in any unseasoned horse. When I described the country to Jim he jumped at the chance to camp on the mountain.

To prepare for the trip we gathered a few food items from our mothers' cupboards, putting them in gunny sacks, along with a change of clothes, a few pots and pans, and some matches. We planned to subsist mainly on fish and game that we would reap from the mountain.

Jim furnished the pack horse, a spindly, spoiled bay that was used to having his own way with Jim's nine-year-old sister. We saddled him with a Decker pack saddle, placed the gunny sacks and sleeping bags in the center of it, and tied the rope around and through the D-rings. I don't know what we did wrong, but as soon as the last knot was tied, the horse put his head between his legs and bucked on the run down the road. We ran after him with our saddle horses and drove him into the corral before we gathered the gunny sacks and sleeping bags that he had scattered along the way. On the second packing attempt he stood still. When we finished, we put our rifles in our scabbards and we were soon crossing the flat below Printers Creek with the bay following along behind.

As we started the climb through the pastures below Petty Mountain where my dad and I had driven the sheep, Jim noticed that he had lost his lariat from the saddle. He told me to go ahead of him to find a camping spot, and he would follow my tracks to join me later. I rode on alone through the immensity of steep pasture land until I passed the old sheep corrals. I then found a thicket of dwarfed alpine that led into a clear, flat spot on top of the ridge. On one edge was a brushy draw that looked like it might contain water. A closer look, after I tied the pack horse to a tree, revealed a pool of spring water at the bottom of a sloping depression on the mountain top. It would make a perfect camping spot. A gentle breeze skimmed across the ridge to disappear into the finger ridges below as I rode back to the pack horse.

The pack horse had just been untied when Jim rode up with his lariat back on his saddle. When I led him to our camping spot, we were busy for the next hour setting up the tent, gathering firewood, and frying supper from a package of elk steaks and potatoes that we had brought from home. Jim tied his horse and the pack horse over the edge of the hill behind the tent, and my horse was staked out right behind us. When supper was over, the horses grazed in the fading light while the two Daniel Boones crawled into their sleeping bags. We discussed our success with our well-behaved saddle horses before falling asleep at the end of an enjoyable, peaceful day.

Then in the oblivion of a dark, deep sleep, my saddle horse let out a piercing shriek. Rocks pummeled the tent like rain while dirt flew in gusts through the cracks. Jim and I bolted from our beds.

"What is it???" Jim shouted.

"I don't know," I croaked. "Something got the horses. Go see what it is."

"I'll build a fire to keep it away. You go."

"I'm not going anywhere. Let's both build a fire."

While Jim groped for the matches I grabbed wood shavings and kindling that we had cut for morning, and threw them into a pile outside the tent. I lit the fire, fanning the air frantically to build it up.

"This is fine for us, but what about the horses?" Jim whispered. "They're too far away for the fire to scare the thing away."

"I know. We've got to get 'em over here."

"Yeah, but how?"

"There's only one way. We'll go together to get Eagle and the pack horse, and we'll pick up Annie on the way back. Let's go!"

We dashed out into the dark, following the sound of snorting horses. We ripped their ropes loose from the tree, and pulled three prancing, circling horses toward the tent. When we tied them close to the fire, we saw long scratches on Annie's neck and rump. Without saying a word, we ran to the fire to feed it into a roaring blaze.

"Get your rifle," Jim said. "We'll sit on opposite sides of the fire."

We took our positions as close to the flames as possible, staring into the darkness, seeing nothing. Then I heard Jim's low, constricted voice, barely audible above the crackling fire.

"Watch it. It's out there. Get ready to shoot."

As I turned to look, a glowing pair of eyes circled around the edge of the fire—two luminous dots orbiting around and around. We stayed frozen in our position while the screams of frenzied horses smothered the soft sputtering of a diminishing fire. My rifle was raised, the iron sights following the dots when they came to my side of the fire. Then they stopped in front of me as if they were suspended from invisible strings. I steadied my rifle and squeezed the trigger. A scream ripped through the night as a blue flame shot into the darkness. The underbrush crackled under the weight of a retreating marauder.

"A cat, huh," Jim said as we stood up to look in the direction of the scream.

"Yeah. Let's go check the horses. Do you think there's any chance he'll come back?"

"No, not a cat. We'll see if we can track him in the morning."

Jim wasn't so sure about the cat not returning because he threw more wood on the fire while I walked to the horses. They still snorted and stomped in a state of wild agitation, but I was able to calm Annie enough to look closely at her wounds. She had received only surface scratches just ahead of her withers, and the same on one side of her rump. The cat had apparently jumped on her back, and was bucked off right after he landed.

Jim and I fidgeted by the fire until it dwindled into a bed of hot coals, then we slipped back into our sleeping bags in the pre-dawn morning. When we woke up, the sun was up and bright. We jumped out of our beds to track the cat.

The tracks started just a few feet from the fire, leading to the water pool at the bottom of the draw. We saw that the cat had bathed in the mud to soothe his wounds. Neither of us liked the idea of a wounded cat crawling around the mountain, but we lost his tracks in the underbrush, and we couldn't pick them up again. The camping spot lost its appeal. We agreed to look for another campsite.

Jim built up the fire when we returned to camp while I fried the rest of the elk meat, and sliced bread from a loaf that my mother had sent with us. When breakfast was over we packed up camp, stuffing our gear back into the gunny sacks. We tied them onto the pack horses and turned back to the ridge to ride across the mountain.

Eagle and Annie stepped cautiously over flat rock on the mountain's crest. Each step on untried turf was met with uncertainty with the addition of a rider on their backs. With our bridle lines always ready to rap them to attention, we left the unrestrained miles of nature's spectacle to drop to the canyons, crevices, and networks of the woodlands below.

By early afternoon we dipped sharply through a dense patch of lodge-pole pine and Douglas fir. We had started to switchback west when we saw a stream of sparkling water just beyond the trees. Although we had never been in the particular spot, we knew by the lay of the land that we were at the head of Bill's Creek. Nature had provided us with a perfect spot for our camp. Positioned between the high walls of a steep little draw, a flat piece of ground lay adjacent to a bubbling spring. The water splashed into a sloping, twisting course to the bottom land where it joined the headwaters of Petty Creek. Timber lined the rim of the draw to shelter us from the elements.

By the time our camp was set up it was late afternoon, and rumbling from our stomachs told us that it was time to fix supper. We rummaged through the flour, left-over bread, lard, and potatoes, but nothing looked very appetizing.

"Looks like we'd better get some meat," Jim said.

"You're sure right about that. Let's go in different directions so we'll have a better chance of finding something. I'm getting pretty hungry."

When we climbed back on our horses, Jim turned to follow a game trail down the draw while I climbed back up through the timber toward the meadows. It was just on the edge of the timber, about a mile up the trail, that I saw two ruffled grouse perched on a pine limb, ten feet above me. I tied the horse to a tree and pulled my rifle from the scabbard. With two successive shots, our supper was at my feet. Annie stopped and snorted when I approached with the birds so I skinned them while she settled down, then I put them in the saddle bags for the trip back to camp.

The birds cooled in the creek while I built a fire. A while later, meat and potatoes were sizzling in a frying pan when Jim turned in at the top of the draw, thundering down the trail in a cloud of dust.

"Guess what I found???" he shouted as he sprang from his horse.

Eagle, who wasn't yet used to such violent eruptions, pulled at the lines to get away from his jumping rider and the spitting frying pans at his feet.

"I don't know, but you'd better move over with that horse before he steps in the middle of our supper."

"To heck with supper. I found the wild horses!!!"

"You're kidding! Where?"

"On Wild Horse Lookout!"

The herd of wild horses had been traveling through the Petty Mountain Range for as far back as anyone could remember, but I had never seen them. There were no government restrictions against their availability to anyone who might want them. Farmers in the area often turned their horses in with the wild herd to winter them, saving them from the deformities of inbreeding.

"Hey, do you know that if we catch 'em we can sell 'em?" I said.

"That's what I've been thinking about all the way to camp."

Jim tied up his horse, and while supper simmered in the pans we dreamed of the fortune we were about to make when we broke our herd of wild horses. It was dusk when we finished eating, and it was too late to look for them. We bedded down early to be ready at daylight to start the search.

A built-in radar system woke us up just before daylight the next morning. We decided to skip breakfast. It was just turning daylight when we started out on the trail in back of camp. When we reached the edge of the timber I saw the outline of a young buck feeding in the meadow. I pulled my horse up short and turned him around in Jim's direction. Jim was stopped, looking at the deer.

"Do you think we should get him now while we have the chance? We might be running after those horses all day," I said.

"I guess so. I'm hungry already. I'll get him."

When we got off our horses, Jim handed me his lines. The buck hadn't noticed us when Jim sneaked up close with his rifle to lean against a tree. When he shot, the horses jumped, pulling back. I held the lines tight to keep them under control.

"I got him!" Jim called from behind. "I'll dress him out if you want to go back for the pack horse."

Usually I would tie a deer to the saddle and sit in back of it, but neither of our horses were well broke enough for a trip of that caliber. When I returned from camp with the bay, Jim had the buck ready to load.

"Maybe we should cool the meat in the creek for a while and fry some steaks before we ride out," Jim said when we rode into camp with the deer.

My stomach told me that he had the right idea, so we spent the rest of the morning skinning, cooling, frying, and eating venison. When we finished, it was again too late to bring in the wild horses, but we rode out anyway to locate them.

Back through the pine trees and meadows, up steep canyons and down grassy hillsides, we picked our way back to the mountain's crest, then we followed a sloping, craggy finger ridge for about six miles. We climbed again out of a dusty basin to Wild Horse Lookout Station, a small frame building on stilts that stood on a high, grassy knoll to house the Forest Service fire personnel during fire season. We circled through the little mountain's draws and coulees until we found the horses grazing in tall green grass on the sunny south slope.

There were 23 horses in the herd in varying sizes and colors. I don't know how many horses the entire herd contained because stallions would keep mares bunched in various parts of the country.

We sat dead still on the hill above the herd, but one of them, a big sorrel, caught our scent. He whinnied loud in a warning call, and took off on a dead run with the herd charging down right behind him.

"WOW!" Jim said when the rumbling hoof beats faded in the distance. "How're we going to catch 'em with these half-wild horses we're riding?"

"I don't know. We'll have to think of something"

That night in camp we carefully conceived plans for our new horse business. We would go back to the ranch to trade Eagle and Annie for well-broke horses. We would make wooden pack boxes so we could carry back corral-building tools. When we were back on the mountain, we would camp not far from the lookout where we would fall timber to build a set of corrals into which we would drive the wild horses. One by one we'd break them to lead, and then take them back to the ranch in a string to break them to ride.

But before we did all that we were overwhelmed with the temptation to capture at least one horse before we left. We didn't know exactly what we would do with it after it was caught, but we thought that between the two of us we would have it gentle enough by the end of the day to lead it back to the ranch.

We found the horses early the next morning at the top of the same coulee. We dismounted, squatting in the grass to work out a capture plan.

"This is perfect." Jim said in an excited whisper. "Eagle's bigger than your mare so he'll be better for roping. I'll take him to the bottom of the coulee and hide in the brush. You ride to the top to scare 'em down. When they come past me, I'll rope one. As soon as you can get stopped, get your rope around it, too. We'll need more than one of us to hold it."

I waited until Jim was well hidden at the bottom of the coulee before I started up. I rode slowly away from the rim until I was almost at the top. Then I spurred my horse hard. She took off in a surprised leap, and when she was at the top, I turned her around and hollered, "Yeeeahhh!!!" The wild horses screeched in panic, turning for the bottom. Annie and I raced down behind them with my lariat circling overhead.

Jim was ready at the bottom with his lariat dallied around the saddle horn. With one hand he had pulled Eagle's head around to hold his nose so the horse couldn't make noise. In his other hand was his lariat, whirling in a big circle overhead.

The first horse, a big bay, reached Jim's hiding spot. When he tossed out the rope it flew in a perfect circle, dropping on the horse's neck He let go of Eagle's head and spurred him. The frightened gray horse reared. The bay ran on while the rope pulled taut. I reached Jim just as he and his saddle flew through the air. The wild horse led on down the mountain with Jim's rope flying from his neck like a flag.

"Do you think we should try it again?" I asked. "Maybe Annie will do better."

"Maybe we'd better wait 'til we get some better horses. There's no point in messing up again."

In the face of defeat we rode back the next day to the ranch. As hard as it was to believe, my dad wasn't impressed with our capture plan, so the wild horses were left a while longer to their freedom. It was a let down for us at the time, but the camping adventure hadn't been wasted. We had a little more survival experience behind us, and I had made a discovery. It wouldn't be the last time that I camped at Bill's Creek.

10

"Have you ever considered outfitting for big game hunters?" Bill Shaw asked thoughtfully as we rode slowly through the West Fork behind a bunch of cows.

"You mean you think that I should get paid to take people hunting?"

"Why not? It's being done, you know."

"Yes, but by people who know what they're doing."

"Oh, you know what you're doing. You already have enough clients, including me, to be in business full time. You just aren't getting paid for it. Think about it for a while, and we'll talk about it the next time I come up here."

If Bill was serious about his thoughts for my future I wouldn't be given much time to think before he returned. He had been a regular visitor to the ranch for a year, since the day that he first showed us his ideas for our meadow sprinkler system. Bill had been contacted when my dad decided to rebuild his herd. After the sheep were sold, the timber on our land was again used as a source of income, and the enterprise resulted in a need for a new method of irrigation.

When Harpers logged the land they cut only choice trees, leaving behind two-million board feet of marketable timber. In those days so much prime timber was available in the country that no logging company would have contracted for the leftovers. My dad set up his logging operation on a limited basis, hiring just one or two fallers at a time, experienced men who were in between more permanent jobs. And so that I could some day join the ranks of the experienced, I was put to work as an advance faller before the regular cutters arrived.

In the last year of the Harper operation, a few of the timber fallers had acquired motorized saws that were prehistoric front runners to modern chain saws. With a 40-inch blade and a gas motor that weighed about 45 pounds, it was still necessary for two men to run them. But by the early 1950s the size of the machines had been reduced so that one man could handle them. Compared to the saws of today, however, they were heavy, cumbersome, and almost powerless.

I was fifteen-years-old when my dad brought home one of the awkward tools, and by nature I was in a hurry to get things done. No one on the ranch could show me how to use it so I picked it up and learned the hard way. I wanted to make the trees fall fast, and they did, but often in the opposite direction from what I had planned. In my zeal I would cut clear through the trunk instead of letting it hold the stump, thus allowing the tree to fall in any direction. Fortunately my legs had grown very long by then. Without that advantage, plus my experience of running through trees and underbrush, my youthful timber-falling career may have ended in disaster.

But I made it through my off-and-on assistance throughout the three-year operation, and the profit from the timber was enough to cover the outstanding debts against the ranch. Then in the same manner that my grandpa had started his herd when he homesteaded, my dad rebuilt his own herd by taking in cattle on shares.

Since the hay meadow had lain fallow for five years it would need reseeding to produce a sufficient hay crop. We had always irrigated our porous meadow ground by flooding the land from irrigation ditches, but the force of flowing water would wash away young seedlings so a sprinkler irrigation system was needed.

When my dad returned to the ranch from Missoula after shopping for sprinklers, he was filled with news about the owner of a new irrigation company.

"Nice young fella by the name of Bill Shaw. He just opened his doors for business. He came over here from Ephrata, Washington. Likes the mountains better. He wants to do some hunting up here. I think you'll like him. Anyway, he'll be out tomorrow."

Early the next morning Bill bounced into the kitchen, brimming with vitality, looking a decade younger than his thirty-two years. His hair was sandy red, his square face was covered with light freckles, and from head to toe he had a wholesome, all-American look. From the minute that he walked through the door he was as enthusiastic about the beauty of Petty Creek as he was about setting up his sprinklers.

"You know that most people spend a lifetime dreaming about living on a place like this. We're going to fix you up with a sprinkler system that'll increase that hay crop out there so you can feed all the cows you need to, to make this ranch a big success."

It was typical salesmanship but it was also sincerely Bill. It would have been impossible to hold down Bill's enthusiasm for anything that struck his fancy.

A short time later Bill brought out his family to meet us, and my mother struck up an immediate friendship with his wife, Alice. She was a soft-spoken, friendly lady and a perfect, steadfast mate for the ebullient, enterprising Bill. Through the course of the evening Alice mentioned that they were renting a house in Missoula, but they wanted a permanent home away from town somewhere in the mountains. My mother told her that a place on the river at the mouth of the canyon was for sale, and within a month the Shaws became our neighbors.

From the time that they moved into their new home Bill spent most of his free time riding with me and learning how to hunt the area.

"How do you do it?" he asked one day after we sneaked up to look at a bull elk that was bedded down in a timbered flat just above the Petty Mountain pastures. When we had ridden half way up the mountain I had told him where we might find a single big bull, and he was impressed when the prediction came true.

"It's no mystery. I've lived here all my life and I know the country. I could ask you the same question about engineering an irrigation system."

"But that's a whole different thing. I have maps, pictures, and sets of instructions to show me what to do. You don't have anything but a mountain of dry grass in front of you and a few trees scattered here and there."

"These mountains are filled with maps and pictures, too, Bill, and I got my instructions along the way from a lot of good teachers. My dad was first, and then came John Adams, a hunting friend of mine from a long time ago. It's too bad you weren't here before John quit hunting out of Ed's Creek every fall."

"It couldn't have been that long ago. How old are you, anyway?"

"Nineteen. I guess it wasn't that long ago. It just seems like it."

I told Bill then about the Indians settling into their camps before the new canyon road was built, how I became acquainted with them, and how their way of life was such a natural part of the country.

"Like the Indians, I learned to hunt because it was necessary," I explained. "I paid close attention to my teachers because I knew that some day I would be the provider. It turned out that way, too. By the time I was ten, I was responsible for bringing home the meat, and I was well schooled in the conservation of ammunition. It was a one bullet for one deer situation. Anything else and I was taken to the woodshed. It really hurt my feelings. As hard as I tried, I wasn't the best marksman in the world at age ten. We didn't hunt for sport or because we thought venison or elk meat would make a nice change in out diet. It was for survival. You may not believe this, but we've never butchered a beef for our own use. I asked my dad once, a long time ago, why we never ate beef. He barked, 'Cuz we sell the beef to pay for the spuds to go with the elk meat, that's why!' So now you know why I can tell you where the elk are bedded down."

Bill's face clouded into a puzzled look.

"How did the Indians get by with taking all those animals when they weren't on the reservation? Weren't they subject to game laws?"

"You bet they were, the same as the white man—one deer and one elk every season. But they were also under the jurisdiction of Clay Holman, that rare breed of game warden who knows game and understands the needs of people. I'm surprised you haven't met him yet. He spends almost as much time up here as you do."

"Is he still the game warden in this area?"

"No. He retired three years ago."

As I talked to Bill about Clay it seemed odd to think of him as retired. Like Louie Albert, Clay had always been a natural part of the ranch, and his retirement didn't alter that situation. Clay was in his early fifties when I first remember him—lean and well muscled with gray hair, broad shoulders, and big bones. He carried Indian blood from somewhere in his ancestry that surfaced in his high cheek bones, his stoic manner of speech, and his natural inclination toward the management of wildlife. He wore a uniform because the state insisted on it, but he topped it with a cowboy hat that had seen as many weather extremes as his lined and ruddy face.

Clay took me into the woods with him from the time that I was very young, and he never missed an opportunity to pass on his expertise. He was a skilled tracker, and from his trapping days he had learned to skin an animal faster than anyone I have ever seen. He told me once, after we had killed a deer, that he was forced to work fast.

"Let me show you how to dress this deer in a hurry and not get blood above your wrists," he said.

When I asked him about the advantage of bloodless arms he said that was the way to keep from getting caught. He said that was why he was a game warden. They couldn't catch him poaching so they decided to put him on their side. He was half kidding, but there was truth to it also. Clay believed that regardless of set rules, animals were to be utilized when their numbers weren't in jeopardy. I asked him once if he ever worried about trouble from his superiors when they discovered that the Indians were hunting so openly.

"No, I don't," he answered. 'Some of us old timers in the department have the same opinion on that subject, and the young ones that don't agree with us leave us alone— for now anyway. But even if they didn't, I would still run my territory like I do now. Look at the facts. For hundreds of years many Indians hunted here every fall, and there was always enough game. Basically the game population hasn't changed, and how many of them hunt here now? Two families, and you, and the people that you hunt for. Plus a few road hunters that seldom get anything. That leaves a lot of animals for the people who need the meat, and in my opinion the Indians need wild meat a lot worse than they need government handouts. A game warden's job isn't to worry about who gets what. His job is to see that the wildlife balance is maintained."

Clay never spoke without meaning exactly what he said. He took his job very seriously when wild life was misused. Early one morning when he stopped at the ranch he could barely pull himself out of his car. He had broken his hips, pelvis, and part of his spine many years before in a mine cave in. The pain that he suffered was evident in the way he walked and mounted a horse. I never heard him complain, but that morning when he hobbled into the kitchen he said,

"Make the coffee hot this morning. I need something to loosen me up."

"What happened?" my dad asked. "You look like you've been run over by a thrashing machine."

"I spent the night in the Bitterroot, laying in tall grass along a fence. A couple of young fellas who've been on an elk-killing spree have been one step ahead of me for a long time. I caught 'em in a herd last night so it was worth it. The soreness will go away."

Clay wouldn't tolerate the killing of game for no apparent reason, wasting of wild meat, or selling game for profit. As he neared retirement age he spoke often about the changing policies of the Fish and Game Department.

"Us older fellas got our experience in the woods," he said. "The new ones are getting it all from books. It seems like there's more interest now in arresting people than in taking care of animals. Sixty-five or not, it's time for me to get out of this business. I don't belong to their ways."

I told Bill then that John Adams died from a heart attack during the same year that Clay retired. So of the original five families that I remember, only Pinto McClure still camped on the ranch to hunt the next fall, and Mrs. Big Sam came with him. She was ancient then, but she still clung to the old ways. When we butchered a beef for someone, she hobbled with a walking stick all the way down from Gus Creek to pick up tripe to eat in camp. She wouldn't let me help her when she carried it back in a gunny sack.

She and Pinto had been in camp for only a few days when we saw the smoke signal that meant that the hunt had been successful. On the following day the new game warden drove up the canyon to arrest Pinto for illegal possession of game. That officially ended the Flathead fall trek to Petty Creek. We didn't see Pinto again. The hunter of the old tradition and the old breed of game warden phased out together."

"The more you tell me about your life here and the more I learn about the country," Bill said, "the more I think you should start a tradition of your own. You're in a unique position up here for guiding hunters. Most outfitters have to lease land for camps, and transport their horses. You've got it all right here. You might not put up your hunters in teepees, but I believe a lot of people would pay you well to guide them through these mountains in search of elk. I'd like to form a partnership with you, but the sprinkler business is growing, and I don't have time for both. I'd sure be around to assist in any way I could, though."

"It's not a bad idea, but I don't know if it would work. To be honest with you, I've thought about it—briefly. I know my dad wouldn't go for it though. He's got his own ideas about the ranch, Bill, and I don't seem to fit into them much except for plodding along with the work that's here. He can be pretty stubborn. He can't seem to get the ranch on its feet, and he's changed a lot through the years. Struggling along with one arm hasn't helped his disposition either. He's frustrated, but he won't listen to advice from anybody, especially me."

"I've noticed the tension at your house. It's too bad. I'll tell you what. Before you talk to your dad, why don't you mention it to this game warden you've been telling me about. He seems to be on pretty stable ground with your family. Maybe he'll have some ideas."

I thought continually after that about Bill's advice. He was right. The opportunity was right at my feet. At his suggestion I kept the idea to myself, though, until the next time that Clay stopped at the ranch.

"I can't think of anybody I would rather pay to take me hunting than you, if that's the only way I knew how to get meat," Clay said.

"Thanks, but if I decide to do this my dad would never okay it."

"If that's all that's bothering you, don't give it another thought. We'll let Mac pave the way, and I'll be right there behind him. I don't think that's going to be a problem. And remember, Roger, if you do decide to go ahead with it, you'll have more people then you'll probably want who'll be standing by to give you a hand."

11

Mac Maycumber—our right arm on the ranch. If anyone could talk my dad into anything it would be Mac.

It was two weeks or so after my conversation with Clay that I approached Mac with the subject. I went to the bunkhouse after supper one night when he was there alone. When I knocked on the door he looked up from his newspaper that was spread out on the kitchen table. He motioned for me to come in, removed his glasses, and leaned back in the chair.

"What brings you here? Haven't you had enough of me today?" he asked.

He flashed his amiable smile, crinkling the corners of his eyes until they almost touched his bushy, black eyebrows.

"I have something to talk to you about. Bill Shaw and Clay have mentioned that they think I should go into the outfitting business."

"I know."

"You do? Why didn't you say something?"

"I've been waiting for you to do that. I thought you needed a little time to think about it."

"I did, and I really want to do it. What do you think?"

"I think it would be about the best thing that ever happened to this ranch."

"But there's so much to do, Mac. I wouldn't know where to start."

"Well, what do you think you have me here for? We always get put where we are for a reason. Maybe that's why I'm here. Besides, I'd enjoy getting back into the packing business for a while. The charts say I'm ready to retire, but I don't think so. One last fling in the mountains is an appealing idea."

Mac had given me the response for which I hoped. Seated there in his relaxed manner, dressed as always in his flannel shirt and baggy jeans, he once again was ready to help out where he was needed. It had been like that for the three years that he had been with us. No matter where you put the affable, easy going cowboy, he was able to do the job, drawing from his lifetime experience as a hunting guide, packer, rancher, cook, wrangler, logger, and sheep herder. His light-hearted approach to life helped reduce tension on the ranch, his casual sense of humor lightened our work load.

Mac's once handsome face had been blemished by the removal of half his lower lip during a cancer operation, but somehow it never really showed, especially with the touch of dignity that was added with his thick head of salt and pepper hair. He had been a recent widower when he came to us, but he spoke little of his loss.

"There's the problem of my dad. I don't think I'd ever find the nerve to bring it up to him," I said.

"You don't have to. Bill and Clay and I already have it figured out. I think we've been working on this idea harder than you have. You're a natural for this business and so's the ranch. You've paid your dues picking rocks and chasing your dad's cows. It's time for something else to happen. The bugs will work themselves out."

It was about a week after my conversation with Mac that my dad and I were alone at supper. I hadn't talked again to Mac or anyone else about the hunting business, so I was caught off guard when my dad brought it up.

"Mac tells me you two are thinking about starting an outfitting business."

"Oh, he mentioned it once. Matter of fact so did Bill Shaw, but I didn't really think much about it."

"That's good, because you're not doing it. I won't have all that craziness on my ranch. You're too young for something like that anyway. Just because you can ride horses and shoot a gun doesn't mean you know anything about running a business. You wouldn't know the first thing about what to do with those big shots from all over the country. Your Uncle Dan outfitted, you know, and all he ever got out of it was a bunch of skinny horses."

"That's kind of what I thought about it, too."

The next day I told Mac about the conversation.

"You did everything just right. I think this is going to be easier than I thought," he said. "I'm going to say something at supper tonight. If it's necessary, ride along with the conversation like you did last night."

That evening I sat nervously through the first part of the meal. While Mac talked about fixing fence and haying, he suddenly switched gears, saying,

"Oh, by the way, Mose. Clay and I were talking the other day about how we'd get things together if we were going to start a hunting business. It takes quite a lot of money to get all the equipment, and then we couldn't be sure that we'd have any hunters. Would you go ahead and buy the equipment anyway?"

"Hell, no. I'd make damn sure I had some hunters first."

"Oh. How would you go about getting them?"

"I'd advertise in an outdoor magazine."

"Hey, that's a good idea. Which one would be best?"

"I don't know. *Outdoor Life's* the biggest one."

"Hmmmmm. Just suppose we put in an ad for a hunting business up here. What kind of response do you think we'd get?"

" None. Who'd want to hunt up here except the people we already know?"

"Probably no one. It might be kind interesting to see, though, just for the fun of it."

"Go ahead and waste your money if you want to."

And so began the hunting business on Petty Creek. My mother and I worked up an ad for *Outdoor Life* magazine, and requests for information began to sift in through the mail. We went about it quietly without discussing it with my dad. He picked up the mail in Alberton every day so he was aware of the response, but he either grunted now and then when he put the envelopes on the table or he made statements like,

"Don't think this means they want to hunt here. People answer ads because they like to get something in the mail."

To answer the requests, Mac suggested that we send a brochure along with the letters of information. We worked out a small brochure describing hunting in our country, completing it with pictures of packed horses and trophy animals. Then Mac started making rifle scabbards from leather that I had on hand. Things had begun to solidify and I developed a severe case of apprehension.

"What if you're making scabbards for nothing, Mac. What if nobody likes the brochures?"

"They liked the ad well enough to respond didn't they?"

"Yes, but they probably answered every ad in every magazine. They'll be more choosy when it's time to make a decision."

"You just hold on here. You'll see that it's going to work."

"But what about my dad? I don't think he really believes that we're planning to go through with this."

"No, he doesn't. But he's being led so subtly that he's already accepted the idea without knowing it. There's a lot going on behind your back. We're dropping broad hints about *when* the business gets going, asking his advice on this and that. With Clay and Bill and I bombarding him all the time, he thinks that he thought of the whole thing, and he's starting to like the idea. I'd say that at this point it's all based on deposits for trips coming in. I know Mose well enough to know that when he sees that people are willing to pay, you're officially on your way."

"I hope you're right. I'm starting to think *when* myself. I'm not counting on anything, but in case it happens, on top of everything else I'm going to need about 15 more dependable horses. That's going to be a lot of horse breaking between now and then. I'd better be getting them down from the hills. I know of six for sure that I want to start working with. If you were twenty years younger, Mac, I'd give the job to you. They need someone with your experience. I've never worked with any quite that wild."

12

The six wild horses that I told Mac about had been brought to my attention by Lloyd Gilman, a tall, dark-haired, former school mate whose dad ran a hunting lodge in Powell, Idaho. Lloyd and I had shared horse pasture on Petty Mountain for the previous three years, ever since the government destroyed the wild horses and opened the land to the public. For a small fee to the Forest Service, we were allowed to keep our stock there on an annual basis. Together we pastured 90 head, leaving them there year around to multiply on their own. We brought them down each spring to work them all at the same time, and Lloyd took home those of his that he wanted to keep.

When we had ridden up the mountain at the end of the first year of sharing the pasture, I noticed six, big, two-year-olds in Lloyd's herd that were grazing by themselves near a water hole.

"What do you think of them?" Lloyd asked when we rode close enough to get a good look at them.

"I'm not sure yet, but I can tell they're awfully big. What do you plan to do with them?"

"I think I'll just let them grow for awhile. I bought them on a whim at the sale last summer. They're out of draft mares and a saddle stud so they should make good pack horses if we decide to keep them. Five of them are studs. I'd like to castrate them when we get them down."

Lloyd's two-year-old horses turned out to be a handful that spring when we drove them to the ranch, and the studs were worse when we roped and tied them for castration. With a year of freedom behind them in their young lives, they weren't about to give in without protest to the invasion of their privacy. By the time we turned them back into the mountains, I'm sure that they hadn't gained any more affection for us.

They grew for the next two years without being touched again. After we drove them to the ranch as four-year-olds, I spoke to Lloyd about them.

"When are you going to do something with those big colts? They're four years old now, and they're not getting any gentler up there. Do you realize how many extra trips we made around the mountain because of them?"

"I know, but I don't have time to mess with them, and I don't think I want to. Why don't you break them for half? They're big enough to make good pack horses for you if you decide to outfit. You can take whichever three you want. If they're too much to handle, forget the whole thing. Either break 'em or I'll sell 'em for canners. They sure aren't doing me any good the way they are."

"I'll think about it and let you know."

It was early summer when I decided to work with the six horses. I brought them to the ranch with the help of my brother. (If I haven't mentioned Pierre in these pages it's not because I wasn't fond of him. It's because he was a little brother who didn't fit significantly into my life until he was able to be of assistance). When they were corralled I turned loose my saddle horse and walked over to assess the job that lay ahead of me. It was going to be a challenging one if nothing else. They were so wild it looked like a pen filled with oversize elk. When I approached them they ran for the other side of the corral to jump over the poles. Had it been anything but a small round corral, they probably would have made it. When their efforts failed they ran head-on into the rails then screamed and pawed the ground.

As I watched them I found that I was drawn to one of the geldings, a chunky, 1,300 pound sorrel, the wildest one of the bunch. Every time another horse touched his hind legs he whirled and kicked. When any of them tried to stand still he cleared a path through the middle of them, wildly bucking and kicking. But he was as beautiful as he was wild. Sunlight played on his twisting body, turning his deep gold coat into burnished copper. His mane, which was the exact color as the rest of him, was long and thick like a draft horse, so that he gleamed with gold from one end to the other. His only other color was a strip of white that slipped down his face from under his forelocks to intensify the fire in his eyes.

"Okay, Goldie," I said half out loud. "You first."

I got my lariat from the barn and very slowly opened the corral gate to step inside. The horses turned savage. Corral poles creaked as they raged through the pen to escape. I twirled my rope overhead, swinging it in the direction of the corral while I ducked flying hooves. When I found a hole through the middle of them my rope found its target, snaring the gold horse by the front legs. As he went down he kicked his hind foot under the rope so that three of his feet were bound together. I held my end of the rope taut, moving in to throw a double half hitch over his three feet. He was secure then so I could work on his head.

With a piece of soft rope I tied a bowline knot around his neck, then I built a hackamore over his head. When I had him tied to the corral post I untied his feet. He jumped up and pulled back, shaking his big neck. His mane flew from side to side while he squealed and reared forward, pawing the air and striking the corral poles. It was useless to go further until he played himself out.

Next I chose a well-marked chestnut pinto and tied him up at a safe distance from the sorrel's hind feet. The only mare, a big, snaky chestnut, was next in line. When the three of them were tied, I decided that they were enough to handle at one time so I turned the other three back into the hills.

"Get them to trust you first no matter how long it takes," my grandpa had said many times when I started breaking horses. "When you've got an outlaw on your hands, don't start working him until he knows you're his friend."

That thought ran through my mind as I lay in bed that night, listening to the colts pulling back, jumping ahead, pawing and striking the poles with their front feet. I had broken many horses by then. At age sixteen I had my own business, breaking them mostly on shares to build up my own herd, but I had not yet encountered a horse that was as afraid of a man as were the three in the corral. I searched through my reserve of observation and teaching from Grandpa.

"Don't ever give in. Plan ahead. Always have an alternative up your sleeve before he gets the best of you," Grandpa had told me when I was young.

As I think about that advice, I remember an incident when Grandpa practiced what he preached.

I was only five years old that summer, but I remember well the small horse that Grandpa was breaking, a soundly-built dapple gray mare with a short back and a long, thin neck. Grandpa was 80 years old then, and my aunts and uncles felt that it was time for him to quit breaking horses, at least the difficult ones, but he wouldn't hear of it. The mare was little but she was crafty. She kept every muscle tense when he rode her, waiting for the opportunity to buck, rear, or turn away.

One morning Grandpa had left with the horse before I got out of bed. When I finished breakfast I ran out to play until he returned. I was behind the blacksmith shop when I saw the horse trotting down the road with Grandpa standing in perfect balance in the stirrups, riding tall as always, as straight as a string. When I jumped out to greet him, the frightened mare bolted sideways, the whole width of the road. Her legs were bent and she almost touched the ground on her side. Anyone—just anyone-would have been on the ground, but Grandpa landed a blow under her belly with the leather lashes of a quirt that he carried in his free hand. In one flowing motion the horse was upright again, prancing straight down the road with her head held high and a look of wild-eyed surprise on her face. Grandpa hadn't changed positions in the saddle. He still stood tall with a smile on his face as he greeted me with his cheerful good morning. It was moments such as those that made me long for the day that I would be able to step into his shoes. But when the opportunity was there with the three wild colts, I wasn't sure I wanted the job.

Early the next morning I was relieved to see that the horses were quiet. But when I walked toward the corral with a bale of hay, the fury started all over again. As hungry as they were, the sorrel and the pinto pulled back, rearing when I pushed hay to them under the poles. The mare lunged toward me, trying to strike me with her front feet. Since they weren't going to eat, I would try to get them to drink.

The pinto was the least active of the three, so to maneuver him to the creek I saddled a good roping horse named Jerry. When I rode into the corral, the presence of my saddle horse calmed the pinto somewhat. I carefully untied his halter rope while I was still on Jerry. I dallied the rope around the saddle horn and turned the pinto's head to the side. Jerry stepped forward at my command, but the pinto pulled back, jumping sideways. Jerry kept tugging until the big horse took a few, halting steps. We proceeded in such a manner for 40 yards until we reached the creek, then the pinto dropped his head for a long drink. On the way back he was less reluctant to follow, planting his feet in resistance only about half as often. When we were back in the corral, I wrapped his rope around the post, tying a knot while I was still on my horse.

Next I rode near the mare. She reared and lunged, snorting and striking at me with her big front feet. I stepped off my horse on the opposite side of the mare, reaching over his back to untie her rope. When the knot slipped loose, I tied a double half hitch over the saddle horn and walked toward the creek, leading my horse. When the mare squealed, reared, and swung from side to side, I held Jerry still. Each time she stopped for a breather I pulled him forward. It was a slow trip, but we eventually made it to the creek and back again, and the mare had her drink.

When the sorrel's rope was untied, I was surprised to see his reaction to being led. I expected to see him whip through the corral in a frenzy, but instead he planted his four feet in the ground. Jerry strained to pull him but the sorrel outweighed him by 300 pounds, and he couldn't make him move. I tried from both the saddle and by leading Jerry to urge the sorrel forward, but he stiffened like a statue with his big neck stretched forward, and a look of wide-eyed defiance on his face. Okay, Goldie, I thought, I'm not going to frighten you into anything. You win this round, but by tomorrow you'll be thirsty enough to give in. The rest of the day I gave them small amounts of hay at intervals and talked to them soothingly in between their fits.

On the following day I led the pinto and the mare to the creek in the same manner as before. When I went back for the sorrel, I was again surprised at his reaction. Instead of planting his feet in defiance, he led easily behind Jerry. They had had all the time that they needed to realize that I wasn't going to hurt them, and since the sorrel had shown such a positive change in behavior, I decided to start working with him.

Because I couldn't even approach the horse let alone touch him, I drove him with my saddle horse into the hold chute so he would be forced to stand still. I tied his head short, then I reached through the poles to pet him on the neck. When my hand touched him he shook so hard he rattled the heavy, tamarack poles. I talked to him while I rubbed my hand slowly over his neck, then I started to work down his back. When I touched his shoulder, his hind legs flew up. As my hand worked its way down, I wondered how long the solid chute planks could accept the blows without cracking. I let go of his shoulder and went back to his neck, speaking softly as I rubbed him in slow, circular motion. The kicking stopped, so I touched his shoulder again. The huge flank muscles rippled, his hind feet flew high in the air and crashed to the floor in continual, thudding rhythm. He would have to learn that pressure on his back wasn't going to hurt him.

Leaving Goldie in the chute, I brought back a pack saddle from the barn. I showed it to him, letting him smell it, and then I climbed on the chute, carefully laying the blanket on his back. Progress had been made. He stood still, but his muscles quivered in convulsive waves from head to tail. I petted him on the neck again to reassure him. When he stopped shaking, I climbed back to his hind legs and slipped the britchen over his hind quarters. The leather strap touched his back legs and his feet flew with such force that he broke the quarter strap. I would have to think of a way to make continual, gentle contact with his hind quarters until he understood that a touch wouldn't hurt him.

I tied a gunny sack on the end of a rope, filled it half full of hay, then tied it on a cross bar above the horse. When he kicked, the bag would swing back, hitting him on the hind legs without hurting him. I gave the bag a gentle push. When it touched him, he kicked so hard I could hear his joints popping from the back of his neck to his tail. I let him kick until his golden coat glistened with sweat, then I released the bag. I petted him from the neck up, offering him grain from my hand, which he accepted. He was tired enough then to be led by hand to the corral.

"Remember that you aren't strong enough to control a big horse if he wants to fight, so you have to tire him before you work with him," Grandpa had told me. "You'll start with a bad handicap if he gets the best of you in the beginning."

I thought about Grandpa's advice before I turned Goldie loose in the corral. By morning he would have regained his strength. I was afraid we'd be back where we started, so to keep the edge off I tied two bales of hay to the pack saddle, and left them on through the night. It didn't help. In the morning when I tried to catch him, he bucked through the corral with the hay on his back.

I got out my lariat again, roped him by the neck, and tied him to the fence. He decided then that we were friends again, and he accepted grain from my hand. But when I tried to touch him beyond his neck, he whirled and kicked. I would have to leave the bales on until the next day. I kept him tied, petting him off and on throughout the day while I worked on breaking the pinto and the mare to lead. I led them first with my saddle horse. By evening they would take a few steps while I was on the ground. The corral had at last become, if not a home for gentle horses, at least a place that you could enter, believing that you had a chance of leaving in one piece.

The following morning Goldie stood still while I removed the hay bales and the pack saddle because he was tired enough not to protest. I fed him grain again, and then I very carefully slipped the riding saddle on his back. He didn't move. I poured more grain to him while I stroked him around his head before I gingerly reached underneath him to take hold of the cinch. He tensed but he didn't move when I pulled the latigo strap, inch by careful inch, to tighten the cinch. I felt that my streak of good luck couldn't go on forever so I left him standing with the saddle on while I praised him throughout the morning along with feeding him grain.

By afternoon I knew by the look in Goldie's eyes that it was a good time to try to ride him. Before attempting to mount an unbroken horse, I had always driven them on the ground in the same manner that you drive a work horse, to get him used to turning in both directions, stopping and starting. But with Goldie's fear of anything touching his hind legs, that would be impossible. So while the horse was still tied to the fence, I put my foot in the stirrup and very slowly put a little weight on it. His eyes sprang open like saucers and his whole body tensed, but he stood rigid while I slipped on and off his back. Then I slowly lowered myself into the saddle, talking softly to him and stroking his neck. I leaned over, untied the hackamore rope, and carefully settled back into the saddle. Every movement was in slow motion, accompanied by soft tones and gentle words. Next I pulled his head to the side, nudging him with my feet. He didn't move. When I gently kicked him he stepped around. I let him take only three or four steps before I pulled back on the lines, calling "whoa." When he stopped I stroked his neck again. We started out a second time, following the same routine. Within an hour he would stop and start at my commands. He was ready to take out on the road.

While I was still on his back I leaned down to unlatch the gate, then I urged him out of the corral in the direction of the West Fork. When we reached the mouth of the canyon I nudged him into more speed, and he willingly broke into a trot. It was too early to coax him into a lope. If he had any plans to buck, he would break loose when he broke into a run.

Earlier in the day my dad had asked me to meet him at the house in the afternoon to help him move cattle that were four miles from the ranch on the other side of Gus Creek. It was time to go so I turned Goldie around to trot him home. My dad was saddling his horse at the hitch rail when I rode up. I pulled Goldie to a stop, smiling down at my dad. I knew that he wasn't expecting to see me still on the big horse.

"You're not going to ride that wild-eyed thing up there are you?" he said, looking up in astonishment.

A favorite expression of Grandpa's came to mind. "He won't get broke standing in a corral," I said, and off we went.

While we rode to the cattle range I made Goldie move right along with my dad's horse so he wouldn't get in the habit of following. I could feel his muscles relax as he traveled with another horse. When we reached the cows my dad sorted the ones that he wanted with his good, little cow horse while I moved around the outside of the herd with Goldie to keep the cows bunched. When we started back for the ranch with the cows, Goldie moved confidently beneath me as if he looked forward to returning home. I was pleased with his progress, but I didn't relax for a minute. I knew that he could break loose at any time for any reason.

We hadn't gone over half a mile with the cows when I heard a rattle under the horse. Goldie stopped dead still, shaking as he had when the pack saddle touched him in the hold chute. I looked down to see a patch of barbwire hidden under tall grass—huge, tangled and unyielding. There were few seasoned horses that would stand still when they found themselves in hidden wire. It was always a license for a colt to run wild. My mind raced to make a decision. If Goldie jumped when I tried to get off I would be in the path of his kicking feet while he tried to free himself. If I stayed on while he tried to thrash his way out we would both be tangled in the flesh-tearing barbs. I had no choice but to hope that he remained still while I dismounted.

When I grabbed the saddle horn it was shaking from the ripples of the quivering horse.

"Easy, Goldie, easy," I repeated at almost a whisper while I placed my foot cautiously on the ground. I gingerly reached for the halter rope, stepping forward. All the while Goldie stood still - tense, wild-eyed, and shaking.

I had never touched the horse's feet, and I knew that then was the wrong time to try. I saw that if he turned to the left he would have a narrow trail for his hind feet to step through between two billowing stretches of wire. I pulled gently on his halter rope, talking incessantly while the trembling horse followed my lead, picking up his feet one by one, gingerly setting them down when he was sure of his footing. Within minutes he was free.

There was something about that horse. He was going to be a good one.

My relief in clearing the wire was cut short when I realized I would have to get on the horse again—either that or walk back to the ranch. I hadn't been out of the saddle since I first got on that morning. It would feel different to him to have me mount in the open. I took hold of the side of his bridle to keep control of his head when I pulled myself up. I eased myself into the saddle so carefully that it wouldn't have moved if it wasn't cinched. When I pressed my knees into Goldie's sides he broke into a smooth trot to catch up with the herd and my dad's horse.

Days passed by and Goldie learned to neck rein, back up, stop and start with verbal commands, and to break into a lope when I signaled with my knees. I know that he enjoyed our riding time together. He trotted over to meet me whenever I approached him with the saddle. When I gave him the command to go he took off briskly with his head held high. I could soon pick up all four of his feet. When I put shoes on him for the first time he barely flinched. But he couldn't control his fear of his hind quarters. Nothing and no one could touch them, including even a chicken that walked behind him and received a death blow from his hind feet. I was beginning to worry that he wouldn't get over it. I couldn't include him in the pack string with that kicking problem.

In one way Goldie's fear was an asset for me. When I rode fence I didn't have to tie him when I stopped to drive staples. In any situation when I needed to get off for a while I just let the lines hang down beside him. He wouldn't move, thinking that they might drag behind him and touch his hind legs.

Goldie and I were on our way through the hay meadow one evening when I heard a shot in the lower field. I rode in that direction to find that my brother had shot a bear on a hillside across the meadow. Pierre had grown into a tall, sandy-haired adolescent who had inherited the family's love for the outdoors, and especially for hunting. I was wearing overshoes so I told Pierre that he could ride Goldie across the creek to see if he got his bear. I would wade through the water and carry his rifle for him. I assured him that he wouldn't have any problems with the horse if he was careful not to touch his hind quarters. I warned him strongly against it, explaining what happened to the chicken that happened by the back side of the horse.

Pierre was a good rider by then. He handed me his rifle, then swung his leg high over Goldie's back when he mounted. They rode through the meadow as if they had been together for a long time. No one but me had ever ridden the horse so I was relieved to see his reaction to a new rider. He had come a long way since he stood shaking in the chute just one month before. It gave me hope to think that some day we might find a solution to his kicking problem.

On the way back over the meadow, Pierre rode through the creek. When they reached the other side, instead of giving the horse to me, he leaned forward, pressing his knees into Goldie's sides. The horse broke into a beautiful lope through the meadow and onto soft, loose ground that sloped onto a bench in the middle of the field. It was the first time that I had seen the animal in action. As he ran, strong muscles rippled under a coat of shining copper. His thick mane flew in the wind, golden strands cascading from the proud posture of a head held high. His feet landed gracefully under his powerful body, his tail jetted behind to soften his billowing frame into a graceful curve. He flew like a flag of solid burnished gold. I thought to myself, you belong here, Goldie. Somehow I'll see that you stay.

As I admired the horse, Pierre pulled him to a stop at the top of the hill. Then he swung his leg over the saddle to dismount, brushing his foot on Goldie's rear end. Before there was time to blink, Goldie had streaked over the hill. Through the dust I saw that Pierre had lost his balance and fallen out of the saddle with one foot in the stirrup. If he was hung up, Goldie would kick him relentlessly. There was little chance that Pierre would be alive, but I would get into position to shoot the horse.

When I reached the top of the hill, Goldie was ripping through the plowed field, filling the air with a cloud of dust so thick that I could see him only as a shadow. I couldn't see if my brother was still in the stirrup. I put a shell in the rifle and raised it to my shoulder, following the running horse through the scope. I had to wait for a clear picture of Goldie or Pierre could be on the receiving end of the rifle. I tried to aim for his neck to shoot as far away from my brother as I could. Then Goldie moved onto solid ground and his head emerged through the dust. I calculated the speed of the bullet against the running horse. My finger tightened on the trigger … and just then Pierre stumbled through the dust that Goldie had left in his trail.

"I don't know why I hit him with my foot," he panted as he staggered in my direction."

"You know something, partner? I don't care why you hit him with your foot. It's just good to see you here in one piece."

"Boy, I'm sure glad that you didn't shoot your horse. I tried not to let him run away so he'd be spoiled. When I started to fall, I grabbed onto the side of the bridle with one hand and hung onto the saddle horn with the other one. I tried to stop him, but he just kept running and kicking at me all the time."

"How did you stay out of the way of his hind feet?"

"I guess I was too far forward. His feet wouldn't reach that far. I held on as long as I could, but I think I just bounced off his side. I don't remember letting go."

"That wasn't a bad job for such a scrawny kid. In fact you did everything just right. Maybe I've been bringing you up right after all."

From that moment on I didn't even whisper across Goldie's hind quarters. My pant leg brushed him once when I mounted, and he shot out for 600 yards before I could get him under control. It was dangerous to keep him on the ranch with all the visitors we had. If I couldn't solve this problem, the only alternative I could see was to keep him in a box stall for the rest of his life. Even that wouldn't work because I didn't have time to exercise him on a regular basis. I didn't know what his future would be, but for the time being I took advantage of his able assistance.

When it was time to bring in the milk cows every morning, I jumped on Goldie bareback. Without a bridle, a halter or anything to guide him, he pranced off to find the cows, and then he herded them back to the milking corral. When I wanted him to stop, I reached down and pressed my hand on the front of his neck. At roundup time he ran through the mountains after cattle and horses all day long, and at night, if there was a need to use him again, he was ready to go. He never said no and he never showed a sign of wearing down.

Goldie and I had been together for four months when Lloyd and some of his hands brought down the horses that they needed for hunting season. I wasn't home at the time, but Lloyd had been following Goldie's progress throughout the summer, and he tried him out for the horse chase. I returned to the ranch just in time to learn the outcome.

Lloyd was aware of Goldie's kicking so he was careful not to touch him with his foot when he mounted. But every rider has a different feel to a horse. Whatever Goldie's reason was, he bucked Lloyd off right in the gate and continued on up the road to Printer's Creek before Lloyd could herd him back to the corral with his pickup. When Lloyd got on the second time, he was ready for the horse, and he rode it out when Goldie tried again to throw him. He wore off the edge then by loping the horse five miles down the road and back. Not many horses could have gone on after that, but Lloyd immediately turned Goldie toward Petty Mountain. They found their horses not far from Lookout Mountain. The rest of the day they ran up and down the ridges, gathering the herd together, heading for home in late afternoon.

Just before dark, I heard the horses clipping down the road so I stationed myself a few yards above the corral gate to guide them in. After they turned into the corral, Lloyd rode up behind them on a tired, sweat-stained Goldie. He jumped off the horse, leaving him standing in the corral with the saddle on. The bridle lines hung down in front of him. Lloyd stomped toward me with his arm pointing back in the direction of the corral.

"How the hell do you ride that outlaw? He tried twice to get me off. The first time he made it!"

"He's never bucked with me, but if he had I couldn't have stayed with him. It would take a hell of a cowboy to ride him."

"Yeah. I found that out."

"I don't know what to tell you. He's a good horse. You've found that out. But as much as I want to keep him I can't have him on the ranch, and I can't do anything more for him."

"I'll talk to my dad, and see what he thinks. We'll be over in the morning to get the horses."

When Lloyd left, I walked back to the corral. Goldie was standing about 50 feet from the gate. The lines hung from his drooping head. He was sweaty and gaunt. When I opened the gate his head popped up. He nickered when he saw who it was, turning around to meet me. Then he realized that the lines were hanging. He made a quarter turn, and with tiny, careful steps he side stepped all the way over to me, shaking his head at intervals to keep the lines in front of him. A lump welled in my throat.

"Damn, Goldie. Why don't you stop your kicking?" I said as I petted him.

Lloyd and his dad, Muggins, drove up in the stock truck the next morning just as Goldie and I came down the road with the milk cows. I waved as I rode by, riding the horse with nothing on him as I always did. When the cows were in the corral, we crossed the grazing meadow to the Gilman's truck. I reached down to touch Goldie on the neck, and he stopped as I slid to the ground. He walked off to graze as I crawled through the fence.

"Hi, Muggins. I haven't seen you for a long time," I said.

He answered while gazing past me in Goldie's direction.

"That horse sure turned into a beautiful animal. You've done a good job with him." He turned to Lloyd and said, "Are you sure that's the horse you rode yesterday? He doesn't look very wild to me. I don't know about you, but I'm taking him home."

I don't know what I was hoping because I knew I couldn't keep the horse, but my heart sank. I guess I was hoping for a miracle. I helped them load their horses in the truck before I crossed the meadow to get Goldie. When we returned he clomped willingly up the ramp and into the truck. As I slammed the tailgate behind him he held his head high to see over the rails. The wind caught his golden mane when the truck disappeared around the turn. I swallowed hard. I somehow knew that he wasn't going to make it in his new home.

It wasn't until two weeks later that Lloyd found the courage to ride Goldie again. As soon as he got on, the horse not only bucked him off, but he pitched him straight over their seven-foot corral fence. Lloyd never rode him again. He traded him the next week to a rodeo outfit in Missoula.

Goldie's career as a bareback bucking horse started the following spring. He soon earned a reputation as one of the best. No one could stay with him for the eight-second count. When he was used the following summer at the annual KO Rodeo in Missoula, I was there to see my horse perform.

The golden giant thundered out of the chute with a sun-fishing, high-kicking buck while the cowboy fought to keep his balance. Three seconds into the ride, Goldie spun into a twisting turn, throwing his legs high in the air. The rider slipped to the side and Goldie suddenly dropped straight to the ground. The crowd gasped in unison as they rose to their feet. Silence fell over the stadium. The rider rolled off, unhurt, but Goldie lay motionless in a crumpled heap. Officials ran to examine the horse. The voice on the loudspeaker announced that he was dead. The rodeo continued after Goldie was dragged away.

An autopsy later revealed that he died of a heart attack. I could have told them that at the time if anyone had asked. I believe they scared him to death.

When I think about Goldie now it's not as I last saw him. I see him standing patiently near a fence with his bridle lines hanging down beside him, and I watch him fly down the mountain behind a herd of horses. I think of him trailing the milk cows, glistening with gold in the gathering dusk, with nothing to guide him but his desire to please, and I see him side step across the corral to meet me. Then a deep sense of fulfillment surrounds me to know that an animal that was once terrified of a man learned to trust me as a friend.

By fall, Lloyd's other five horses were broke for pack animals or saddle horses. I kept only the pinto and I sold the other two. While I broke horses, Mac kept busy making rifle scabbards, and I continued to wonder if he was wasting his time. Through the winter I still broke horses to sell or trade or keep for myself. Whether I went into the business or not, I could always use good trading stock.

It wasn't until early spring that the first deposit came in. Mac had told me that if the inquiries sounded promising I should follow up the mailed information with a phone call. I did, and a man from New Jersey was the first to book a reservation. I almost framed it. I knew that would be the only one I would receive. But week by week reservations were made. By the end of summer the season was almost filled.

With the deposit money I bought equipment—tents, stoves, cots, lanterns, kitchen tools. Gunny sacks were no longer acceptable for packing equipment in and out of camp so I bought pack saddles, mantie canvasses, and ropes, and Mac and I built pack boxes to go along with them. There were saddles and bridles to buy, blankets, halters, shoes, halter ropes, and nose bags for the horses. The deposit money didn't cover it all. I stayed busy breaking horses to keep, to trade for equipment, or to sell.

I can't pinpoint the moment that my dad accepted the idea of a hunting business, but when a few deposits had come in, Mac and I openly discussed our plans. My dad gradually offered opinions, although never with wholehearted approval. But I would hear from other sources that he was pleased with the prospect of people from all over the country visiting the ranch. He couldn't help but get caught up in the excitement. It hovered over the place as almost everyone who visited became involved in the venture with their ideas, questions, and offers to help.

Deposits were still coming in when help was lined up for the season, and the new equipment was stacked and stored in every available corner on the ranch, Twenty five horses were ready to go and so were we. It was time then to find our camping spots.

13

In the early stages of planning for the guide business, I had thought that it would be colorful to use a string of mules for pack animals. It would add a certain amount of charm to the western image to be seated on a saddle horse with a lead rope in my hand and a long string of packed mules winding over the mountain trails behind me. Now there is a growing trend to use mules for riding, but at that time they were used mainly as pack animals by outfitters and prospectors. I had had no working contact with the animals, but I would have an entire year to learn their habits before the season started. It was only a thought, and I mentioned it one evening to my dad. I wasn't expecting a violent reaction to the idea, so I was startled when he bellered in response,

"Mules??? It's bad enough that you think you have to turn this place upside down as it is. Now you want to bring in a bunch of those moth-eaten calf killers. I won't have 'em on my place! If you're going to have a string of long ears in that damn business of yours, you can find yourself another place to outfit from!!!"

"Let's forget about it, Dad. I'll get along fine with my horses."

The mules weren't mentioned again as our plans continued to develop. In June, when the opening of an early season was just a little over two months away, Mac and I decided one night at the supper table that it was time to find our camping spots. We planned a pack trip of several days, starting the following week. Barney Quinlan, a friend of ours who would help us guide through the season, would join us.

As Mac and I discussed our plans, my dad was unusually quiet, and throughout the following week he was less vocal than usual about the hunting business. I knew that an idea of some sort was brewing inside of him so I kept our conversations in areas other than hunting.

Then two days before the trip was to begin he said that he would attend the auction at the sale barn in Missoula. He sometimes returned from the weekly sale with an animal or two, but he mainly went to keep in touch with market prices and to visit with the area ranchers. He asked me, as he climbed into the stock truck, if I needed anything from town for the trip. I told him that everything was in order, and with a nod for a reply he drove off.

Whenever my dad went to Missoula he made a day of it. When he returned that evening my mother, brother, and I were sitting at the kitchen table.

"Hurry up and finish your supper," he grumbled at me when he opened the screen door. "I've got some stock out there for you to unload."

"What did you buy?" I asked.

"Mules."

"Mules? What for?"

"For you."

"For me?"

He trudged across the floor and laid his hat on the wood box. "Yeah, for you.
You never heard your mother say she wanted any did you?"

"No, I guess not."

"I'm going to wash up. Put my plate on, Mom, I'm hungry."

My mother and I exchanged glances while Pierre continued to eat with the deep concentration of adolescent boys. Above the splashing of water in the bathroom sink, my dad's voice boomed out,

"I got 'em now because I thought you might want to try 'em out on your pack trip."

"Good. Thanks." I turned to my mother. "Is he kidding?"

"Your guess is as good as mine. Why don't you go out and see. I'll keep your plate on the stove."

The stock truck was parked at the loading chute with several pairs of various-colored long ears poking above the top rail. When I lifted the tailgate, five heads turned curiously toward me. They were not the matched mules that I had envisioned.

I untied their halter ropes, and they clipped confidently down the ramp and into the corral. I threw them hay before I stood back to assess my new collection of pack animals.

A gentle, big, black jenny munched hay lazily in a corner of the corral. Next to her stood an old, short-legged, white jack whose long head and big bones were the same size as the large mules. Beside him was a big, brown jack who kicked at me as I walked by. The motley group was rounded out by two jennies, one of them tall and gangly, and the other with a chunky build like a quarter horse. I placed them mentally into the line of pack horses and I couldn't decide if they should be interspersed, lead, or bring up the rear. Any way I thought of them, they didn't add a thing to the appearance of my string of big, well-built pack horses.

When I walked back into the kitchen my dad looked up from his supper plate, beaming.

"That's all the mules they had at the sale so I couldn't get any to match. But they're all experienced pack mules."

"They look like a fine bunch to me. I'll saddle them tomorrow to see how they do. It'll be good to have Mac on the trip to show me the ropes. Thanks. We'll put them to good use."

My dad had chosen his own way to let me know that he wanted the business to succeed.

Two days later, while Mac and I carried our equipment to the hitch rail, Barney Quinlan drove up. He got out of his pickup, standing with his hands on his hips as he looked at the saddled mules.

"Well, I'll be dammed," he said as he strolled to the hitch rail with his giant stride.

"Yeah, me too. I hope you're ready to start loading mules because this is our freight outfit for the trip. Don't worry, they're all broke. Only one of them is a little crabby."

"What happened to that string of matching mules you used to talk about?"

"It's a long story. I'll tell you about it later. Just start packing."

While Barney shook his head at the comical assortment of mules, I thought how fortunate we were to have him with us for the season.

I had met Barney two years before on a high, windy ridge in Burdette Creek on the south side of Deer Peak. I had been hunting by myself, almost frozen to the saddle from the penetrating cold of a high-velocity wind. I stopped to build a fire, and as it blazed precariously in the screaming gale, I noticed a lone rider traveling slowly up the bald-face mountain below. His big, bay horse leaned into the hillside with his tail and mane flying straight out to the side of him. The rider was crunched into the saddle with his head turned away from the wind. One of his hands was holding the lines and the other was fixed firmly on top of his hat.

As the horse plodded closer to the top, I could see that he was carrying a very big man who was headed my way. When they came to a stop at a short distance from the fire, a huge pair of blue eyes popped up from the protection of an upturned jacket collar.

"Hi. Do you mind if I use your fire for a minute?" the man asked in a clear, deep voice.

"Help yourself, partner. I think you need it. You look like I felt a few minutes ago."

"It's so cold I was going to turn back until I saw your fire. I didn't think I had enough fingers left to stop and build one."

Barney removed his gloves and rubbed his big, ham-like hands close to the flame while we introduced ourselves. As the conversation moved along, a rapport developed between us that kept us seated by the fire until the wind died down and the flames burned vividly in a gathering dusk.

"Why don't you ride to the ranch with me and meet my folks?" I said. "I'll drive you to your pickup and you can bring it back to the house to load your horse. By that time my mom will have supper ready. You must be about as ready for fried elk steak as I am."

"Thanks. You must be a mind reader."

As time went on and I watched unsuspecting elk succumb to the power of Barney's

300 Weatherby Magnum, I wondered if his hunting success resulted from skill or if the sight of him simply froze the elk in their tracks. Barney had the classic look of a powerful, rugged, western hero, standing 6 feet 5 inches tall with big, broad shoulders and narrow hips. A quiet, tensile strength radiated from his lean, big-boned frame. High cheek bones and a long, narrow jaw framed immense blue eyes that penetrated your thoughts with alarming awareness.

When Barney and I sat close together by the fire on our first meeting I thought it would be a good idea to never cross the man. It was an unnecessary thought because the heart of a lamb beat under his tough exterior. He was in his early thirties when I met him. If he had ever harbored aggressive feelings toward anyone he had worked them out in his youth when he won the Golden Gloves title for the state of Montana.

Barney was with us to show us his favorite hunting spot in Irish Basin, just on the Montana side of the Idaho border. He thought that it would make a good hunting camp for the fall, and since Mac and I had never been there he was eager to point out the way. He had scheduled his job with the Milwaukee Railroad so that he could spend half the fall season guiding hunters. He had been able to take off just a few days for the pack trip that we were about to take.

By mid-morning the mules were packed and we were ready to go. With Barney and me in the lead, and Mac bringing up the rear to make sure that the packs rode intact, we started up behind the house in the direction of Deer Peak. The sun shone bright after a pouring summer rain, saturating the woods with a steamy smell of wet grass and pine. The mules tripped along behind us like the trail veterans that they were. The big, black gentle one was the first in line, followed by the short, white jack with the big head. Next came the tall, gangling jenny, then the chunky little brown. And finally, so that there would be peace in the string, the kicking jack that we had aptly named Kicking Jack, was last in line so he had nothing to target with his hind feet but the trail behind him.

When we had gone a short distance I turned around to check them.

"We might not have the prettiest string in the country," I said to Barney, "but it looks like we won't be eating scrambled eggs when we get there."

"I was just thinking about the mules myself. They make it look like you're really serious about your work, like you're not just interested in how things look."

"Thanks, but when the hunters get here the string will consist of a good looking bunch of stout and able horses."

We turned south at the base of Deer Peak, riding through thick grass that waved up the sides of the pointed mountain in rippling tones of green. We descended then across an open ridge through Slaughter House Gulch, a steep, brushy elk paradise that had been given that name because of the numbers of elk that Pinto McClure took from the area. From Slaughter House Ridge we dropped into the north fork of Burdette Creek. A consuming fire that swept through western Montana and Idaho in 1910 had cleared Burdette of mature timber, leaving the steep canyon filled with alder brush and lodgepole draws that made good cover and browse for game. In the heat of the summer sun the south and west slopes were carpeted with rich, green bunch grass that ascended gracefully like a lawn, with golden sunflowers scattered among the blades.

As our saddle horses switch backed down through the brushy, steep terrain, stepping over fallen trees and circumventing tangled undergrowth, we heard Mac holler from behind. I stopped my horse to look back and see Kicking Jack on the hill above me, standing still and helpless with a billowing pack of duffle ready to slide over his head. I gave the line to Barney, and ran back to help Mac.

"Look at that," he said when we got hold of the pack. "All that's holding his load on is his ears."

Besides the duffle, the mule had been loaded with heavy pack boxes, and the britchen snapped on the descent. We untied Jack from the mule in front of him, carefully turning him uphill so we could wiggle the pack back into place. Mac always carried a pocket full of rawhide strings so we used some of them to tie the britchen together, and we were on our way again.

After a fast trip down the remaining half mile of the steep hillside, the canyon opened into twenty acres of flat ground with a creek running through the middle of it. In the center of the flat, a ten-acre meadow of white clover and red top would provide good horse feed. On the southern edge, a thick stand of long, straight lodge-pole would make perfect tent and corral poles. Tamarack snags that were ready to be used for firewood interspersed the entire area. I pulled my horse to a stop.

"I think we just found our camp," I said.

We hobbled the horses and mules so they could graze in the meadow while we set up camp for the night. When Mac started supper, I slipped off to the meandering creek and caught several small fish to eat for breakfast the next morning. When I returned, Mac had a good supper ready of elk steak, potatoes, and green beans. When we finished eating we rinsed our dishes in the creek before crawling into our sleeping bags for a long sleep.

When I woke up at daylight the next morning I lay in the warmth of the rising sun for a long time, gazing up through needled branches of the big pine that dominates most of the Fish Creek drainage. It was in the first rays of morning light, when my thoughts were as still as the changing day, that I was most aware of the pungent scent of pine that filled Petty Creek and all the surrounding mountains. In Fish Creek it was especially pervasive because of the size and numbers of trees. My thoughts wandered back in time when only Flatheads hunted our mountains. It was the Indians who were responsible for the size of the trees. Before the days of the white man, they burned their hunting grounds after the fall hunt to eliminate the under brush and small trees, thus insuring a ground cover of thick grass that would keep the elk and deer in the area. I could almost see the teepees that may have been raised in the clearing where we lay in our sleeping bags, and I felt like an intruder onto sacred ground.

But I was brought into the present by the stirring of Mac and Barney who were ready for the day to begin as soon as they opened their eyes.

"It's about time to get those mules back in a line," Barney said as he rolled his long frame out of the sleeping bag.

Mac hopped out of his bed, pulled on his pants and ambled, yawning, to the pack box that carried the groceries. "You guys better hurry because I only call once for breakfast," he said.

We had only our duffle left to put on Kicking Jack when we heard Mac's call. Taking him at his word we left the pile where it lay and strolled toward the crackling sound of frying fish. Steam poured from a pan filled with golden brown trout, and a frying pan of eggs, sunny side up, stayed warm on a flat rock beside the camp fire.

"I don't know if it's this outdoor living or your talent in the kitchen that makes your cooking look this good, Mac, but I don't think that my mom could have done a better job in her kitchen," I said.

"It comes from a lot of years of looking forward to the end of long, hungry days."

When breakfast ended and the mules were packed, we saddled our horses to ride for Fish Creek. We followed an old, unused Forest Service trail that was littered with fallen trees so we were forced to dismount through much of the morning to chop logs out of our way. By noon we stumbled onto an almost deserted little ranch near the county road that runs through the bottom of the Fish Creek drainage. An attractive but not-so-friendly lady in her thirties came out of the small, weathered farm house to ask us to move along on our way. With all the diplomacy I could muster I was able to extract from her the name of the owner of the place. She said that she was only camped there for the summer and then the place would be vacant. I questioned her because it looked like a good spot for a base camp for the regular season with its log bunkhouse, corrals, water for the horses, and the house that could be used for a cook house. I would check into leasing it from the owner.

We crossed Fish Creek after leaving the little ranch, to begin the ascent to Cash Creek where we would camp for the night. As we climbed higher through the hot, shadowed silence of the big timber, the grassy bottom lands were replaced by thick beds of brown pine and fir needles that snapped beneath our horses' feet. From years of habit, we climbed through the hills in silence, noting every detail of our surroundings. When we needed the information we would remember the draw and benches, the game trails, the areas that provided cover, and the open meadows where game would browse.

By early evening our horses stepped into the rocky thread of silver that was Cash Creek at its junction with the wider banks of Fish Creek. We stopped to camp for the night. When the mules and horses were unsaddled, Barney and I left Mac to set up his kitchen while we set out in opposite directions of the two creeks to catch our supper. Barney decided to fish downstream in Fish Creek so I climbed the steep, rocky terrain beside the small stream. I walked about a mile before stopping to fish my way back. My creel held a supply of lady mites, a tiny, tied fly with a red belly and a gray body made of deer hair. I had hardly hit the water with my first cast when a fish grabbed the bait. Two hours later I was back in camp with forty, fat trout for our supper.

When I walked past the feeding horses I could see through the trees that Barney was sitting on a log with his head bowed in deep contemplation. I approached him cautiously with my string of fish.

"How did you do, Barney?"

"I got three."

"That's too bad. What were you using?"

"Rock worms."

"That must have been the problem. I couldn't have beat the fish away from my mites."

"No, that wasn't the problem. The problem was a bear. The biggest one I've ever seen."

"You mean you got chased away from your fishing hole by a bear?"

"No, I didn't get chased. I ran. Don't laugh. He was as big as a Brahma bull. The way he charged out of the brush right behind me, I'm surprised I'm not still running. The next time I meet a bear, I'd better have something more than a fishing pole to defend myself."

I could see that Barney was in no mood for jokes so I sat down to listen to the details of his adventure. His big eyes stared vacantly ahead as he told his story. He hadn't recovered yet from a moment of honest terror. He said that the bear ran through the brush right behind him while he was fishing. When he slipped around to see what the noise was, the lumbering animal was only 15 feet from him.

"It must have been a big one, Barney," I said. "Most of the bear in this country are the size you could pick up and throw away with those hands of yours."

We talked of other things then to get Barney's mind off his bear until Mac bellowed out with his dinner call.

When we reached the camp fire we found pans of fried trout that were a golden brown like Mac had fixed them that morning. We piled them onto our plates, along with heaps of fried potatoes, sat down on a log, and dived into the steaming meal. When I was well into eating the fourth fish, I noticed a strange lump in the middle of it. I had been too hungry to notice that anything was amiss in the first three.

"Am I imagining things, Mac, or did you forget to clean these fish?"

"No, I didn't forget. I always cook the meat the way it's given to me. I've always thought that's the way the people wanted it cooked."

I had been catching them so fast that evening that I decided to clean them when I returned to camp. But Barney's bear story got in the way. While I listened to Barney's story I didn't think for one minute that Mac was dipping intact fish in the flour. That was the last time that I gave Mac an unclean piece of meat to cook—fish or fowl.

When we woke up the next morning, Mac decided to stay in camp so Barney and I saddled our horses to ride for his hunting spot in Irish Basin. About a mile out of camp I spied in the trail a hind bear track at least 14 inches long that Barney, who was riding in the lead, had passed by.

"It's not that I doubted the size of your bear last night, Barney," I called out to him, "but I really believe you now. Come look at this thing. He had to weigh seven to eight hundred pounds."

"Yes, I know. Let's make some tracks of our own before my horse gets a whiff of him and does the same thing I did last night."

Leaving the stands of Ponderosa Pine behind, we soon reached the edge of the high country. The forest setting gradually transformed from a bold denseness to a delicate lacing of cropped meadows and slender spires of spruce and white pine. An electric atmosphere pervades the high country. A visitor can feel in the clear, warm air the impending violent change in climate that nature will inflict upon its peaks. As the hunting season approached, we could be riding through deep snow even before the usual heavy frost had tinseled the delicate cover of the alpine mountains.

Two hours out of camp, as Barney and I cleared a stand of white pine to break into a violet and bluebell meadow, a surprised herd of elk raised their heads from a hillside salt lick, not 50 yards east of us. As we sat still on our horses to watch them, many of them lowered their heads again to lick the salt. Barney turned to me with a grin that crinkled the corners of his big eyes. He raised his arms with three fingers spread out on one hand and five on the other. Thirty-five animals were in the bunch—big bulls that maneuvered their spreading racks adeptly as they mingled through the herd to find a new place to lick, graceful cows whose heads bobbed in our direction in concern for their young, and the young members of the herd who romped playfully at the edge of the feeding adults. As always, I watched the animals as if I had discovered the perfection of the natural world for the first time.

When we left the meadow we began a steep ascent that would last for the next two hours. Many young trees had fallen under the power of winter winds and heavy snow. The horses picked their way over the slender logs and prickly branches as they switch- backed up the steep terrain. We rested them often, using the time to plan for the season ahead.

"I like your country, Barney, and I see its potential. But do you think some of the customers who have never been on a horse can handle it?"

"Probably not. But think of the stories they'll have to tell when they get home. They'll love it. Besides, we'll be out of here before the snow gets thirty feet deep."

"I guess you're right. I like the idea of staying here on top of the world. When the snow is belly deep on the horses, we'll move back down to Fish Creek, and the hunters that come after that will never know what they missed."

A final, almost perpendicular rock wall brought us to the rim of Irish Basin. Seven-hundred feet below, the basin floor was sheltered on three sides by a bowl of rough, granite slabs, as if a child had molded it from clay. Thick at the bottom, tapering into an oval knife-edged ridge, the rough-hewn rock was streaked with pink and blue feldspar. White quartz crystals hung like daggers of ice from cracks in the ragged surface. At the open end, tall spruce and white pine enclosed the 200-acre grassy floor. Before the snow was deep, elk would press through the thick timber to feed in the meadow.

"I'm glad you decided to join us, Barney. You know how to pick your camps," I said.

We rode down and picked out a camping spot on the edge of the timber at the basin's open end, and then we climbed to the heights of Montana Ridge where peaks and basins, abundant meadows, and dwarfed timber stretched out below for as far as we could see. It was late afternoon by then, and the thought of biting into one of Mac's suppers overpowered our desire to see more country.

"I'm so hungry I don't even care if Mac doesn't clean the fish tonight," Barney said as the horses bounced from rock to rock on their way back to camp.

The next day it was time for Barney to return to his job. He had planned to leave at first light, but when Mac and I picked up our axes to cut poles, the temptation for Barney to stay a while longer overpowered his better judgment, and he joined us for the morning as we fell young trees for tent, corral, and feeder poles. We would return to the ranch that night to pick up the tools that we needed to complete the building project.

It was long after dark when the three of us rode up to the hitch rail at the house. My mother rushed out with her usual greeting.

"Thank heaven you made it back," she said before disappearing into the kitchen. Barney was overdue at home so we said goodbye at the gate before going inside.

With the areas firmly in our minds, we made mental notes of everything that we would need to complete our camps. I was not an experienced packer. I couldn't imagine that my stock was adequate in numbers to carry up that much equipment unless they pounded the trail all season. Mac assured me that we would have the Irish Basin camp complete with one trip, and there would be a two-week interval to plan for the regular season.

"Just remember, you have more stock than you thought you'd have with the addition of your five, fine mules."

"You're right, Mac. They'll be included in the string. I can't hurt my dad's feelings. He's a hard one to figure sometimes, isn't he?"

As good as it felt to be back in my bed, my mind raced all night long through the details of the season ahead. By daylight, I decided that I would trust my capable friend to fill in for my lack of experience.

After breakfast the next morning we loaded Kicking Jack with a fresh supply of groceries and our building tools. In an attempt to gentle the mule into a more acceptable animal he had become our chief cargo carrier. When the pack was complete we saddled our horses and left the ranch for Irish Basin.

It took us five days to complete the camp. Jack pulled our fallen lodge pole to the center of the meadow, which we enclosed with a round corral. In the center of the corral we built log feed racks for twenty-five horses and mules. Saddle racks were tacked between trees on the meadow's edge, and poles for tents were leaned against other trees. Tamarack snags were cut, split, and piled for firewood—enough to last for weeks. And then the season was almost upon us. In three days our first hunters would arrive.

Twenty-five horses and mules lined the hitch rail at the ranch when Mac and I carried out the lanterns, heating stoves, sacks of grain, hay bales, ropes, nosebags, shoeing equipment, tables and chairs, a cook stove, groceries and cots. It was early afternoon by the time our ropes were slung around the last pack. We tied the horses and mules together with their halter ropes, each rope fastened to the pack saddle of the animal in front, until they all faced in the same direction like a parade of ships whose billowing sails had puffed out from a forceful wind. Mac held the rope of the lead horse. I took the rope from his outstretched hand, nudging my saddle horse ahead. The rope pulled tight and the lead horse stepped forward, pulling the rest of the string into a jerking, then steady forward motion. The line of horses and mules bowed into a horseshoe turn until I was even with Mac who trailed behind the string.

I was twenty one years old then, and I could hardly contain my excitement. I'm sure that Mac read my thoughts.

"Beats working for a living, doesn't it," he said as he followed the string up the road, grinning through the dust.

The fall sky was blue and sunny and the air was crisp that day as we trailed over the ridges for Irish Basin. I felt like we belonged on a picture post card when we rode the last half mile into camp. New mantic canvasses glistened white in the sun as the horses slowly wound up the steep switchback trail, and bubbling waterfalls stair stepped along the way.

In two days the once-bare meadow was set up with a first-rate camp. Even stacks of split wood stood beside a gleaming white cook tent. Three sleeping tents spread out along the creek with their own piles of wood beside them. Twenty-five pack animals pulled hay from the feeder, and coffee steamed on the stove in the cook tent. It was the day that the hunters would arrive at the ranch. I would ride down to bring them back the following morning.

"We'll see you tomorrow afternoon, Mac, and I'll be ready for a big supper," I said as I rode out of camp.

"It'll be ready, but try to remember that this time you'll have paying customers who'll be hungry, too, so leave something in the dish after your turn."

"I'll try to remember," I called as my horse stepped up his pace on the trail home. And to myself I added, And thanks, Mac ... for everything.

14

As I rode to the ranch, I knew that time had slipped away from me through the busy morning, and that the hunters would have arrived by the time I got back to the house. I was nervous about meeting the first clients, but I wasn't concerned about their welfare in my absence. My mother would feed them and welcome them with her gift of hospitality, and my dad would be offering detailed accounts of what they could expect through the week. And on top of that, as they clustered around the kitchen table with mugs of hot coffee in front of them, they would also be entertained by the life force of whatever group he joined—our guide for the week—Danny Jansic.

Danny was the last person I had thought of as a guide when we were putting the business together. In fact I hadn't thought of him at all. I was dumbfounded when he appeared at the ranch in early spring to say that he was interested in guiding on a part time basis.

"Danny, I know you're a good hunter but how can you guide when you don't know a thing about horses?" I asked when he made his proposal.

"I thought that would be an asset. I wouldn't come in with a lot of pre-conceived notions about how things should be done."

Danny's engaging wit threw me off balance again. It was always that way when the unpredictable policeman from Anaconda stopped by.

It had been only a year or so since a friend of mine from Anaconda had brought Danny to the ranch, and it had only been a few times since then that Danny had traveled our way. But each time he paid us a visit he was welcomed by all as a long-lost member of the family. It was the cultivated charm of the tall, dark young man that opened doors for him wherever he went.

When he sat on the wood box that day and said that he wanted to guide, he and I both knew that that is exactly what he'd be doing. But I had to carry the suspense a little further.

"You don't have time to learn to ride that well. Do you have any idea what it's like to take care of a bunch of hunters who have never been on a horse?"

Danny's long, rangy body shifted positions. He drew up his bony knees, rested his elbows on them and looked at me intently.

. "No, I don't. But I think you're about to tell me."

"Okay, I won't put us through it. Let's go for a ride and see how you do. I'll give you a gentle horse."

"There isn't time for me to learn if I start with gentle horses. How about giving me one that isn't broke?"

"Okay, Danny, you win. But don't sniffle to me when you roll down the mountain underneath a half ton of horse."

I didn't give Danny an unbroken horse that day, but I did bring out a big chestnut, a Morgan-Thoroughbred cross that I had ridden only a few times. The colt was good about standing still when I got off and on, and I didn't think that he would buck for anyone. But he was high spirited and he'd run away at the drop of a hat. As long as Danny could hold on he'd be all right. At the same time, the horse might possibly set him straight in the area of over confidence. I held the horse at the hitch rail for Danny while he mounted. When I was seated in my saddle I glanced back at the pair. The horse stood still and relaxed, and Danny sat confidently in the saddle, smiling with boyish charm.

"Okay, Danny, let's go. Your horse has a tendency to run away so stay behind me for a while," I said.

When we started out on the road to the West Fork I turned around to check out a commotion behind me. Danny had taken my advice about holding the horse in check. One of his hands gripped the saddle horn and the other pulled the lines so tight that the horse's lower jaw dropped open onto his chest. The animal tried to raise his head and pranced wildly. The amiable smile was gone from Danny's face.

"Ease up on the lines," I shouted. "That poor horse thinks you put him in a straight jacket. He's going to explode any minute."

Danny put a little less tension on the lines, and the horse followed along quietly until we turned from the road into the timber. Then Danny called from behind.

"We're getting along great back here now. What will happen if I relax the lines some more?"

"I don't know. Why don't you try it and find out? Only let up just a little bit."

Danny let the lines drop and the horse shot forward, almost out from under him. By the time I reached him, Danny had pulled the chestnut's mouth into an open-jaw position again. The horse reared high with a wild shriek. When he came down I grabbed the side of his bridle, pulling him forward beside my horse.

"Do you want me to ride him for a while?" I asked.

"Why would you do that? We were just starting to have fun."

I showed Danny how much tension to keep on the lines, and I told him to stay right beside me so that the horse wouldn't worry about being left behind.

"We'll stay this way until the road starts up, and then we'll trot for a while to tire your horse. Maybe then you'll be able to talk to him a little bit. I gave you what you asked for. You've got a lot of horse under you there."

"I could tell that right away and I like him. How much will you take for him after I get him broke?"

After a mile of head shaking and prancing from the chestnut, I was happy to see the road start to rise. I told Danny that I would trot my horse up the hill, and if he loosened the lines slowly his horse would follow. When I gave my horse a quiet kick, Danny's horse shot forward again into a dead run. He wouldn't run for long when the road got steep so I stayed back until the horse wound down.

"Where have you been?" Danny asked when I rode up behind him. "You should get a fast horse like mine."

Since the chestnut was tired from his uphill run, I thought it was a good time for a cross-country trip through the timber. When we started out he picked his way calmly through the trees until he got his second wind. Then it was back to the prancing, and he added to it log jumping, running under low-hanging limbs, fighting to turn around for home, running sideways into trees, and everything that he could think of, except bucking, to get Danny off his back.

But Danny's confidence was fortified each time the horse tried, and lost. He screamed, pulled on the lines, kicked him, ducked under limbs, rolled in the saddle, and bounced high in the air. Finally the chestnut decided that he had met his match and he kept a steady pace at my horse's side all the way back to the ranch. I couldn't help but praise Danny's performance.

"You may not be the most graceful student I've ever had, but you take the prize for guts," I said.

"I won't have any trouble with the hunters, anyway."

"No, I don't suppose you will."

So that was the first step in Danny's career as a hunting guide, and the second step was taking place in the kitchen as I rode for home from Irish Basin. Under his care would be his brother-in-law from Helena, another fellow from that city, and an elderly man who would drive his car from somewhere in the Midwest. I tried to visualize the group, and I assumed that Danny would by then have them reveling in stories and laughter. When I entered the kitchen though, the atmosphere was not as I had expected. An air of restraint hovered over the group. I was perplexed because the two men from Helena impressed me as friendly, relaxed people who would blend well with Danny's lively personality. When I met the third man, however, I understood the reason for the general atmosphere of constraint. Danny had injected an air of refinement into the conversation in deference to a dignified elderly gentleman, a retired Army colonel who was in his eighties. I had talked to the man on the phone so I knew he was an older person, but I had no idea that he had seen that many winters.

As he greeted me with a smile and a warm, firm, hand shake, telling me of his attraction to our country, I felt an overwhelming responsibility to see that he took home an elk. For all the vigor that he displayed in that hand shake, he wouldn't be able to ride through the mountains on horseback for many more hunting seasons.

One of my mother's big breakfasts awaited us when we woke up the next morning. When we finished eating we put the hunters' duffle and rifles in back of the pickup for the drive to Fish Creek. It was such a long distance to Irish Basin, we decided to drive to the base camp and ride horse back from there.

When the pack horses were loaded at the Fish Creek camp and the riding horses were saddled, I stayed close to the Colonel in case he needed help with mounting. But the moment that he put his foot in the stirrup, I could tell that he was no stranger to horses.

"You handle your horse as if you've had lots of experience," I said.

"Oh my, yes, but not for many years. I was in the cavalry for a long time and I loved every minute of it. That's one of the reasons why I've been looking forward to this trip so much. I haven't been on a horse since I left the Army, and for some reason I felt like I just had to get back in the saddle. I can't tell you how good it feels to be riding through such beautiful country on this nice little horse. I know it's going to feel even better when we find all those elk that your father's been telling me about."

"We'll certainly do our best to find them."

When we rode up the steep switchback trail into camp, Chappy, the horse that the Colonel was riding, slid back from time to time through the slide rock. When I watched the Colonel gently urge the horse forward with relaxed confidence I continued to gain affection for the fine, old gentleman. We had ridden for ten miles and he wouldn't stop once to rest.

Mac was all ready for us when we pulled up to the hitch rail behind the cook tent. He came out to greet us, wearing his baggy jeans and plaid, flannel shirt.

"Glad you made it up here to our billy goat country, fellas," he said. "Let me take your horses so you can go in for a cup of coffee. I'll be back in a minute, and I'll catch your names then."

We entered the cook tent to find coffee steaming on the stove. Beside it, a big pot of stew bubbled and a pan of raised biscuits was ready to pop in the oven. The table was set with a mug beside each plate, and a big bowl of jam made the centerpiece. As long as you gave him clean groceries to work with, you couldn't find a finer camp cook in the country than Mac. After gorging ourselves, we stretched out happily beside the stoves in the sleeping tents. Mac had built fires in them while we ate so the tents were comfortably warm.

Shortly before daylight the next morning, an elk bugled with a long, loud call that twisted through the peaks and valleys. A good omen, I thought, as I saddled little Chappy for the Colonel. The gentleman will have his elk. When we finished saddling the horses, I stopped by the sleeping tents to wake the hunters. Then I went into the cook tent to join Danny for a cup of coffee while Mac put the finishing touches on our breakfast.

"I haven't had a chance to tell you how proud I am of the good manners you're showing for the Colonel, Danny," I said.

"It's good to live like the other half once in a while. Besides, he's worth the effort. I really like that man."

"So do I, and that's why I'm going to hunt with him today. I'm afraid you might slip back into your old self," I said with a smile.

We started out that morning with Danny and his two hunters traveling in the direction of Montana Ridge while I took the Colonel through the Cash Creek area. I was glad that I had such impressive country to show my client because I couldn't find an elk to show him, not even one through the whole, long day. We rode for miles through all the basins that Barney and I had covered the week before. We saw their bedding ground, and the sign was no more than two days old, but the elk had disappeared.

We rode hard through the mountains for the next three days, and the Colonel never complained. I knew he was tired, and I tried to ride through easy country, but he wanted his elk. All that we could do was keep searching.

Then on the fourth day he called to me as we rode down a steep hill.

"In the Army we used to stop every two hours and dismount. This certainly is a lot harder riding."

My heart almost broke when I turned around to see that fine old man hanging limp in his saddle, bracing his hands on the saddle horn to take the pressure off his legs.

"Don't worry, Colonel. One way or another you're going to have an elk to take home."

"Do you think that you could get one for me? I don't think I can go any farther, and I just can't go home without one."

It's against Fish and Game rules to shoot game for anyone, but what could I do when that grand old man looked at me through a tired, lined face with a request like that. He knew that he was on his last hunt, and I vowed on the spot that he would have an elk in back of his station wagon when he left Petty Creek.

When we returned to camp Danny's two hunters told us that they had to leave the following day. They had had a good time and they were experienced hunters so they understood that game will sometimes vanish. They reserved a spot for the next year, later in the season. After hearing the news that they were leaving, I told Danny that the Colonel would stay in camp the next day and that he and I were going together to find him an elk, come hell or high water. Those were prophetic words. By the end of the following day we were right in the middle of both.

Danny's hunters told us the next morning that they would ride back to the ranch by themselves so that we could be on our way to find the Colonel's elk. Leaving Mac to see them off, we said goodbye to them from camp, and then we left for the lower end of Burdette Creek. We would traverse the country on the way down, and stay at the base camp in Fish Creek that night. I asked Mac if he had left any food at the base camp. He assured me that he had stored enough staples and canned food to last for the season.

Since Danny and I were going to be alone, I asked him if he thought he could handle a barely green-broke horse. It would be a good time to give the animal some experience. Danny was ready and eager, so I picked out a big bay named King, and for myself I chose an even bigger 19-year-old buckskin work hose that had never been broke to ride. We started out with the typical thrills that go along with green-broke horses, but Danny had learned a lot since his first ride through the West Fork, and he kept the horse under control.

We rode hard all the way down without success in finding an elk. By the time we reached camp it was dark. We were so hungry that we spent the last two miles planning a menu from the food that we imagined was in the cupboards.

"I'll unsaddle the horses while you go in and start supper," Danny said when we pulled up to the hitch rail. "I don't care what you fix, but make sure there's plenty of it."

Mac had left several lanterns on the kitchen counter so I lit one to shed light on the cupboards. The first cupboard revealed an unopened case of canned corn on the shelf. The second cupboard was bare, as was the third, and all the rest. I assumed that Mac had stacked the food somewhere else in the house so I began a search around the kitchen floor and on through the living room.

"Why is that light flickering all over the house?" Danny said as he entered the dark kitchen. "I thought you'd be in here covering the stove with kettles by now."

"So did I. There's plenty of kettles in the cupboards if you want to get them out. I'll keep looking around 'til I find the food to put in them."

"What do you mean, find the food?"

"There's nothing in the kitchen but a case of corn. The rest of it must be somewhere else."

"To hell with the kettles. I'll help you find the food."

Danny and I crept through the house with our lanterns for several minutes, climbing up the stairs, into the bedrooms and closets, checking the bath tub, the medicine cabinet, and searching every corner of the house.

"Is there a wood shed to look in?" Danny finally asked.

"Yeah, go check it out. I'll start opening the corn."

I had started a fire in the stove and I was opening the first can of corn when Danny came back in the kitchen.

"Do you think Mac did this to us on purpose?" he asked.

"No, Danny. Mac just had a lot to think about, and he forgot what he put in which camp."

"Oh, well, if we divide what we've got between supper tonight and breakfast in the morning, that will give us three cans of corn apiece at each meal. By supper time tomorrow, we'll be back in Irish Basin with an elk.

"I don't know. The way things have been going I'm not going to count on it. I'm limiting us to two."

We were on the trail early the next morning after eating the second set of canned corn. About five miles out of camp an elk bugled again, not very far away. It was still too dark to see so we stopped our horses to wait for daylight. When the hazy outline of ridges took solid form, I saw the shadowed figure of a feeding elk about 600 yards away. It was a long shot but we needed him so I fired. We crossed the canyon, but we couldn't find a trace of him and the pressure was on.

As we rode up and down the ridges, we found ourselves on an almost perpendicular mountain of slide rock without a trail to help us reach the top. The horses fought their way through the boulders without balking until Danny's horse suddenly lowered his head to begin one of the most powerful displays of bucking I have ever seen. He had run a stick between his hind legs and through the double cinch, and if it took a crumbling of the entire mountain to break loose, it looked like that's exactly what he would do.

"Steer the horse toward me!" I hollered at Danny, but he could do nothing but hang on. King fish-tailed, stumbled, slid backward, and fell, over and over again. I fought my way through rolling rock to ride as close to him as I dared. Suddenly, Danny miraculously guided the animal into the back of Buck. When the motion stopped, and the two horses stood trembling on the mountainside, Danny's face was white, and he shook from head to toe. He was also speechless for the first time since I'd met him.

"Well, he's learning, Danny, and so are you, and that's what counts," I said.

Danny was too shaken for a comeback.

We rode on, making a big circle through the country, until we were back on the rim of the canyon where I had shot at the elk. We had just stopped our horses to survey the area when another bugle sounded from across the canyon. Startled, we looked at each other hopefully. Quickly, we dismounted and tied our horses to a tree. With our rifles in our hands, we crept down through the lodge pole, crouched, ready to shoot, barely making a sound in the dry pine needles under our feet. An old beaver dam provided a bridge for us when we reached a high, swift creek at the bottom of the canyon. We found firm footing in the center of it, and we crossed to begin the ascent. Then a twig snapped under my foot. A spike bull jumped up through a patch of alder brush in front of us, and I got him. The search was over. We would soon return to the Colonel with his prize.

The bull was small enough for Buck to carry out whole so the Colonel could see his animal intact. Danny dressed him out while I ran back up the hill to get Buck. After we crossed the beaver dam, the horse caught the elk's scent and snorted. I tied him to a tree as he pranced nervously from side to side. He was a big, willing horse, but at age 19 it was going to take some getting used to, to have an elk slung on his back.

I tied him shorter and stroked him while Danny dragged the elk toward him. As his nervousness gradually disappeared, we continued to speak in soothing tones while we lifted the elk beside him. He kicked with his hind feet, swinging his hind quarters as far away as possible. We kept talking and stroking while we lifted the elk closer to him until we convinced him that it wasn't going to hurt him. When it was finally draped over the saddle I made sure that it was tied so that the horns couldn't tine him. Then I started down the hill, leading Buck and his elk. Danny came along behind me, leading his saddle horse.

The elk had been shot just before dark. By the time we reached the bottom of the canyon it was black dark. We could see nothing, neither our horses nor our hands in front of our face. I knew I was close to the bottom when I heard the sound of the swift-running creek. My foot slipped down and hit rocky ground as freezing water gushed inside my boot. Buck snorted and pawed behind me while I crawled slowly along the bank, feeling the water with my hand to find the beaver dam. When I felt a bed of sticks I knew that we were at the dam, and I could only hope that we would stay in the center where it might be sound enough to hold a 1,300-pound horse and his 250 pound elk.

Danny managed to pull his horse over the pile of watery sticks, but when I started over the dam Buck planted his feet. I tugged and snapped the rope at him until he finally lurched forward. We moved along that way for some distance with Buck pulling back then lunging, causing me to fall face down with every few steps. Then the horse could not be budged. I could tell by the position of the lead rope that he had either fallen or he was mired.

I crawled back to him, groping ahead of me so I wouldn't stumble into him and fall into the current. When my hand touched his nose, I reached back for his neck and felt a pile of sticks. Only his head was above water.

"Tie up your horse and get over here, fast, or we're going to lose Buck!" I hollered.

Danny told me when he found the dam. I talked while he crossed so he could judge his distance.

"We'll have to get the elk off before we can help him out of here," I said when he reached my side. "I've been trying to work these knots under water but the rope is swollen and I can't move them. My hands are so numb I can hardly feel a thing."

We worked together under water on one knot at a time while we lay in sticks along side the horse. I wasn't keeping track of time, but it was a long while later when the last knot gave way. We heaved the elk from the horse's back, skidding it over the water to the bank. (Elk float because they have hollow hair.)

To release Buck from the mire, we would need the help of King. When Danny brought the horse across the dam I tied one end of my lariat in a bowline knot around Buck's neck and dallied the other end around King's saddle horn. Danny pulled on his horse while I snapped him from behind with a rope. King pulled forward with all the strength he could muster, but it wasn't enough to raise the mired Buck. Danny led him back over the dam.

In a last effort to save Buck, I inched my way through the water to his rear while Danny took hold of the halter rope. By then we had displaced so much of the dam's surface that only Buck's nose was above water. We pushed and pulled together in rocking rhythmic motion until our strength was gone. We rested for a minute, and then we repeated the procedure many times until the ground around him gradually gave way. Eventually he had enough freedom to work his feet. While we pushed and pulled, he scrambled with increasing force until he finally lunged to the top. Danny pulled him forward immediately. I held my breath, listening to mud slurp around King's big feet as they walked away.

"We're on the bank, out of your way," Danny finally called.

When I reached the other side, Buck was tied to a tree a few feet from the dam. We found the elk, and by groping along we carried it up the bank.

"We won't have any trouble finding the horse," I said. "I can almost feel him shaking from here."

"He's not shaking any harder than I am. It's been a long time since that last can of corn."

We made our way to the horse, and lifted the elk onto his saddle. He was too tired to protest through the long session of tying it on with a stiff, water-soaked rope and our frozen fingers.

"It'll stay," I said when the last knot was tied. "Let's find the trail back to camp. If I don't start walking pretty soon, I might freeze standing up."

When my feet reached the trail I realized that we had another obstacle to overcome.

"Danny, how am I going to lead this horse down the trail when I can't see where I'm going?" I asked.

"We'll let my horse see for you. I'll ride ahead and talk to you so you can follow my voice."

"Okay. Start talking."

"I'm on my horse and we're starting out. Did I ever tell you how I got hired by the police department?"

"Oh, come on. Keep it light. Sing a song or something."

"I don't think you'd like that. I ride horses better than I sing. I'll tell you about the girls in Anaconda."

"Before you do that, tell me why we aren't on the trail. I'm following your voice and I'm going uphill."

"King, why did you leave the trail? Okay, I've turned him around and we're going down. I think we're on the trail now. He's leveled out. Are you following?"

"We're coming. Keep talking."

Danny chattered on until I felt myself going up again.

"It isn't working, Danny. Your horse isn't trail wise yet. Turn him around and stop when you think you're back where you belong. I've got another idea."

Buck and I stepped our way back down.

"This horse can stay on the trail. We'll put him in the lead and I'll hold onto his tail for a guide. You can ride your horse. He'll follow."

"Okay. Let's give it a try."

"Come on, old fella. Take us home," I said. "You're not pulling logs this time, only me. Giddup!"

As the tired horse stepped out at a fast walk, I thought how good it must feel to him to lead at his own pace after crawling behind me through the night with an elk on his back.

"We should have thought of this earlier!" I called cheerfully. "This horse knows what he's doing. Are you following okay?"

"We're right behind your voice."

"What a relief it is to be moving. How far …

My question hung in mid-air over the sound of a big SPLAT! I had fallen head first into Buck's hind feet. He jumped forward, grazing my forehead with the cleats in his shoes. I hollered, "WHOOAA!" When the horse stopped, I stood up and talked to him while I worked my way to his head. I grabbed his halter before he changed his mind about staying in Fish Creek.

"That was a close one. I forgot about the windfalls. We're going to have to do it the hard way," I said.

Leading our horses, we spent the night feeling our way down the trail, inch by inch. It was daylight when we reached the cabin at Fish Creek. Together we lifted the elk off of Buck and hung it from the porch rafters. Danny took the horses to the corral while I went inside to open the four remaining cans of corn.

"Don't bother to heat the corn," Danny said when he came into the kitchen. "I have to get back to Anaconda to restore law and order."

"You're a fine looking marshal."

Danny's eyes were red, his whiskers were half an inch long, and he was covered from head to toe with elk blood and mud. Since his brother-in-law had returned to Helena without him I wondered about the success of his plan to hitch hike to Missoula, and then take a bus to Anaconda.

"You know, Danny, if I was the driver of a car or a bus that you were trying to board, I might have my doubts about letting you on."

"That's because you have trouble seeing a diamond in the rough. I'll probably be back in Anaconda before you get to Irish Basin."

We gulped our corn in silence.

"A bad start means a good finish," Danny said when he took his last mouthful of corn. "I'm sure sorry I can't be with you when you tell the Colonel about his elk. I can't say it's been a terrific week, but then it hasn't been the worst week I've spent, either. Hang on to my sleeping bag. I'll see you when the snow flies."

Danny walked down the trail to the Fish Creek road. I got up wearily and strolled to the corral to saddle a fresh horse. Before riding out of camp, I stopped by the hanging elk and extracted the four teeth that were often used in making jewelry. When I reached the Fish Creek Road, a Forest Service truck was just leaving the trail junction with Danny as his passenger. Danny smiled through the window with a smug look. I waved him on his way.

I was half way up the switchback trail into camp when the Colonel stepped out of the tent. He waved, watching intently as we climbed. When I was close enough to see the expression on his face, it was one of deep concern. He disappeared into the tent, reappearing a moment later with a jacket on. I rode up to him, stopped my horse, and reached into my pocket for the elk teeth.

"Danny had to leave, Colonel, but he sends you his regards. We thought you might like to have these while we ride back to Fish Creek to pick up your elk," I said.

His face shone like a new silver dollar as he reached for the teeth. Every minute of the day before had been worth it, and I knew that I had found my niche. In front of me was a happy old Colonel with an elk to take home, and ahead was six more weeks of adventure. I could hardly wait for the regular season to begin.

15

ow are we going to get him up the mountain? It's too far to walk," I said to Barney that first morning of the regular season. We were ready to leave the base camp for Irish Basin with our two likable, middle-aged hunters from Wisconsin, and we had run into a snag. I had spent much of the previous year thinking of solutions to every possible problem that might arise, but I didn't anticipate this one in my wildest imagination.

When the hunters arrived the day before, one of them told me that he had never ridden horse back. I had several gentle horses for non-riders, one of which was Chappy, the little palomino that the Colonel had ridden.

"Don't worry, George," I told him. "I have just the horse for you. He's small and he'll be content to follow along behind the others. All you'll have to do is sit in the saddle."

George looked at me gratefully, but a flutter of skepticism crossed his face.

When all the horses were saddled, I led Chappy to the back of the line and held him while George mounted. I showed him how to hold the lines loosely and told him that when we started out, Chappy would follow without any command. Barney led us down the trail and I rode in front of George.

When we had gone just a few yards I turned around to see how the horse and rider were getting along. Chappy had stayed behind at the hitch rail.

"Give him a little kick, George," I said.

George kicked, but Chappy didn't move.

"A little harder!"

George kicked harder, and Chappy nibbled on the hitch rail. I turned my horse and rode behind him.

"I'll ride back here, George," I said. "I'll give Chappy a little slap with my lines to start him moving. Don't worry. He won't do anything but walk ahead."

I tapped him from behind, and the horse moved down the trail and into the timber.

"Pull on the lines, George," I said.

George pulled but the horse continued to walk through the trees. I rode up beside him and took hold of his bridle to stop him.

"There. Now follow me," I said. "He'll want to get back to the other horses now."

I started back to the trail but Chappy refused to budge. Barney left his hunter on the trail and rode up beside us.

"Is Chappy on the warpath this morning?" he asked.

"I don't know what kind of bee he has in his bonnet. He won't do a thing for George."

"Why don't we go back and get another horse?"

I took Barney's advice and went back to camp for a big bay named Slim. If any horse would take care of George he was the one. I hadn't chosen him in the beginning because I thought his height might intimidate the wary hunter. But all by himself, Slim had carried tiny children around the meadow, and he had taken more people on their first ride than any of my horses. No matter how inexperienced the rider, he responded to every makeshift command. If anyone started to fall, he slowed gradually to a stop until they regained their balance. He would be a valuable asset to a hunting business.

George mounted Slim and the drama unfolded as before. To this day I have no idea what made the horses respond as they did. It never happened again. When I saw that the situation was hopeless I took Barney to the side, pleading with him for a solution.

"Why don't I lead his horse with my saddle horse? Slim's so big we'll put him back on Chappy so he'll be more comfortable," he said.

"He'll probably feel ridiculous."

"All we can do is ask him. It looks to me like he doesn't have a choice if he wants to hunt."

With a sigh of relief, George agreed to the plan. When he was once again settled on Chappy, Barney picked up the lead rope to ride in front, with the little horse and his rider following along as if it had always been the natural way to travel through the mountains.

By the time we reached Irish Basin, a drenching rain had soaked us to the skin. The deluge continued so violently for the next three days I could hold my hand a foot away from the ceiling and feel the spray penetrate the canvas to the inside. We couldn't hunt, but after the soaking we received on the way up, the hunters were happy to stay inside where it was warm and dry. By the third night the rain stopped, and we woke up the next morning to a mountain country covered with snow.

Elk tracks led everywhere when we rode out the next morning. Barney led George and Chappy in one direction, and my hunter and I rode the opposite way. We had been gone for about an hour when shots rang from Barney's side of the mountain. When we rode back to camp to see if they had been successful, we found Barney starting out down the trail with two pack horses behind him. He had led George straight to an elk. My hunter wanted to go along to help pack the animal on the horses so we all rode down together.

It was early evening when we returned to camp with our packed horses. We had just reached the camp meadow when five elk crept out of the alders to feed. My hunter got one of them, and the week had been a success.

It was time then to pack out camp before we were buried in snow. Barney took the hunters and their elk to the ranch. He would return with the pickup the next day to the Burdette Creek junction. By evening, Mac and I had everything ready to go, and we loaded the horses and mules at daylight the following morning. As we led them down through falling snow, branches bowed low beside the trail, already burdened with a heavy winter coat. Beyond them was a screen of white and the silence of a winter forest.

When we reached the pickup it was almost dark so we scrambled to unload the packs. We needed daylight to arrange the equipment so that it would all fit in one load. Though dark overcame us we managed to get it all in. Barney started for home with the pickup wheels spinning in the two feet of powder snow that covered the road. Mac and I pushed to start it rolling, but it only slid sideways before it stalled. Barney poked his head out of the window.

"Any suggestions?" he asked.

When I had ridden down the trail behind the pack string I noticed that the horses and mules packed the snow into a hard surface. I thought that if we divided them into two strings, Mac and I could each lead half of them on opposite sides of the road, tire width apart. With ten animals to make a trail through the snow, the road might be firm enough to drive on. Barney agreed to try so Mac and I divided the string. We climbed into our cold, wet saddles, and moved out into the dark with our animals trailing behind. We could hear the motor's faint purr when Barney started the pickup. A weak illumination from the headlights made visible the flakes of falling snow as they touched the ground. Other than that, only silence and darkness surrounded us.

"It's peaceful riding through the dark on a snowy night, isn't it, Mac," I said.

"I guess so, if that's the way you want to look at it. It's a good thing you enjoy it.

If you stay in this business very long you'll be doing a lot more of it."

We rode on for a short distance and then the soft light at our feet disappeared.

"Barney isn't with us any more. Hold the horses and I'll see what the problem is," I said.

I rode back down the road to find Barney stuck in the snow. The horses weren't able to pack it hard enough. We took shovels from the pickup and started to dig. All through the night the truck moved along in jerks as we added a few more feet with our shovels. For a while the truck would make it over the trail, and then we would have to stop the horses to dig again. When we reached the highway, Barney was able to make it on his own. Mac and I led the pack strings over the ridge to the ranch. It was daylight when we tied up the horses at the house.

I didn't think that I could lift a pack box until I was fortified with food so we left the animals at the hitch rail and went inside for breakfast. Only one hunter was registered for the week, and he was due to arrive that morning.

It wasn't snowing at the ranch so when we unloaded the horses and mules, Barney and Mac laid out tents to dry while I carried pack boxes to store in the shed. I had just started my third trip across the driveway when a new station wagon pulled up to the house. Assuming that it was our hunter, I set down the box and walked up to greet him. A short, slightly-built, dark-haired man who was about forty years old leaped out of the car and scurried toward me. His lips were pressed tight in a grimace and his small, black eyes blazed with fire.

"Hello. I'm Roger Longpre," I said.

He stopped abruptly in front of me.

"I'm going to be hunting this week. Is anybody else coming?"

He spoke so fast I could hardly understand him.

"No, you'll have your own personally guided tour of Petty Creek this week."

"That's good. I'm not a well man. I'll need special food and special attention while I'm here."

"That's what I'm here to provide. Let's go in the house—ah—I don't believe I caught your name."

"Harold. You should have known that already."

"Yes, I'm sorry, Harold. You must be hungry after your long trip."

"Yes, I am, but all I can have is a glass of milk. I have bad ulcers and they're acting up. I came all the way from New Jersey, you know."

"Yes, I know. I'm glad that you landed here because our good Guernsey milk will fix up your stomach in nothing flat."

Harold! The name and the state suddenly rang a bell. This was my first reservation, the one I almost framed. As we walked to the house I turned around to wink at Barney who was kneeling beside a tent in an open-mouthed stare.

I left my client to the care of my mother while I gathered up Coco, a big, strong pack horse who would carry Harold's gear into Burdette. Barney walked out to the meadow with me.

"It looks like you picked the right time to go home," I said.

"I'm not so sure. I feel guilty leaving you with that guy. I sure hope you find him an elk in a hurry."

"If it gets too tough I'll send up smoke signals. You can come back to bail me out."

When Coco was saddled I went back to the house.

"If you'll come out to your car, Harold, you can show me what you want to take with you into camp," I said.

Harold scurried again out the door, and when I got to the station wagon he had the back of it open. He pointed nervously to five suitcases and a three-foot-long box.

"Do you want to take all of these?" I asked.

"Yes, I certainly do."

"What about this wooden box?"

"Mercy me, yes."

I started to lift it out of the car, but I was immediately interrupted.

"Here, here! Don't lift that out. Let me do it. That's my medicine chest. I don't see how that horse is going to get it up there without breaking everything," he said as he pushed me out of the way.

"You don't need to worry. He carries eggs clear across the mountains and not one has ever been broken. Are there any glass bottles in your chest?"

"Heavens no! I wouldn't think of putting the chest on a horse if the bottles were made of glass. But I'm still worried."

"Why don't we open it? I'll stuff your socks in between some of the bottles to keep them from rattling around."

When Harold opened his medicine chest I started to believe that the man had legitimate complaints about his health. No one that took that many pills and potions could possibly stay well. He must have had armies of antibodies in his system that were lined up and ready to attack the regiments of invading medicines.

On the trip to camp I was given the complete history of Harold's lifetime series of aches and pains. He did have diabetes, and I was sorry about that, but his headaches, the ulcers, the chronic kidney problem, the hemorrhoids, and the rheumatism made me think there was more than just a bit of hypochondria involved in his medical history. Mac had already left for Burdette. I wasn't looking forward to inflicting upon him this chronic complainer with his special dietary needs.

"Mac, come out and meet Harold," I called when we rode up to the cook tent. I thought that it would be best for Harold to unload his health problems on Mac before he went inside and found something cooking."

"Welcome, Harold. I …

"What is that I smell cooking?" Harold interrupted.

"Just a big pot of stew. That's always the first meal."

"Does it have spices in it?"

Before Mac answered I excused myself, telling Harold that I would put his horse away while he and Mac got acquainted. I had listened to the man for 15 miles. When I returned to the tent, Mac looked at me with an expression of deep pain.

"Harold was just telling me about his diabetes and some of his other health problems. He was able to eat a small amount of stew. Now he's tired and ready for bed. I'll go right out and start a fire in his sleeping tent. Did you put his duffle in there?"

"You bet. Everything's ready and waiting."

"Before you start a fire, bring me the wooden box that's in there," Harold said. "My pills are in it. I need several of them right away."

Harold took his pills, and I tucked him into bed. When I returned to the cook tent I collapsed into a chair.

"A week of this, Mac? A whole week???" I said.

"You're doing fine and you're learning what patience in its purest form is all about. Just keep telling yourself that it's only one week out of your life, and then it'll be back to business as usual."

"Well, it's not going to be a whole week. One way or another I'm going to find a way to send Harold home early."

It had been over 36 hours since Mac and I had slept. I ate a plate of stew and we both went straight to our sleeping tents. I had just settled into my sleeping bag when Harold burst into my tent.

"I want you to come out here to hold the flashlight for me. My kidneys are bothering me so I'm afraid I'll have to urinate often tonight."

That was the beginning of the first trip out into the night. On the third one he decided that I should move into his tent so that he wouldn't have to stumble in the dark to find me.

It became clear after the second day of hunting that Harold wasn't going to go home with an elk. He wouldn't leave his medicine chest long enough to find one. The riding was too hard on him, as was sitting on the ground to watch the bottom of canyons. Everything was too hard on him, including Mac's cooking. But on the third day a big buck popped out of the bushes across a canyon from us, not more that one-half mile from camp. The deer was unaware of us, which gave Harold ample time to shoot, and he got his buck. He said that it would be too tiring for him to ride across the canyon so he waited, seated on his hemorrhoid pad, while I brought back the deer. The trip allowed me quiet time away from Harold's chatter, and I came up with a brilliant idea to entice him to leave.

"That's a beautiful animal," I said when I rode up with the deer draped across the saddle."

"Yes, I hope you dressed him properly so he doesn't spoil."

"Never fear, Harold, he's in good shape."

"What took you so long? I've been in terrible pain sitting here all this time, and it's past time to take my kidney pills."

"Since you mention that subject, Harold, I want you to know how much I admire the way you're able to carry on out here when most men in your condition would crumble. But I'm afraid that if you keep pushing yourself this way something bad might happen to you, and the blame would all be mine. So, since you have such a nice buck to take home, I have a set of seven-point elk horns that I would be happy to add to your trophy."

"You'd give me a set of elk horns that big for nothing?"

"You bet I would. And I'll even go a step farther. I know you're too tired to ride to the ranch, so we'll ride together to the bottom of the trail at Fish Creek. You can wait for me there with the deer while I go to the ranch for the pickup. How does that sound?"

"It sounds all right to me. Like you said, I've been under a terrible strain, and it's only right that you help me out."

When I got back to the ranch I ran into the house and hollered,

"Brace yourself, Mom, and fix a big bowl of bread and milk. I'm taking the pickup to Fish Creek to get Harold."

When he left the next morning, Harold instructed me to tie the deer, intact, on top of his car next to the elk rack. The buck wasn't skinned or bagged. It would ride through sun and rain all the way to New Jersey so that the entire United States of America would know that Harold bagged a buck in Montana. I was thankful that he lived too far away to invite me for supper.

Harold later wrote to us many times to book a trip for the following year and to request that we sell him five acres at the end of the grazing meadow for his retirement. His letters were never answered.

With the nightmare of catering to Harold behind us, we would enjoy every minute of the third week of the season when five capable outdoorsmen from Nevada joined us. I would learn something new every week about our hunters' expectations for a successful trip. The Nevadans showed me that they can have as much fun getting ready for the hunt as they do hunting itself.

Barney had joined us again, and Danny stayed through the week to guide. We woke up on the first morning in camp to brilliant sunshine that was so bright we couldn't see into the north slopes of the alder patches where the elk would feed and bed down. I suggested to the men that we move camp to the log bunk house so we could hunt in areas where the sun wouldn't be a problem, and they all agreed. I told them to relax while we packed the horses, but they all asked if they could help. They carried cots and lanterns to the hitch rail, and helped pack groceries in boxes. Some of them caught and led the horses from the corrals, and saddled them with pack saddles after watching how it was done. We enjoyed an atmosphere of relaxed camaraderie through both the preparation for the trip and the ride to the ranch. When everything was unloaded, and they were settled in the bunkhouse for the night, they were invigorated and even more excited about the upcoming hunt.

After the pack horses were unloaded that day, Barney and I took them along with the saddle horses and their feed to the bottom of Petty Mountain so that they would be ready to take us up early in the morning. The sun wouldn't be a problem on the east side of the mountain. I had a good feeling that we'd find success.

When we had ridden with the hunters past the old Casper wild horse camp and through the sheep meadows, I spied four bulls bedded down in the bottom of a canyon. Danny and Barney placed the men along the rim of the canyon while I rode to the bottom to drive out the elk. When the bulls thundered up the canyon, three of the hunters each got one. While Danny rode down the mountain for the pack horses, all the men helped dress the animals and then load them on the horses. A happy bunch of Nevadans rode with us back to the ranch. Every one wanted to trade their horse-weary legs for some footwork the next day so we hiked into the West Fork. By evening the last two men had their elk, and the joy of success swept though the bunkhouse that night.

When the last week of the season arrived, eight hunters from the Midwest were on hand to share with us the beauty of a sparkling, frozen Petty Creek country. We tried for two days to hunt horseback, but a slippery skiff of new snow covered the ice, and the horses fell on the steep terrain where the elk would be found. We abandoned riding and hunted on foot. We were too far away to reach elk ground, but every hunter got a deer, several nice bucks included. The Midwesterners were a congenial, fun-loving group that enjoyed every minute of their hunt. Before they left, several of them reserved a spot for the following season.

When our eight hunters left for home at the end of the week, my first season as an outfitter was over. As the last car disappeared around the bend, I watched into the silence as I had so many years before when another group of hunters trailed out of sight through the canyon walls. Many things had changed since then. Not one of the men who were with us that season needed the meat to survive, and trappings from the modern world had been added for their comfort. But I believe that the contrast between Petty Creek and the life they left behind was as significant for them as was my association with the Flatheads. In both cases, we buried for a time the artificiality of a progressive society for the challenge of uniting with the elements.

"When you're young like you it's a let down for a while after they leave," Mac said as he walked up behind me. "That's one of the advantages of putting on years. All I am is tired and glad to have peace again for a while."

I turned around to look at my friend, and saw his weariness through his drooping stance and the deepened lines in his face.

"You've put in a season, haven't you, Mac. Why don't you head for the bunk house and sleep for a while. Camp won't blow away overnight. We'll wait until tomorrow to pack it out."

I felt the need to be busy then so I walked to the tack shed and started a fire in the stove. I placed some riding saddles close to the fire to warm them, and set a can of hardened bear grease on the stove. When it melted I poured some onto a saddle. Thoughts of my season with the hunters raced through my mind as I rubbed the life-giving liquid into the weathered leather. I didn't notice that the fire was dying until I shivered in winter's gathering dusk. Mac and my dad would soon scatter hay to the cows, and my mother would be busy with her pans of frying meat.

I set aside the saddles, and tiredness overtook me. I strolled across the frozen field to the house, looking forward to supper in my mother's kitchen and a warm night's sleep in my bed. A year was a long time until the next season, but I would begin in the morning to lay out my plans.

16

Two weeks after the end of hunting season we were enjoying the warmth of the fire one evening while we ate supper by the light of kerosene lamp. Then the door opened to let in a cold wind and….. Danny Jansic.

"Come on in or blow in if it's easier, but leave the blizzard outside," my dad said to Danny; chuckling to himself while Danny stomped the snow off his boots before slamming the door against the wind.

My mother jumped up from the table. "Sit right down here and I'll put on a plate for you. You must be starved," she said.

"There's no hurry, Stella. I'll just sit on the wood box here and thaw for a while.

I've been waiting for this moment ever since I left Anaconda. The roads are in such bad shape I wondered if I'd ever see that welcome light shine through your kitchen window."

"I guess you know by now that anyone with any sense is staying home this weekend. What are you doing here?" I asked.

"I had some ideas to talk over with you for hunting next year and, well, I just got lonesome for Petty Creek.

Danny had enjoyed the season as much as I had, and he felt the urge, blizzard or not, to come back to hash it all over. We talked long into the night about our time with the Colonel, and all of the season, and he wanted to know every detail of every day that he wasn't there. We agreed, as we re-lived the long trips to Burdette and Irish Basin, that our camps were too spread out and that we needed to find one new location for the next year.

"Bill's Creek! It's perfect!" I blurted out when we talked about the bull elk that our Nevada hunters got on Petty Mountain. "I passed by it on our way up with the hunters, but other than that I haven't been there since it was used as a base camp for a wild horse roundup, and that was several years ago. Why didn't I think of it sooner?

We can hunt Petty Mountain until the snow drives the elk down, then we'll hunt from the ranch. We can still cover Burdette from here, and we've got the West Fork, Slaughterhouse, and all the country we'll need. There won't be enough room in the bunkhouse. We'll have to build permanent sleeping quarters and a cook house somewhere down here."

"Sounds good. When do we start?"

"Do you think you can wait until spring thaw?"

"Maybe, but on the condition that your mom will do the cooking for your helpers."

As soon as the ground thawed the next spring, the sound of saws and hammers rang through Petty Creek. The numbers of builders had increased since the first bunk house was built. Besides the help of my uncles, friends drifted in to contribute their time. An air of excitement filled Petty Creek all spring. For all of us who loved the country, it was a satisfying feeling to watch the buildings take shape, knowing that we could make a living by sharing it with people from every corner of the land. So with many hands and much advice, a red shake bunk house with white trim and a matching cook house were complete by fall, standing side by side opposite the ranch house on the edge of the grazing meadow. Small and efficient, the cook house contained all the conveniences for the preparation of diversified menus, and the bunk house slept twelve with two complete bathrooms.

When the buildings were completely furnished, hunting season was two weeks away and it was time to set up camp on Petty Mountain. It would be a different beginning than the previous year because my partner from the season before was no longer with us. With promises to make frequent visits back to the ranch, Mac had said good bye to us at winter's end when he left for the city of Spokane, Washington to set up housekeeping with a new Mrs. Maycumber.

"I'll be hearing the elk bugle next fall clear from Spokane and I'll know you'll be having a good season," he said when he got into his car to leave.

"It might be a good one, but it won't be the same without you, Mac. Are you sure we can't change your mind about bringing that bride of yours back here to live?"

"No, I'm ready to be turned out to pasture now, but this isn't the end forever. I'll be sneaking on back from time to time. I can't spend my whole life in an easy chair, but for the times when I'm enjoying the relaxation it'll be good to know you're up there carrying on where I left off. And now I'm going to take off before I change my mind. Tap 'er light, young man."

His car kicked up dust as he sped down the driveway, then he braked to a quick halt just before reaching the gate. As his head poked out the window he said,

"And watch that young Jansic! I don't know if I can trust the two of you without me there to look after you!"

"Don't worry. If we get in any trouble, somebody'll see to it that we have plenty of corn in camp."

His car disappeared around the bend, and my corral builder, camp cook, packer, and friend retired to a well-deserved rest.

Even if Mac had stayed on the ranch it would have taken more than the two of us to set up camp because we were booked to capacity with six to ten hunters registered for each of the six weeks. I felt fortunate, in the absence of Mac, to have in the family my shirt-tail cousin, Art Scheffer, who would take the packing responsibility for the entire season.

Since I had developed an attachment during the previous season to my mismatched mules, I acquired eight more of the animals through the year. In appearance the new ones were more evenly matched than the first bunch, but in disposition and degree of experience they were as diversified from each other as the first five were varied in size and color. When the thirteen animals were put together, their temperaments covered the spectrum of mule behavior—some good, some bad, some gentle, some wild, and I was happy to give them all to my cousin, Art Scheffer, who had acquired from the Longpre side of the family the experience and the talent for handling them.

Art was born in the saddle, and to complement his ability to handle stock he was given a classic cowboy appearance, even to a distinguishing limp that he acquired in his teenage years when a horse reared over backward on him, shattering his left leg and much of his spine. He was 5 feet, 6 inches tall, and wiry, with an exaggerated square set in his shoulders to compensate for the stiffness in his back. His blue eyes gazed stoically through the lean, angular bone structure of his always tanned face, stamping him as the strong, silent type who is more at home with his horses than in the company of idle conversationalists.

Art would begin the season by packing in tents and building tools. I would start setting up camp with Ernie Deschamp, a nephew from my mother's side of the family, who had inherited a placid approach to life that characterized most of the Heberts. He was a few years older than I with a slow, almost drawling manner of speech, a thick head of black hair, and narrow, dark eyes that twinkled in a never-ending smile. He was also handy with a horse and a gun.

Ernie had taken time off from work to help me for the week, and he would guide off and on through the season. So when the mules were packed with everything that we would need until Art could return with another load, the three left for Bill's creek—Art in the lead with his thirteen mules lined out behind him, and Ernie and I trailing behind in their dust..

Seven miles later, when we turned from the county road into the timber at the mouth of Bill's Creek, I rode ahead of Art to lead the way up the six-mile trail to the camp site. We climbed gradually upward on a winding trail that was enclosed by thick stands of pine and fir. Then a sharp ascent for a mile was followed by another gradual rise where the familiar timber of Petty Creek transformed into gnarled ghost-like appendages. An open meadow on the timbers' edge had left the trees unprotected from the careening winds of the high country so that their tops were lopped and their limbs were branched out in contorted form. Gray moss draped like matted hair from the bare limbs. An eerie silence accompanied our ride through the cheerless land-scape until the open sky peeked through from the timbers' edge. For a brief moment we glimpsed the ridges beyond until the trail turned west at a sharp angle, and we were enclosed in the draw that would lead us to the head of Bill's Creek.

"Well, what do you think?" I asked Ernie when he circled around the mules to the flat spot where we would erect the tents. Ernie looked carefully around the area.

"Not bad," he said as he led his horse across the trail to the creek. The horse lowered his head for a long drink. "I liked it here as soon as we rode in, and now I know it's a good spot because my horse likes the water. The only thing that bothers me is that I can't see out."

"That won't bother you a bit when you come into this protection at midnight after you've led your mules with their elk quarters for 15 miles across those windy, below-zero ridges."

While we talked about the best place to put the corral, I realized that Art was still sitting on his horse with the string of mules lined up on the trail behind him.

"You're holding up traffic," I said. "Why don't you ride up just a little farther and join us?"

Art led the mules down the bank into a circle around the campsite. He stopped his horse in front of us, but he still sat in the saddle with the lead rope in his hand.

"Now that you're here, don't you want to get off your horse?" I asked.

"Not until I'm sure that this is where we'll be unloading."

"This is it, but even if it wasn't wouldn't you want to get off to stretch?"

"I get all the exercise I need while I'm riding."

Ernie had been watching Art thoughtfully throughout the dialogue.

"Now I know who your remind me of," he said suddenly as if he had made a great discovery. "Joe Big Sam."

"I haven't had the pleasure of meeting him."

"That's because he's been dead for a long time. He used to hunt up here when I was a little kid. I barely remember him. In fact, I probably wouldn't except that he was so big and fat he could hardly sit on his horse. Mose told me that once he managed to pile on he didn't get off again until he got back to camp, and that impressed me at the time. I'll admit you don't look anything like him, but you do spend a lot of time on your horse. Maybe we could call you Little Sam."

So Little Sam, shortened later to just Sam, is the name by which Art was known to the hunters all through the years.

While Ernie re-named Art, I looked at the mules standing in the middle of the draw. Their billowing packs made them look like a circle of teepees in an Indian camp.

"You two can go ahead and tell Indian stories, but I'm going to unload these mules," I said.

One by one we untied the ropes that held building tools, tents, pack boxes, and stoves. When the last pack was on the ground, Art climbed back on his horse. I handed him the lead rope and the circle of mules slowly straightened into a line as they climbed back onto the trail. Art would be back the next day with additional supplies and hay. Every season, all by himself, he would pack in 400 bales of hay, and all the food, tents, and equipment. He made a load a day from the ranch, saddling and unsaddling, loading and unloading thirteen mules, and traveling 14 miles on the road and 12 miles on the trail. Throughout the season he packed game into camp for the hunters, and helped wherever he was needed. We had a good partner in Art, the silent cowboy with a dry wit who was seldom seen without a horse underneath him and a string of mules trailing along behind.

When Art and his mules had disappeared into the timber, Ernie and I were left in the quiet of the draw with a mountainous pile of packed equipment in front of us.

"Well, let's get on it," I said. "We don't have all that much daylight left to get this unpacked and put where it belongs."

"You're right. We don't have much daylight left. But why do we have to unpack it all before sunset?"

"Because sunset is the end of the day, and you're supposed to have everything done by then."

"If we do everything by tonight we won't have anything to do tomorrow. Why don't we just do as much as we can without getting excited about it, and save the rest for another day."

Deep-smiling, black-eyed Ernie began to open boxes, chatting amiably in his slow, relaxed manner. To judge the results of Ernie's work output by the manner in which he labored would be a mistake. Like the Indians, it always looked like little was being accomplished until the final tally was in. Ernie did everything fast and slow at the same time.

So with my cousin beside me at the campsite, it was in a relaxed atmosphere that we leveled ground at Bill's Creek to make flat surfaces for our tents. Three days and many shovels full of dirt later, we had raised five flat spots in the middle of the draw, one close to the creek for the 16 by 20 foot cook tent and four smaller areas for sleeping tents that would be staggered down the hill below it. While we worked, Ernie talked unendingly about furnishing the cook tent. It had been a pet project of his since we first developed our ideas for camping on Petty Mountain, and we had it almost equipped before we left the ranch.

A small, like-new cook stove had been dismantled so that it could be carried up on two mules, and sheets of plywood for a table had been hinged together and folded into a size that could be packed on one animal. We had loaded pine lumber for a wood box onto one mule, and we draped mill felt for the tent floor over several pack saddles. With all this equipment piled in front of the tent, Ernie began furnishing his dream kitchen while I cut lodge pole to make corrals.

To begin, he placed the cook stove next to the tent entrance. When it was polished to an ebony shine, he inserted a gleaming new stove pipe that reached through the chimney hole in the tent top. He built a wood box from the lumber to set beside the stove, and filled it with kindling. Together we constructed a pole frame for the table top which he set in the middle of the tent. He then hewed wooden benches out of logs for each side of the table. In his cupboard corner he stacked three sets of pack boxes, three deep, so that nine separate cubicles held the staples that we had carried up. Kerosene lanterns hung from the ceiling pole to light the interior while Ernie tacked mill felt on the benches and spread it from corner to corner on the floor. Lantern flames cast shadowy designs onto the tent walls when Ernie curled up to sleep in his kitchen that night, as happy as a pack rat in a full nest.

I knew that Ernie wouldn't want smudges on his stove before the season opened so I had started supper earlier that evening on our open fire in time to have it ready for Art's return. Besides his hay-laden mules to keep him company, Art would also have with him Roy and Mary Rigaby, our cooks for the season. I had met the Rigabys, a retired couple from Florida, when they stopped by the ranch several years before to inquire about hunting in the area. I spent some time guiding them through the mountains on horse back, and since then they returned every fall to hunt. They were a cheerful couple who looked alike with their small, lean frames and pleasant, rosy faces. They had never worked as camp cooks, but there was no doubt in my mind that they would do an excellent job.

We were all ready for bed early that night. Ernie and I had been sharing a sleeping tent, but since he wanted to nest in his cooking palace, Art put his sleeping bag in with me, and the Rigabys retired to the tent just below Ernie. I fell into a deep sleep as soon as I crawled into the warmth of my sleeping bag, and I remained that way until a shrieking howl made me bolt straight out of bed.

"What was it???" I called to Art.

Art turned over in his sleeping bag, muttering, "It was Ernie. He said there's a bear up there."

By then I was awake enough to understand Ernie when he yelled,

"Bring a gun!!! There's a bear up here!!!"

With nothing on by my shorts, I groped in the dark under a pile of saddle blankets until I found my rifle. I clutched it against me and ran to the tent flap, but I slammed into the opposite wall and fell flat on my face. I crawled around the perimeter, stumbling over Art as I tried to raise the bottom of the tent to crawl underneath it. When I finally found the flap I stumbled out into the cold, stubbing my toes on the little stumps from the trees that we had cut. Then I saw in the beam of Ernie's flashlight a small animal just outside his tent. It was black with a brown nose, and in that light, looking uphill, it looked as if it might be a mule.

"Are you sure that isn't one of the mules?" I called to Ernie.

"Mule, hell! It's a bear. Get him out of here!!!"

I took Ernie's word for it and shot. I heard the animal drop, then roll down the hill. And then the sound of another scream … followed by the sight of Roy and Mary Rigaby squirting out of their tent like a water gun , little Mary in the lead in her flannel nightie. The bear had rolled down the hill right through the back of their tent.

When it was determined that the Rigabys were unharmed, Ernie ambled down the hill with his flashlight. I followed him with my rifle, feeling grateful for a lighted path to guide my sore feet. He beamed the light into the tent, and we saw that the bear was dead. In the silence that was broken only be the clicking of my chattering teeth, Ernie said,

"Kindling doesn't make a very good bear gun. I think I'll ask Art to bring up a pistol."

With the bear taken care of and the cook tent ready for occupancy by the camp cooks, Ernie was free to help me with our camp construction. I had already started on the corrals with the help of Buck, the green-broke buckskin that mired in the beaver dam the year before. Buck had come a long way in one season, evolving into a gentle saddle horse, a high-life, willing work horse, and a steady, dependable pack horse. When he pulled lodge pole to the corral site, as soon as the chain was unhitched from his log he would whip around and stamp back up the hill, ready to snake the next one down to the creek. With the help of Buck we soon had our logs in place for corral poles, mangers, and saddle racks.

In the ten days since we had turned from the Petty Mountain meadow into the Bill's Creek headwaters, the setting had changed from a steep, tree-filled little canyon into a camp that looked like a tent town out of a history book. I walked down the trail to the bottom of the draw to see it as the hunters would when they rode into camp. Above me a big sound corral with a wide swinging gate surrounded the creek where it began to twist its way down the mountain. Two lodge-pole mangers, notched with an axe to fit snugly together, stood at either end of the corral. Just beyond the corral were sturdy, yellow-pine hitch rails. Beside them, nailed between trees, were the poles that held our riding saddles.

Small white tents were scattered through the upper draw, protected by stands of pine and fir on either bank. Above them, smoke puffed through the chimney of the cook tent which had taken its place already as the center of camp life.

When the season opened, the hunters couldn't quite believe what we had put together. It was all so new and sturdy it resembled a painting more than a working camp. Ernie beamed with pride when compliments rolled in for the cook tent, and the hunters thought that they were in a hotel room when they found cots, felt-covered floors, and wood stoves in their sleeping tents.

Mary's cooking was the highlight of every day. She baked bread, pies, and cakes while Roy hauled water for her, cut stove wood, filled lanterns, and kept the mangers filled with hay and the nosebags filled with grain. When the snow drove us down to the ranch the Rigabys settled happily into the luxury of the cook-house kitchen.

Guides were added to take care of the increased numbers of hunters. Seventeen to twenty people lived in camp throughout the season. We worked hard, sometimes right around the clock, and we had close to a 100 per cent success rate for elk. It didn't seem to matter to any of us how many hours we put in each day. We were right where we wanted to be, doing what we wanted to do. We didn't have time clocks on Petty Mountain—only satisfaction for a job well done. We had established our business and made it a success.

17

"Roger, I'd like you to meet Gator Bob," Barney said from somewhere behind me. It was the day in between—the busy time when you assist one group of hunters on their way home while the new group arrives. I had just dropped the last elk quarter into the pickup of one of the departing clients. When I slammed the tailgate shut I turned around to see who Barney had introduced. A tall, dark, broad-shouldered, middle-aged man with black hair just graying at the temples stood before me. A big smile spread across his face, and his hand was outstretched to take mine.

"Gator Bob?" I inquired.

"Tha's right, boy, Gatah Bob, but y'all can all me jus' Gatah."

He wrung my hand until it almost dropped off.

"Do y'all know how Ah got that name?" he asked.

"No, I don't believe I do."

"Ah got it because Ah'm the best alligatah huntah in all of Loueesiana. Tell me, how many elk do y'all think y'all took out of these mountains?"

"I don't have any idea, to be honest with you."

"Well, Ah reckon it's been quite a few, but Ah'll tell y'all right now that it's a drop in the bucket compared to the alligatahs Ah've taken out of my country."

"I'm sure it is, Gatah..er...uh...Gator."

"And besides that, we don't jus' shoot our gatahs the way y'all do yuh elk. We wrestle 'em. If Ah had the hide of every alligatah Ah've wrestled, Ah could paper the walls of my whole house with 'em."

"Well, I'll tell you, Gator, I'm really looking forward to hearing more about your alligator hunting, so I'll just say goodbye to these people and then I'll be with you. Barney will take you to the bunk house so you can put away your things."

"That'll be fine, boy. Ah'll rest up a bit to get ready for the elk."

He stuffed a big wad of chewing tobacco in his mouth and walked away. As I watched the tall, well-dressed southerner saunter back to Barney's pickup, I noticed a matching set of beautiful leather luggage in back of the truck along with big sacks from an expensive outdoor clothing store in Missoula. I knew that my work was cut out for me that last, tiring week of the season. Gator would be crushed if he didn't leave Petty Creek with the finest trophy animal that the mountains could produce.

When I got to the bunkhouse, Gator was well into a supply of Canadian Club whiskey that he had brought with him. He was busy telling stories to some of the hunters so it gave me an opportunity to talk to Barney alone.

"Keep Gator entertained tonight, will you, Barney? You've had time away, and I'm bushed. After supper I'm going to the house for the night. I can tell I've got a week ahead full of Gator, and I'd like to retreat for a few hours.

"Sure. I don't think it's going to be much of a job. He seems to be entertaining him-self without any assistance."

"Good. I'm going to the house to wash up. I'll see you at supper."

By the time we sat down to eat in the cook house, Gator didn't seem to care if anyone listened to him or not. I talked with the other hunters during the meal while Gator lectured to the room at large on the finer points of alligator hunting. When enough time had passed that I could politely excuse myself, I said good night to the boys before heading to the house for the night.

It was so icy the next morning that we couldn't hunt on horseback so I took Gator under my wing, and we left for Gus Creek on foot. I was glad that we weren't riding because he was so puffed out with his new, warm clothes that I couldn't imagine how he could mount a horse. Earlier, when I had picked up my rifle before leaving, I walked over to Gator as he pulled on his new, down-filled mittens.

"It might be hard to get those mittens off in time to shoot, Gator. Do you have gloves that you could wear instead?

"Don't y'all worry about me, boy. Ain't nothin' gonna stop me from movin' like lightenin' when Ah see an elk. If an alligatah can't keep away from me, an elk doesn't have a chance."

For a man who liked to talk as much as Gator did, I was surprised that he walked along at a fast clip in total silence when we climbed the hill behind the house. We hiked cross country for half a mile until we turned onto an old logging road where we would check a water hole for game. Three hundred yards later we rounded the first bend in the road to find a big mule-deer buck with a beautiful four-point rack. He was standing in the middle of the road, not 50 yards away. The burden of Gator's mittens flashed through my mind. I was afraid that the buck would run before he got them off. But the animal stood still, and so did Gator, as if he was frozen to the ground.

"Shoot, Gator," I whispered.

A desperate voice croaked back, "No-no-no. Y'all shoot him."

I glanced at Gator and saw a grimacing, pained expression on his face. The Fish and Game rules hadn't changed about shooting game for other people, but then they hadn't been responsible for Gator, either. I couldn't let the buck just slip away so I raised my rifle slowly, and I got him. Gator immediately turned into his former enthusiastic self. Looking like a big, red marshmallow in his down-filled outfit he ran up the road for his prize.

"Jus' look at that animal," he said jubilantly. "Did y'all ever think Ah'd get one this soon? Ah'm gonna have him mounted jus' as soon as Ah get back. Wait'll the boys at home see what happens when Ah get turned loose up north."

That night in the bunk house Gator related the story over and over again of how he shot his buck. I'm convinced that by the second time he told it he believed it himself. But whatever he wanted to believe, I was just relieved that he had a trophy, and I hoped that an elk would come as easily.

The following morning at breakfast I had just started to give Gator a strategy for our elk hunt for the day when he interrupted me.

"If y'all don't mind, Ah think Ah'll stay inside today. Where Ah come from we've got thin blood and it jus' don't take to these cold mountains. Next year when Ah come back Ah'm gonna' make sure Ah've got all the warm clothes Ah need."

I wondered how he would manage to wear more clothes at one time than he already had. I assumed that there was a reason other than the cold that was keeping him indoors. When I came back from hunting that night my suspicions were confirmed. With a trophy safe in his pocket, Gator spent the day at his second favorite sport—drinking whisky. I walked into the bunk house that night to find him in the posture for which we will always remember him best—a dark, swarthy figure slumped in the corner, talking about alligators while tobacco dripped down his shirt like a pair of suspenders. Gator loved his tobacco as much as he loved his whiskey, and when he drank heavily he chewed until the juice ran down his shirt in quantities to match the size of his alligator stories. He was happy to tell his tales to himself if no one cared to listen, so camp life went on as usual while Gator tramped through the swamps alone.

By the end of the week Gator managed to sober up to make the trip home. Before he left he made his reservation for the early part of the season for the following year. He told us that we wouldn't have to bother picking him up at the airport. He would find his own way to the ranch.

It was the second week of the following season when he was due to arrive, and I looked forward to seeing him. We had sent off the last hunter when a big, brand-new car pulled into the driveway. Gator stepped out from behind the wheel.

"Damn, it's good to see y'all again," he said as he wrung my hand in his firm grasp. "But those elk aren't gonna be happy to see me cuz Ah've had a whole year to get ready for 'em."

"Did you drive all the way out here, Gator?"

"No, boy. Ah rented that at the Missoula Airport. Got the biggest one they had."

"Well, everyone's here, and there's still time to get to camp. Lay out everything you want to take and we'll do our best to pack it on the mules."

It was Art who packed Gator's clothes, and I had forgotten about my hunter telling me that this year he was going to be prepared for the cold. However, the next morning at breakfast my memory was jarred. The temperature had plummeted to below zero during the night and two feet of frozen snow lay on the ground. I had just come into the cook tent after saddling horses for the day when Gator lumbered through the door.

"Remember how Ah told y'all Ah'd be warm this year? Well, Ah'm a man of my word, and Ah want y'all to see how Ah'm fixed up."

He pulled up the leg of his expensive wool trousers to show me the wool underwear that he had bought. Above the top of his big, fuzzy boot was an electric sock that plugged into a battery in his back pocket. He wore a fat, down vest over his soft wool shirt, and over the vest he somehow managed to put on a new down jacket. Thick furry mittens covered his hands and on his head was a brand-new ten gallon hat.

"If that outfit doesn't get 'em, Gator, nothing will." I said.

It took all the dexterity I had to load Gator on a big, gentle horse that I had picked out for him. He rolled around inside his clothes while the horse plodded along, way behind mine. When the horse trotted to catch up, Gator hung on to the saddle horn, bouncing like a ball while tobacco juice dripped from his mouth in rhythmic jerks. We rode on in such a manner until we reached the higher ridges above camp just as the sun rose over the distant peaks. Below us, three bunches of elk stood in an open park, waiting for the sun to warm them. For the second time in a row, a trophy was laid at our feet.

I held onto Gator while he rolled off his horse, then I tied the animals so that we could slip down to the elk on foot. Once again, Gator walked silently through the woods, treading lightly to keep from crunching over the frozen snow. When we were within shooting range I looked in his direction. He quickly averted my gaze, which told me that he wanted me to shoot. I raised my rifle, took quick aim, squeezed the trigger—and nothing happened. It was so cold that the cosmoline in the spring of the firing pin had frozen. I had bought the gun new that fall and this was the first cold snap in which it had been used. Gator held out his rifle for me to take.

"Look, Gator," I whispered. You've got a whole herd of elk right in front of you, and a brand-new 300 Weatherby Magnum to shoot with, and there's absolutely no reason why you can't get your own elk."

He stared at me in perplexed silence for a moment, and then he drew back his rifle, took aim, and fired. Then he fired again and again and again in the middle of the herd until he emptied his rifle. When the last animal ran out of sight my heart sank. Gator must have felt disgraced.

"Well, that's the way it goes sometimes," I said. "Let's move on and see if we have better luck next time."

We got back on our horses and rode west across the open ridge. The air was crispy blue from the cold and the horses were white with frosty hair. A twenty-mile-an-hour wind cut my face with every puff. I was afraid that if I moved in the saddle my body would break like an icicle. I pulled my horse to a stop, waiting for Gator to catch up with me.

"I'm going to stop for a while and build a fire," I said.

"Now isn't that jus' like a Yahnkee. Here Ah'm from the south and Ah'm as warm as toast, an' y'all 're the one that's freezin."

"That's probably because I forgot my electric socks."

When the fire blazed and my hands thawed, I backed up to the flame to warm the other side. I had just felt the warmth penetrate my back when Gator yelled,

"Y'all 're on fire!"

I dropped to the ground while Gator threw snow on me. When the excitement was over, the north wind was blowing through an eight-inch hole in my jacket, right through to my skin.

"Elk or no elk, we're going back to camp, so don't say another word," I said.

Gator was loaded on his horse and I had just mounted mine when I saw a big bull elk walking through the bottom of a canyon below us. I coaxed Gator to shoot, but he pleaded with me so pathetically that I took his rifle and got his bull.

"Ah'll make a deal with y'all," Gator said when we rode back to camp for the pack horses. "Since Ah got me my elk, Ah'll stay in camp the rest of the week and y'all can have my 'lectric socks."

We picked up the pack animals in camp, and Gator willingly rode back with me to help load them with the elk quarters. When we returned, the meat was frozen solid so we didn't hang it as usual. All week long the hunters' frozen quarters were stacked beside the creek like cord wood.

When his hunt was over, Gator retired to the cook tent with his Canadian Club and snoose. For several days he relaxed in camp until Art and one of the hunters rode in one day for pack mules. The hunter had downed an elk on Black Mountain, about three miles from camp. When Gator heard that they would be riding for that short a distance, he decided to join them to get some fresh air. Art warned him that it might be a rough trip because they had to ride through brushy country that was covered with snow.

"Y'all don't need to worry about me. Ah always dress for the weather."

I formed my doubts about the outcome of the trip. Art had only one weakness in his packer-guide position. He could never find Black Mountain. We took a lot of game from that area, but no matter how many trips Art made, he always got lost, either coming or going or both. It was a mental block that he developed for some unexplainable reason, and he accepted his handicap without complaint. But for him to be lost with Gator in tow made my heart sink. I tried to talk Gator out of going, but his mind was made up.

"If we're gonna be ridin' through brush, Ah'd better get mah rain gear on," Gator said as he stuffed a wad of chewing tobacco in his mouth. He lumbered across the tent to get his rubber rain pants and jacket when Art walked up to me.

"If I have to take him with me, you're at least going to load him on the horse. He's wearing more clothes than I have in my whole closet."

It amazes me still that Gator was able to move at all with his heavy rubber pants and jacket over all his other clothes. I almost had to lift him into the saddle while Art held the horse.

"See if you can't help Art find Black Mountain, Gator," I called when the group rode out of camp. Then I ducked back in the tent before Art had a chance to turn around.

At the same time that Art returned to camp that day, I had returned with my hunter for pack animals. He had gotten his elk many miles from camp so when we returned with the meat, Gator and Art were already in the cook tent. When the meat was put away I walked to the tent to thaw out. I had just pulled back the flap when Gator jumped out of his chair.

"Have Ah ever got somethin' for y'all to see," he said before he scooted to the back of the tent.

In seconds he came skipping back, holding up some shreds of rubber that had once been his pants and some strings that had formerly been a jacket.

"What d' y'all think the boys down home will say when they see what happened when I rode through the blizzard?"

Art sat at the table staring stoically into space. When Gator held up his pants, Art reached for Gator's bottle of Canadian Club and took a long, slow drink.

"I think this story can be told without me. Good night," he said before he slipped from the tent, favoring his stiff leg.

If Gator's version of the trip had been true as he told it that night, we wouldn't have seen him again until we unburied him in the spring. Art later explained the troubles that they met on the way.

Art had almost made it to the mountain on the first try, but a wrong fork in the trail led them into a brushy area where thick undergrowth and fallen logs were hidden under the snow. As the animals stumbled through the entanglement, Gator fell from his horse. He decided then to walk the rest of the way, letting Art lead his horse. When they started out, Gator immediately ran into problems. He couldn't walk through the snow in his bundles of clothes. He crawled, fell, tripped, and pulled himself from tangled bushes for half a mile until they reached the mountain. When the elk was loaded on the mules, Art told them that he had his bearing then and he would lead them down a brush-free trail back to camp. Gator believed his guide so he allowed himself to be lifted back on his horse.

They had gone only a short distance when they rode into a worse jungle than before. This time Gator's horse fell into the middle of a pile of logs. Gator rolled out of the saddle, scrambling out of the way while the horse struggled to free himself. As the animal thrashed through the fallen trees, he became so entangled that the logs had to be cut with an axe to free him. After that Gator walked for another mile until he was sure that they were on solid ground. By the time he was ready to mount his horse again, his clothes hung in shreds.

Gator had his problems on Petty Creek, but for all his tall tales and his exaggerated self-image, he did go along with whatever plan we laid out for him. I took him on some rough rides through the years, and I found that he had a stout heart under his patent exterior. He may have been ungainly in the mountains, but at his own home he was a successful businessman, a devoted family man, active in city government in his town, and eager to participate in many facets of adventurous living. I always felt that he could accomplish whatever he wished if he could bury his need for notoriety long enough to use his own resources. It wasn't until the tenth year that he hunted with us that my idea was proven true.

In camp that year Gator suffered with a painful, swollen leg. A doctor that often hunted with us happened to be there that week so he examined the leg.

"You have one of the largest blood clots I've ever seen," he told Gator, "and if you don't stay off it completely there's a good chance that you'll be dead before you leave camp. If we were in town I'd put you in the hospital."

"Then it's a good thing we aren't in town, Doc, because Ah came out here to hunt and there's a whole mountain full of elk out there waitin' for me."

Conditions were right that morning for elk to congregate in a big canyon called Madison Gulch. We took all the hunters with us when we started out, with plans to spread out in small groups to hunt along the way. Gator had brought his son-in-law, Jim, with him that year so I took the two of them with me. As we rode down a narrow finger ridge with miles of timber and valleys spread out below us, I saw three bulls passing through the trees about 1,000 yard away. We would have to proceed on foot to remain unnoticed, and I was afraid that Gator would insist on following us down. I knew that Doc had told him the truth about his leg, and it was a frightening responsibility to have him with me.

"I'll help you off your horse, Gator," I said. "Jim and I will tie them up. I know it's hard for you to walk so you stay up here. If we miss, maybe they'll run back up and you can shoot from here.

"Y'all must've read mah mind. That's jus' what Ah plan to do."

Jim and I crept through the timber, but the trees were so dense we couldn't get a clean shot.

"Go ahead and try, Jim," I said. "Maybe you'll be lucky."

Jim aimed his rifle and fired three rapid shots, all of which missed the elk. They ran down a long, open ridge and out of sight. We had just turned to go back up the hill when we heard another shot just above us. Our mouths dropped open. It had to come from Gator, but why would he shoot for the first time ever when the bulls had to be a least 800 yards from his position.

"You don't suppose he hobbled down the ridge, do you?" I said.

"He couldn't have. He really is in terrific pain. Let's get up there."

We scrambled up the hill, and when we reached the edge of the timber we saw Gator standing right where we had left him. He was looking off into the distance, leaning on his rifle which he was using as a cane.

"What are you doing? We thought you had an accident," Jim said.

"Now why would y'all think that. If y'all hear a shot when you're huntin', it usually means somebody's shootin' at game. See, there he is."

Gator pointed to the bottom edge of the timber where a bull elk lay in a grassy field. I knew it had to be a mistake; maybe it was something that had died a few days before and I only imagined that I saw a set of horns.

When Jim and I reached the animal, he was lying still with one shot right through the shoulder. No one but a physicist could have calculated the drop on a bullet traveling that distance. But Gator Bob, who hadn't shot his own game in the ten years that he hunted with us, did it all by himself.

In keeping with tradition, he returned to his Canadian Club and chewing tobacco for the rest of the week. He slumped in the corner of the tent to tell his alligator stories while tobacco juice ran down his chin. He only mentioned his elk when someone asked about it, as if shooting one was too routine to talk about. The pain that throbbed in his leg was never mentioned.

The saying, "He has a lot of gravel in his gizzard," was used in our part of the country for someone who was willing to hang on when the going got rough. It certainly held true for Gator. You just had to dig a little deeper inside of him than in most to find it.

18

When an event runs smoothly it looks effortless to those on the outside, and so it must have appeared to the hunters when they rode into camp each year. A whole years' preparation was necessary for each season as I bought and traded for stock, repaired and replaced tack, mantie canvases, tents and pack saddles, broke horses and mules, and upgraded all equipment. But the big drive to get ready for the season hit us when I brought the horses down from the hills about two weeks before opening day.

We used a total of forty animals, and each of them had to be shod. All the tents, lanterns, cots, and miscellaneous equipment was brought out of storage, and groceries for six weeks were purchased and packed in boxes. All of it, including hay and grain, was packed into camp, and the tents were set up and furnished. We paced ourselves through the two weeks and we enjoyed our work so we were calm, rested, and ready for opening day.

As the seasons rolled by, the initial excitement of the business diminished into a pleasant expectation of adding to our income while we provided a service that we enjoyed. But when the first hunters arrived, that old tingling thrill always came back. Six to ten of them bounced in at a time, filled with questions and raring to go. Their heady anticipation of the hunt couldn't help but rub off on us, and we left for camp that first morning almost as excited as they. The next morning, though, the excitement dwindled when we were faced with the reality of the six weeks of work that lay ahead.

We rolled out of our sleeping bags at 3:30 a.m. to saddle horses and give them grain. We never felt like eating at that hour, but we knew that it would be a long time between meals so we joined the hunters for breakfast. When they finished, we loaded them on their horses, along with their lunches and rifles, and we were on the trail by 5:30 or 6:00.

I checked the weather and ground conditions to calculate where the elk might be that day. Each two hunters went out in different directions with a guide. Most of the time the hunters covered 20 to 30 miles a day on horseback.

Back at camp the cook was busy all day long feeding ten hunters, four guides, and myself, plus friends who dropped in throughout the season. Because cooking was a full time job, a camp tender was hired to chop wood and kindling, haul water, and help with cooking. He also started the fire in the cook tent in the morning and lit the lanterns in each sleeping tent when he woke the hunters. He kept the mangers filled with hay and the nosebags filled with grain. He started fires in the sleeping-tent stoves and lit the lanterns in the tents before the hunters returned at night.

The packer waited in camp, if he wasn't needed elsewhere, until someone came back to tell him where an elk was down. With those miles of ridges, canyons, and open meadows to hunt, we sometimes had one elk down ten miles from camp and another to be loaded fifteen miles in the other direction. It was usually an all day job to bring in an elk, and none of us could be everywhere at once. Many times we would return to camp after dark to learn that we had to head out again.

The cook had a pot of stew on the stove all the time for just such occasions. We would gulp it down, pick up the mules that the camp tender had saddled, and we were off again. If everything went well we would be back with the meat in time to saddle the horses to start another day.

Except for possibly the first week of the season, the ground was covered with snow and it was near zero or colder every day. We climbed into our frozen saddles every morning and started riding, carrying the responsibility of leading the hunters through steep, slick country when most of them could barely handle a horse. If the elk were scarce we pushed for them, riding for miles away from camp until dark and traveling the same distance back. Often I planted the hunters on ridges and rode through the canyons in hopes of flushing out the animals.

When the week ended the hunters were dead tired and glad to be on their way home. We knew exactly how they felt. We packed all their gear and all the week's meat on pack animals, and rode down the trail for the 12-mile trip to the ranch. Then we loaded the meat in their cars or made arrangements for it to be flown. And while we sent the ten men down the canyon road or drove them to the airport, the next group was already waiting in the bunkhouse, full of questions and raring to go. So we smiled, answered politely, loaded them on their horses, and rode back up the trail.

And every time we started out I was grateful to have for a partner the real worker in the outfit, my saddle horse, Happy. The rest of us could take our bows, do our complaining, and when it was over, collect our pay. But Happy worked uncomplainingly all season long for nothing more that his twice-a-day ration of oats. His contribution to the business had turned him into a legend.

Since the first time that I took notice of Happy I felt that he had unusual potential. It was the spring of my 16th year, after we had brought down the horses from the mountain, that a brown, short-legged three year old colt caught my eye. He was out of a good looking Morgan mare and an equally fine Thoroughbred stud, so he should have been tall and stately. In appearance, though, he was just another colt in the bunch with two white legs and a white spot on his face. In spirit, however, he stood out from the rest with a strong, alert, independent look that made me decide to try him out.

When I roped the little horse that day to catch him, he hardly put up a fight. After the halter was on he took halting steps in response to a tug on the rope. In a few minutes he trotted behind me as if he had been leading all his life. Without any preparatory ground work, I put on the saddle and lifted myself in. The horse stood still like a veteran. I kicked him gently and he stepped slowly forward. In a short time he was turning, stopping, and starting as if we had been working together for hours.

The phenomenon was too much to keep to myself so I rode him across the grazing meadow to the house, through the yard gate, and up the walk to the porch.

"Look what we're doing already!" I called to my mother.

She stepped out on the porch. "Why, you shouldn't even have the saddle on him yet," she said, and the horse walked up the steps to greet her.

I pulled him around while my mother followed. When we stopped she reached out to stroke him on the neck.

"What a happy little horse," she said, and Happy had a name.

In only a few days, Happy responded to every command, turning on a dime, stopping and starting with ease, performing like a seasoned saddle horse. I was pleased with his willingness, but disappointed in his basic temperament. He gave in too easily, and he was content to walk around the ranch for hours in lazy circles. The spark of life that had caught my eye was gone.

The horse was too young to be ridden hard, but I thought that a short horse chase in the mountains might kindle a spark in him. Some of the horses had been turned back into the hills not far from the ranch so I set out with Happy to bring them back down. He padded happily through the bottom of the West Fork, but as soon as we began a slight ascent he lay down in the trail, relaxed, content, ready for an afternoon nap. It took a lot of work with the halter rope under his belly to get him up. We continued on until he repeated the performance for the third time. I gave up the horse chase idea, admitting to myself that I had misjudged his potential as a saddle horse. I didn't give up on him though. With his breeding and gentle disposition, he would be an asset to the herd if I used him for a stud.

When we returned to the ranch I turned him in with several mares, and little easygoing Happy transformed before my eyes into a barrel of dynamite, waiting for the fuse to be lit. His tail arched, his head was held high, his whole bearing was one of perpetual motion.

Within days we returned to the West Fork. There was no lying down on the trail that time. He shot straight up through the timber, and when we reached the herd he fought to join them. We had a long session again with the sting of the halter rope, this time to settle him down. When he was under control, I circled around behind the herd while I let out a holler to start the horses moving. Happy dashed down the mountain behind them. Each time they turned back up the canyon, I spurred him to teach him to move out fast and cut them off. After only a few quick turns he understood what I wanted from him. He watched the herd with deep concentration, moving out like lightening to turn them back. I had never seen a horse learn so fast.

Later, when I first used Happy to move cattle, he reacted to herding as he had with the horses. His whole power of concentration was centered on the herd from the moment we got behind them. As we rode along, he would suddenly wheel out before I even noticed that a cow was going to turn. By the time she swung out, he was at her side and she was back where she belonged. With speed from his Thoroughbred side, endurance from his Morgan side, and a thinking power that was all his own, Happy was born for the chase.

It was necessary for the first few months to keep the horse in check. He was still too young to be ridden long and hard. It was difficult to imagine that that much power, stamina, and desire to go could be contained in one little three-year-old animal.

Happy quickly gained a reputation as a remarkable horse, and friends came to watch him bring down the horses in the spring. I had the feeling that even the trees must have dug their roots a little deeper when Happy sailed through them. He was so incensed with the chase that he passed it on to the herd. Thirty to sixty horses thundered down through thick timber, individually trying to cut through the trees. Happy would leap to one side to cut off a horse while he was already calculating his move for the one that had turned back on the other side. I could feel his thought processes in his movements. He darted like a firefly from side to side, down, back, and around, never cutting speed, never losing his concentration. The herd poured out of the hills as one, as if encircled from behind by a raft of riders. But Happy was the only force behind them. I simply sat in the saddle and let him work.

Happy was seven years old when we started the outfitting business, and hunting elk was new to him. But with a year of herding experience behind him, he transferred his ability easily to the new situation. I often drove elk out of canyons for the hunters. After one trip behind them with Happy, I turned the reins over to him to do the job. In country where the brush was so thick it was hard to imagine an elk even walking through it, Happy covered it on a dead run, jumping four-foot logs, landing dead center between two trees with an inch to spare on each side, racing on as if he was in open range. Brushy canyons filled with bottomless holes, hidden logs and rocks, granite walls—somehow he tore his way up, down, and through it all. I heard over and over through the years,

"I didn't think a horse could to it."

I didn't either, until I started riding Happy.

Besides his physical abilities and intelligence, it was his sense of purpose that won for Happy the respect of everyone who associated with him. He had a way about him—a look, a physical bearing, an intangible something that told us that he was ready for the hunting day to begin. We always left camp before daylight, and we didn't always have trails to take us where we were going. But Happy had a built-in radar system to guide us. After we had traveled in daylight a few times to a certain hunting spot, I only started him in that direction when we left camp. He would pick his way through timber, along game trails, across canyons, and over mountains, and by daylight we would be there.

"I couldn't see a thing. How did you get us here?" hunters would ask.

"I didn't," I would answer. "Happy wants to hunt here today."

The length of days never mattered to him, either. He would leave at top speed in the morning, travel all day long, and come in at night at the same pace. He had a motor that never got tired.

Not everyone could ride Happy, but everyone could enjoy him because he was as gentle with the saddle off as he was powerful with it on. At the hitch rail, in the corral or pasture, he maintained his gentle disposition. At the end of the day in hunting camp, the sweat-stained power house soaked up attention from the hunters like a kitten. It was only when you put your foot in the stirrup that he transformed into a jet-propelled rocket that was programmed to target cows, horses, or elk.

I always felt that I couldn't have operated without Happy, but it was about the sixth year in the business that he took on the qualities of a saint. It had been an unusually cold year, but there was little snow on the ground so we stayed on Petty Mountain for the season. On the last day the guides had left with the hunters and their meat, and I was left alone with one last elk to pack out that had been downed that morning. The only pack animals that had been left behind were five, outlaw mules that we had tried, unsuccessfully, to gentle through the season. I picked out the two least offensive ones and left with Happy for the five-mile trip to the elk.

The mules behaved as usual when I loaded the elk quarters—running in circles, kicking at me, trying to buck off the meat. It took much longer than it should have to complete the job, and when I returned to camp for the other three mules, the long, cold day had turned into a whipping-wind, below-zero night. My chaps were frozen solid and I had no feeling in my frost-white hands. I was too stiff and tired to keep order among the commotion behind me while keeping myself out from under tree limbs in the dark, so I once again was relieved that Happy would take us home.

When the mules were all in line I untied Happy's halter rope. He began dancing up and down like a merry-go-round pony, like he always did when he knew it was time to go home. I knew how he felt, and I told him, "Hang on, partner, we're as good as there."

I untied the lead mule's halter rope, stuffed my frozen foot in the stirrup, and heaved my leg over the saddle. In the next instant I was lying on my back in the snow with my foot twisted in the stirrup. The mules were pulling back, running in circles around us, rearing, and tangling themselves in their ropes. I couldn't move to stop them.

An excitable horse like Happy wouldn't stand still in such a situation. I knew it would only be a matter of time before he would be off down the trail on a dead run, dragging me behind. I saw only one chance for myself.

I began talking very quietly to Happy while I slowly rose up to reach for the scabbard and my rifle. I would shoot him if he started to run. The mules circled us, kicking up snow while I spoke softly to my horse. I raised myself so carefully that I barely moved. My hands were numb, the night was dark, and I couldn't find the scabbard. But Happy stood patiently in the middle of the commotion. I don't know how long I lay in the snow with my head raised and my hand circling the air in search of the scabbard. But suddenly my foot fell to the ground.

I gathered the mules and straightened their ropes. When I climbed back into the saddle, Happy didn't move a muscle. When I was seated he waited until my knees nudged his side before he took off at his fast clip, heading for home. By the time we reached the ranch, the cold was gone. A light that shined from a halo over my horse's head had warmed me from head to toe.

Happy was twenty-seven-years old when I hunted sheep with friends in Spanish Peaks, a high, mountainous area near Yellowstone Park. We had all the necessary pack animals and saddle horses to make the trip, but Happy came along as a spare horse because I couldn't imagine leaving for the mountains without him. He had earned his rest so I no longer rode him on strenuous trips.

None of us had been through the rugged mountains, but we were told that Moon Lake would be a good place to camp. From the map we chose a trail that cut through Hell Roaring Canyon because it looked like the best way to go. Peak after peak and basin after basin faced us for thirty miles on the trail that hadn't been used, we found out later, for seventeen years. Windfalls lay across our path every hundred feet and rotting bridges were filled with holes.

It was dark by the time we picked our way to the bottom of the canyon. We crossed the last bridge to start the long climb out when a big buckskin with a 250 pound pack on his back fell over the rim. After we retrieved the horse it was too late to start out again so we camped on the spot for the night. Thunder rolled when we built a fire, lightening flashed, and we spent the night sitting up in driving rain in the bottom of Hell Roaring Canyon.

By daylight the rain had turned to snow. The horses were cold and hungry and so were we. We could see then that the buckskin was too bruised to pack again so the spare horse got the job. Little, short-legged Happy was loaded with an over-size, 250 pound pack that was filled with tents and duffle, and we were on our way again. The canvas caught on every stump along the way, but he never lost a step. His feet slogged through deep mud, but his strength and determination kept him from miring in the ooze. He never broke stride as he pulled himself up steep climbs for another full day.

Forty hours after we started, we reached our camping spot. As I removed the bulging pack from the little horse I was reminded of so many nights before. It was Happy and his iron will that brought me home when I wouldn't have made camp without him.

Happy was such a big part of my life that it was always satisfying to share him with others. Hunters who hadn't been to Petty Creek for a few years would call me from time to time, or stop by when passing through our country, and people that moved away from the area would return for a visit. After initial greetings had ended and inquiries about the ranch were answered, the inevitable question, "And how is Happy?" would be asked.

"As fit as the last time you saw him," I would answer, and then they were deep in memories.

"I never saw a horse like that. Remember the time … " was usually the way it started, and Happy would again be glorified as the legend that he had become.

From time to time I would think of the deep impression made in my early years by the story of Grandpa's Indian killer horse, and I often thought of the legacy that he left me through his love for horses. Grandpa was gone before Happy joined us on the ranch, but it made me feel good to know that in our respective lifetimes we shared a common joy. We had each known the fulfillment of spending an important part of our lives with a horse that couldn't be replaced.

19

All of our advertising through the years to interest sportsmen in coming to Petty Creek centered on hunting deer and elk. But one year we added another species to the list to satisfy one of our hunters. When it was over, I thought that it would have been better to stay within the limits of our level of competency. But trying experiences usually convey character building lessons, and in this one we were to learn the advantage of staying calm under stress. It was through a moose and Ernie Deschamp that the example was set.

There were few moose on Petty Creek, but occasionally one or two wandered east from the swampy areas of the Idaho border into similar terrain in Fish Creek. One year a fellow named Dan drew a permit for a moose along with his elk license. Toward the end of the week Dan had his elk, as did all of the hunters in camp, so Danny, my brother, who had grown up and was able to guide by then, Ernie, and Barney accompanied Dan in his search for a moose. They thought that by covering all corners of Fish Creek they might be lucky enough to find one. I stayed in camp to get a head start on taking the hunters' elk to the ranch, but the story was brought to me in graphic detail.

After descending Petty Mountain, the group rode west through Burdette and into the South Fork of Fish Creek. By early evening they were lucky enough to get on the track of a big bull. They followed his trail along the creek bottom until they found him eating moss in an old beaver dam. It was almost dark, but still light enough that Dan had no trouble getting him.

After the animal was dressed, Pierre started cutting limbs from the nearest tree. Dan questioned him, wondering what his plans were for the tree. When Pierre told him he was going to cover his moose for the night, Dan said that he wanted to take him to camp immediately. Pierre couldn't convince him that coyotes weren't native to the area, and the guides would be back in the morning before magpies were out of bed, so the moose would be safe. However, Dan insisted that his moose be brought home that night.

Guides are in business to please their customers so the group began a long journey through a dark, swampy forest with a bull moose for company. Under ordinary circumstances the moose would have been quartered and dragged with saddle horses. However, there was a beaver dam to cross on the way, and we had learned that using horses to cross dams after dark is not an efficient way to take game out of the woods. Fortunately, a bright moon helped light the trail.

When they got together to decide how to transport the moose, Danny presented the solution, proposing that they cut the moose in half, put ropes around each one, and two of them could pull each half to the road. Dan could follow along, leading a saddle horse. When they reached the road they could rest while Danny rode to the ranch to bring back a pickup.

They slung two ropes around each half, positioning themselves for a long trip to the road, with Ernie and Barney on one half and Danny and Pierre on the other. At the count of three, Ernie and Barney pulled together on the ropes and crashed into each other, leaving the moose half lying in the trail. Ernie realized then that they would have to walk in step.

"I'll count, four steps to the count," he said. "Ready? One-two-three-four, go-two-three-four."

They took several steps in place until the moose slid slowly forward. They then reeled through the timber for a mile, sweeping the shadowed trail with their moose half, stopping every few yards to rest. By the time they reached the beaver dam they were panting from exhaustion.

Remembering his trip over a beaver dam in the dark from the first year of hunting, Danny told them they would have to watch their step because the dam was full of holes which they could fall through at any time. Ernie told him,

"I have plenty of light, so you just watch where you're going, and we'll make out fine."

When Dan had led his saddle horse safely across, Pierre stepped onto the precariously-constructed bridge, feeling the water pool around his ankles. He cleared away a few upended sticks, thinking, he said, that beaver dams were made for beavers, not for hunters who couldn't limit themselves to daylight hours. He had a clear, although short, path on which to drag the moose before more sticks had to be cleared. When they were half way to the other side, their moose-half mired tightly in the mud.

Pierre called to Ernie and Barney for help. They left their moose in his pile of sticks to help Pierre and Danny put sticks in front of the mired moose. Pierre, Ernie and Dan stationed themselves to push from behind. Danny was in front to pull while the rest of them pushed. He braced himself on the rope, counted to three, and lunged. The moose-half surged forward, and Danny fell flat on his face. Then a loud "kersplash" broke through the bubbling creek. Silence followed. Danny ran around the moose in a bent position, holding onto the hide so he wouldn't lose his footing. Pierre and Barney stood behind, looking down into the water. Ernie was missing.

Danny screamed for Ernie. Pierre answered his call with a casual, "Don't worry. He'll be here in a minute."

Then a head rose through the middle of the dam, and a pair of hands grasped the sides of a big water hole. Ernie pulled himself up, creeping onto firm ground. When he gained his footing he wiped his face as he shook the water from his head. He turned around to look at the depths from which he had returned. He hadn't yet spoken when he stared down at the inky circle of water. Neither had anyone else. After a few moments he broke the stillness.

"Now—that there—is a hole," he drawled, and without further conversation the group moved on with their moose.

They could have sworn at the beaver for making flimsy dams or they could have scrambled in fear the rest of the way over it. Instead, from Ernie's influence under stress, they trudged calmly to the other side, traveled on to the road, and apparently more or less enjoyed their time together while they waited for Danny to return with the pickup.

From a confrontation with a bear on top of Petty Mountain to the bottom of a beaver dam in Fish Creek, Ernie was the center of a rippling calm that always managed to lighten the load.

20

Bill Lapel's old ranch above us had been sold again the year that I was preparing for the hunting business. It wasn't a big enough place on which to make a living, but its pretty setting in a timbered draw at the mouth of Bill's Creek was enough to make a lot of people give it a try.

That time it was bought by the Carltons, a large family that pulled together to try to make the ranch work. Bud Carlton worked for the Forest Service for their basic income while his wife, Mary, and the seven little Carltons did their best to keep the ranch going.

Life was tranquil in their home—busy but refreshingly unregulated. As each child grew into a new level of capability, he or she just naturally fell into a designated position of responsibility. While an eight-year-old boy in patched bib overalls squatted at milking time beside the raw-boned family cow, a little three-year old girl in a faded cotton dress would tiptoe across the barnyard, clutching an egg in each hand. The eggs were often broken by the time they reached the kitchen, and the milk pail was filled with almost as much straw as milk, but the children were praised lavishly for their efforts.

I believe that it was that attitude of acceptance from their parents that prompted each of the children to accept their assigned chores with dogged determination to succeed. At least that thought struck me one spring day when I rode by the Carlton ranch and saw their big tractor with a grain drill behind it chugging over the far side of a plowed field. I watched the progress of the machine as I rode along until I saw two tiny heads bobbing just above the fenders. My curiosity was piqued then so I waited until the noisy tractor crept around the turn by the road.

Two little people who could barely peek from behind the steering wheel caught sight of me, and two little brown arms shot up in the air to wave. The operators of the clumsy, demanding equipment were five-year-old Billy and seven-year-old Nancy Carlton.

Nancy was in the driver seat steering the tractor, and Billy stood beside her working the clutch. They didn't stop when the tractor labored by, but they smiled to greet me as they zigzagged down the field with the grain falling out of the drill in spurts.

When the grass sprouted that year it came up in crooked rows with missing patches here and there, but it grew; and the milk cow and handful of cattle had their winter feed. We were lucky to have for neighbors a vanishing breed of family like the Carltons, and we were sorry at the end of five years when they told us that they were moving to town.

The family hadn't yet sold their ranch when they moved, so while it stood vacant I had no need to visit the place. It was with surprise then that I saw their little yellow dog limp down the road by our corral one day about a month after they left. She was only a year old then—a medium-size, fluffy yellow and white English Shepherd cross with a white striped nose and a stub for a tail. I had liked the dog when I visited the family. Like the Carlton children she was quiet and well mannered. When I stopped by their house she would stay away from me until I motioned for her to come. She approached then with a wag of her tail and a lick of my hand before she trotted off to join one of the children or to retreat quietly to a corner of the kitchen.

Had I known that they would leave her behind I would have found a home for her I didn't need or want another dog at the time, but when I kneeled beside the thin little animal, I knew that I couldn't send her away.

"Well, little girl," I said as I stroked her matted coat. "How would you like it if I called you Stubby, and you stayed here with us?"

Stubby approached her new surroundings with reserve, spending most of her time lying quietly by the house. She showed little interest in the other dogs or any of my activities. I coaxed her to follow me, but she would stay by my side for only a short distance before turning back to the house. I knew that she was lonesome for her family, and I tried to think of something to generate for her a new interest in life. It was when I was in the barn one day that I hit upon a possible solution.

We were plagued with mice on the ranch that year, so many that the cats couldn't keep up with them. Whenever I lifted a bale of hay, two to eight brown mice scampered out from under it. As I watched the mice scurry for cover, it struck me that mice and grasshoppers must have been Stubby's only source of food when she lived alone. She had probably left her home when the mouse supply ran out.

The next time that I went to the barn, I coaxed the dog into following me the whole way. When we reached the barn door she all but refused to enter the building. Her little tail drooped and she slinked around outside in big circles. When she finally made up her mind to come in, she ran right to me and sat down. I praised her and told her that I had a surprise for her, and she licked my hand. When I walked to the hay bales she sat still, watching me curiously with her head cocked to one side. I lifted up a corner of a bale, and three mice raced across the floor. Stubby lost all of her reserve. As quick as lightening she pounced on two of them and gobbled them up. Then she stood rigid with fire in her eyes. I lifted another bale and she jumped on the mice as quickly as before. When she had eaten her fill, she still ran after the mice. Stubby had discovered a satisfying means of earning her keep on the ranch, and an introverted little animal assumed a brand-new outgoing personality.

Stubby followed me everywhere after that, but she retained her same obedient nature. She took special pleasure in following along when I rode horse back. She would quiver with excitement whenever I took a halter rope or a saddle out of the shed. One day when I was on my way to catch a horse in the hay meadow, I didn't want her running through the field because the horse was hard to catch. When I walked by the house with a halter rope, Stubby raised her head and her tail bobbed, but she lay back down when she saw that I would be going on alone.

I crawled through the barbwire fence along the road to start out to the horses. I had walked about half the quarter-mile distance through the field when I heard the thud of little feet on the run behind me. Before I had time to turn around, a streak of yellow tore past me, disappearing through the stubble of cut hay. An instant later a herd of horses was racing in big circles through the field, with a little yellow dog flashing in and out of sight behind them. Stubby was on her way to developing another means of earning her keep on the ranch.

A herding instinct had been held in abeyance. When she was denied the pleasure of going with me she must have lost her reticence to act without a command, and her natural instinct took over. When we returned to the house I put a rope around her neck and taught her to come when I whistled. That was the only thing that I ever had to teach her. On her own she turned into the best stock dog I ever had.

So Stubby herded cows, corralled horses, and chased mice, and when she wasn't working she lay quietly by the house until a whistle from me sent her tearing into action. It was hard to believe that there had been a time when I thought that I didn't want her on the ranch.

As Stubby became more attuned to our working life, she became more involved in rewarding herself with horse rides. As time went on she didn't wait for instructions when she saw me carry a saddle from the shed. She'd sprint from the porch to the horses. She sat beside me while I put on the saddle, but her little tail thumped and her whole body quivered. When I was seated on the horse she was off and running, leading the way everywhere we went.

Stubby had been with us for a year when Barney, Mac, and I rode to Irish Basin. She knew that something special was in the air when we saddled the pack horses. From the first steps away from the ranch she covered many times more country than the horses as she charged up and down canyons, splashed through creeks, and explored every peak along the way. Her pace continued until she collapsed into an exhausted heap when we reached the meadow.

With the first stirring out of our sleeping bags the next morning, Stubby jumped into excited anticipation of the day ahead. Her exuberance diminished though with her first steps. Her legs were stiff and her little feet were so sore she could hardly walk. Some of the stiffness worked itself out after she moved around for a while, but she limped quietly along behind the horses when we started out, obviously in pain.

"If I had known this I would have brought another saddle horse for Stubby," I said to Barney as we rode along.

"She can't take a day of walking. Why don't you carry her with you?"

"It looks like I'll have to do that."

I stopped my horse, picked up the dog, and handed her to Barney. When I was back in the saddle Barney handed her to me, and I placed her in front of me on the seat. She showed her gratitude by sitting completely still as we rode together, sliding and rocking while I constantly shifted positions to accommodate her.

The following morning I was stiff and sore from my unnatural position in the saddle, and I decided that it was time that Stubby learn to ride by herself. Kicking Jack may have shown bad manners at times with people, but he didn't seem to be bothered at all by the dog when she ran back and forth behind him. So when we were ready for the return trip I picked up Stubby to place her behind Jack's saddle. With the mule's broad back to use for a brace, she rode from the beginning like a veteran. While Kicking Jack tripped through the mountains, an alert, straight-backed little dog rode confidently on his back with her head held high and her bright little eyes absorbing the countryside.

From that moment and all through hunting season Stubby earned the title of official trail mascot. Every time the pack animals moved out she rode assuredly on the last one in line, keeping watch on the string and looking awfully proud of her riding ability.

It was during the spring of Stubby's second year with us that I started working with an appaloosa stud colt. When I brought the gentle horse to the ranch, he and the dog spent their leisure time romping together through the grazing meadow like two pups. When I rode the horse each evening to give him experience, Stubby would jump on his shoulder when she wanted to ride, and I would pull her into the saddle with me.

After two weeks of our evening routine I saddled the horse one evening just before dark. Stubby didn't come out to meet us so I assumed that she had found a particularly big mouse nest in the barn or some equally interesting pursuit. The horse and I had gone down the road a short distance when I heard the dog running up behind us. I stopped to wait for her. She approached us on the run, leaping to his shoulder as she had done so many times before. The horse must not have seen her or heard her coming. Just before her feet touched his side he whirled and kicked, almost throwing me from the saddle. Stubby dropped to the ground and lay still.

I picked up the unconscious dog and rode home with her in the saddle. She lay motionless all through the night in a box by the kitchen stove. By morning my little trail partner was gone.

It happens that way sometimes. You don't want to let yourself get too attached to an animal.

21

When our horses grazed on Petty Mountain, the grass grew green, dense, and a foot tall every spring. Snow dissolved into the ground like a melting ice cream cone as the mountain replaced its winter white with a coat of sparkling green. It was a whole different world from the fall before, and I enjoyed trailing easily through the warm, open mountain country with a string of happy horses and mules on the way to their summer feed. The season always impressed me with a new appreciation for the miracle of nature's life-giving handiwork, but never had I viewed it with such enthusiasm as the spring that I rode up the mountain with Barney Quinlan's thirteen-year-old boy, Kelly.

The Quinlans had struggled through the experience of adjusting to their loss when Barney's wife died of cancer the fall before. We thought that it might be good for Kelly to spend the summer with us since Barney would have to leave him alone when he worked. He was already like one of the family, as were all the Quinlans, so it helped fill the void in his life to receive my mother's loving care, and to be a part of our ranch life.

Kelly had entered adolescence with a typical growing spurt. His arms and legs dangled from their sockets like rubberized bean poles, and his youthful face displayed a light sprinkling of freckles, a pair of big, sparkling blue eyes, and a winning smile that spread continually from ear to ear.

It was haying season when Kelly arrived at the ranch, and he literally bounded onto the field to help us from his first morning on the job. He wasn't content to wait for the tractor to start. When we reached the hay wagon he ran for the nearest bale, and staggered back at top speed with the hay bouncing beside him as he ran. In a sweeping motion he threw it onto the wagon and ran back across the field again.

"Hey, slow down. The day hasn't even started yet," I said. "I'll lose my helper by dinner time if you keep up this pace."

"No you won't. I want to finish so we can break horses tonight."

"We won't finish these 300 acres today, but we'll ride colts tonight no matter how much we do. That is, if you're not too tired."

"I won't be. I bet I can load as many bales as you."

"I don't doubt it a bit."

It was a combination of the promise to work with colts at the end of the day and the pleasure he felt in contributing to our work life that gave Kelly the desire to please us that summer. It seemed to me that it was just what the boy needed at that time in his life so I let him work at his own tortuous pace.

Kelly wasn't a stranger to horses. Barney had seen to that from the time that he was very small. But his experience in working with colts was limited. He loved horses, and whenever he visited the ranch he was always eager to learn about new ones that I had acquired, what stages of breaking they were in, and how much I had used the ones that he had ridden on his previous visit. So when he came to stay with us I suggested right away that I needed help with colts that I was breaking. Kelly tried to remain subdued, but the sparkle in his eyes and the volley of questions that followed told me that I had pushed the magic button to please him.

For all of Kelly's eagerness in the hay field that first morning, I noticed that after a short time his steps faltered as he stopped to sneeze and rub his eyes. He tried to hide his face from me, but I noticed that it was swollen and his eyes were puffed up and watery. I tried to ignore the condition for his sake, but rather than watch him suffer I signaled for my dad to stop the tractor. When Kelly ran up to the wagon with a hay bale, I stopped him before he could turn back again.

"I didn't know that hay bothered you like this, partner," I said. "Why don't you go back to the house for a while. Maybe you'll feel better after dinner."

The look of self-recrimination that struck Kelly's face cut through me like a knife.

"Am I doing something wrong?" he asked.

"No, Kelly, you're doing everything exactly right. There's just no point in making yourself miserable out here."

"All I'm doing is sneezing a little bit. I'm not miserable."

The puffy, red eyes, the stuffy head, and the violent sneezing were not going to kill Kelly at the moment, but when I looked behind his distorted features I knew that sending him away would break his heart.

"All right," I said. "It takes a man to keep going when the going gets rough, and it looks like that's what I've got for a partner this summer. But the next time that Mose goes to town, I'll have him pick up a face mask for you. Promise me that you'll wear it because if the swelling doesn't go down you might scare the colts to death when we ride tonight."

A grin of relief spread across my young partner's face as he ran to toss the next bale on the wagon.

I had always enjoyed putting quiet miles on green-broke horses in the lengthening stillness of summer evenings, but from the first ride with Kelly at my side, the training of horses took on a magical quality. When he brought a resisting colt under control he would glance in my direction with a self-satisfied grin. Sometimes I praised him openly, sometimes I only nodded approval, and often I remained silent to let him sort out his own thoughts about his achievements. As the days of haying and riding wore on, long and lean Kelly couldn't leave my side for a minute of every long summer day. Freckles sprouted thickly through his deepening tan, and his light brown crew cut turned almost white under a hot summer sun. He was in heaven in the wilds of Petty Creek, and I couldn't help but feel the same way myself with his thrill-a-minute outlook on life bouncing back on me all day.

So when it was time to lead twenty-five head of mules to summer pasture on Petty Mountain, the anticipation of sharing the trip with Kelly made me believe that I was about to embark on the adventure of a lifetime.

Kelly broke into an infectious grin when I told him our plans for the day. When I asked him to lead a green-broke mare up the mountain, I believe he added another foot to his burgeoning height.

"We'll be packing block salt on one of the mules, and we'll need a horse to carry the pack saddle back down," I said. "Would you lead that mare up that we've been working? I'm afraid she'll get the mules excited if I put her in the string."

"Do you mean that nervous sorrel?"

"That's the one."

"Do you think I can handle her?"

"Not only can you handle her, but I think you can do her a lot of good. She needs experience."

Kelly had our horses saddled before I finished my breakfast, and we were on our way to bring down the mules from Ed's Creek. When they were corralled at the ranch we tied them together, head to tail, with brand-new halter ropes that I had just bought. Kelly caught the mare and put on her halter while I loaded the block salt on one of the mules. He was an excited young man when he picked up the pack mare's halter rope as he climbed on his saddle horse to lead the way up the road.

The sun was warm for a June morning. The mules stirred wisps of dust around their feet as they clipped along behind me at the beginning of what promised to be a relaxed and pleasant trip to the cool summer meadows high above the ranch.

Kelly led his horse a short distance ahead of me when we wound our way up the trail, checking back from time to time to let me know what to expect ahead. I thanked him and told him that if he came to heavy windfalls or slide rock across the trail to stop and wait for me. He disappeared from my sight for a while when the trail first turned into the trees. Then, when I rounded the bend, I found him standing at the edge of a big snow drift that spread way up the hillside into the trees, on down through the timber-shaded side of the canyon.

"Is it okay to cross this?" Kelly asked when I stopped my horse and mules behind the mare.

"I don't know yet, but we'll give it a test."

Drifts are deep at that time of the year and they can appear deceptively hard. It's nature's way of storing up a little more water for summer, and you never know just how much melting snow lays under the crusted surface. It was still early in the summer, but the season had been unseasonably warm. It would be wise, I knew, to wait until dark when the snow would freeze solid, but I had already missed too much time away from ranch work. We couldn't circle the drift because the timber was too thick on both sides of the trail.

I dismounted, giving my saddle horse to Kelly to hold for me while I walked across the snow. When I jumped up and down in the middle of it, the snow held firm. I went back for my saddle horse then, and led him across the snow. As I rode him back he barely made a track through the surface. That was encouraging, but it was only one animal. I couldn't be sure if 25 of them would cut through the surface. I knew that Kelly and the mare could make it so I made the decision to move forward.

"Okay, Kelly, you take your mare and go," I said. "Keep riding after you reach the other side of the drift because I'll be coming behind you with the mules. We can't stop in the middle of this thing or we might fall right through. We're going to need a little help from Mother Nature to make it, but I think she'll be on our side."

A look of concern crossed Kelly's face, but he kicked his horse ahead, looking back often to check on the mare. When he reached the middle of the drift, I started slowly forward with the mules. Holding my horse back to a crawling pace, I watched behind me to see how deep a trail the 25 sets of feet would make in the snow. As we crept across the drift, the first mule in line made little tracks in the snow, and each mule in succession softened the surface into deeper ruts. I turned forward to judge the distance to the other side. One hundred yards of snow lay in front of me, and I held my breath. I looked back again just in time to see the last mule in line fall straight down through the crust. As he struggled to regain his footing, his halter rope stretched tight, pulling down the animal in front of him. Then like a row of falling dominoes, a string of thrashing mules disappeared from sight.

I ran my horse across the drift to tie him to the first tree on the trail while Kelly ran back to my side. Together we watched the bed of undulating snow. All the mules were out of sight. The snow bubbled like a boiling cauldron as they struggled beneath the surface to regain their footing. A look of terror was on Kelly's face as he looked silently from the snow to me.

"It's not as bad as it looks," I said. "Those animals are smart. They'll kick like that under the snow until they realize they can't help themselves. Then they'll be still and let us help them. We need to find some big sticks now to use for shovels. As soon as they're quiet we'll dig trails down to them."

By the time we returned with our sticks the forest was quiet again. Birds flew through the trees above us and flies buzzed through the still summer air. Before us lay the drift—still and silent mounds of snow.

"They're ready for us now, Kelly. Let's shovel all the trails first, then we'll bring up the mules. Don't worry about getting close to them. They won't kick again. They'll be fine until we can get them out. They aren't so deep that they don't have air to breathe under there."

For hours Kelly and I dug deep into the snow with our makeshift shovels. Several of the animals had struggled to the bottom. Kelly worked silently, but with intensity, as the snow flew from his burrowing stick. By then I don't think he relied completely on my judgment. His silence spoke of his concern for both himself and the mules.

When all of our trails were made we descended to the first waiting animal. He lay still in his white grave while I brushed away the snow from his halter rope before carefully untying him from the animal beside him. It slowed down the rescue process to untie the swollen knots, but I didn't want to cut the new ropes from the halters. When his head was free I told Kelly to hold the halter rope while I got behind the mule.

When I counted to three, Kelly pulled on the rope while I pushed from behind. Gradually the mule rolled over until he got his feet beneath him. With a lunge he raised up, scrambling up the trail to freedom. With the mule in tow, Kelly stumbled over snow clumps to tie him to a tree while I descended down the trail to untie the next one in line. One by one we repeated the process until 25 mules were tied to trees along the trail to Petty Mountain.

"Well, what do you think of that?" I asked Kelly when the last mule emerged from his tunnel. "Not one broken bone and every rope's intact. I'll bet every pair of cowboys couldn't do a job like that."

"I didn't know anything like that could happen. Wait'll I get home and tell the kids about this!"

Little Kelly never quite forgot that moment. He talked about it all summer long. But when I rode back up the trail in the fall to bring down the mules, I didn't think that our summer adventure had been so exciting. Scars on the trees showed where the mules had kicked the bark, wrapping their halter ropes around the trunks as high as 15 feet from the ground. I was reminded then of my lack of judgment in allowing the mishap to occur.

I had provided a never-to-be-forgotten experience for a young boy, but that wasn't compensation for having led 25 animals to potential destruction. I knew the ways of nature and that she couldn't be outguessed. I tampered with her authority that day and almost lost.

22

Leading mules through dangerous country, fighting bears, and driving thundering herds of horses from mountain tops are the moments in my life on Petty Creek that stand out in memory at story telling time. But they aren't the times that ultimately made the mountains such a unique place to live. The distinctive quality of life there stemmed, I believe, from our appreciation for the wisdom of the proprietor of our land, Mother Nature.

From the beginning, my dad developed a reciprocal relationship with her, always deferring to her authority. The power of her influence was such in the family that Mother Nature was known as the boss lady of the ranch.

"That hay looks ready to cut," my dad would say when yellow, heavy-topped timothy hung low in the summer sun. "But I don't know. I'd better check with the boss lady first, see if she's telling us to wait for a while."

From the time that my dad first settled on Petty Creek he needed a few of nature's elk and deer to feed his family. He took them, but in return he cleared land where the rest of the herds periodically grazed with our cattle, and in winter, occasionally ate hay. As the cattle herd increased, they trespassed onto land that belonged to nature's bears. To compensate for the intrusion the bears took a few of our calves when they were hungry. Nature didn't always seem kind, but she ultimately worked for our welfare. When we struggled through hard winters, we knew that water for our crops would be plentiful in the heat of her summer.

When I was old enough to use nature's resources to make a living I took elk from her mountain, and I used the same land to pasture the horses that I needed for the business. That agreement was fine with Mother Nature. My horses kept the grass grazed down through the summer so that new grass shoots got a good start the next spring. Every year hundreds of acres of grass grew green and thick, and the elk and deer that we left behind were provided with grazing ground. We didn't need to sign contracts with Mother Nature for the use of her land. Common sense told us how to operate under her control.

But while we lived in the security of our reciprocal relationship with nature, people in other parts of the country were defying her authority for the sake of progress, that inherent need of mankind. Handled properly, the development of land and resources can be of great benefit to the human race. But the human condition is such that since the beginning of time, political forces and power structures of competing interest groups have toppled the best grass-roots intentions. To simplify a discussion of complicated, already well documented issues, I will say only that by the time it became obvious that our industrialized society would destroy itself from the misuse of nature's gifts, the government agencies that were in control of our resources had grown large and out of control themselves. Theories for the use of our lands were formed from books and by political forces rather than from an understanding of the land itself.

Our lives on Petty Creek were remote from many of the cares of the world. During my teen-age years I was concerned with changing cattle and timber markets, but I didn't involve myself with the problems of encroaching regulations in our society. Then Clay Holman retired from the Fish and Game Department.

"It's not going to be as easy for you to get your own game any more, but I'm sure you know enough to keep from starving, even if somebody else comes around to check up on you," he said one day when he came to the ranch for his last "official" call. "Just don't feed the new game warden any elk steak in the summer."

Nothing really changed for a while after that because Clay still spent as much time on the ranch as before, and I was too young and confident to understand the significance of his warning. But then Pinto McClure was arrested for illegal possession of game. I couldn't believe that with the abundance of elk and deer on Petty Creek that one Indian would be penalized for providing for himself in the way that had been natural to his people for thousands of years. Our logging roads and the people that used them had driven away most of the Indians. The government trespassed on the natural right of a last survivor of the old way. Gradually, the same forces would intrude upon me.

When the Gilmans' horses and mine were pastured on Petty Mountain, the elk and deer population in the area grew steadily even though my hunters harvested many of the animals each fall. Then I was told by the Forest Service that the horses were taking too much feed from the mountain, and the elk would perish unless the problem was brought under control. We were cut down at first from almost 200 head to 70 head. More animals were eliminated each year until none at all were allowed to graze. The elk and deer alone couldn't crop the land sufficiently to allow new grass shoots to flourish in the spring so hundreds of acres of yellow grass lay rotting on Petty Mountain, and the elk and deer population decreased. Theorists had outguessed Mother Nature's land use plan.

In the lower hills, few game animals ever roamed the area. Only a little snow falls there so winter pasture was available for many horses. But when summer pasture was prohibited on the mountain, winter pasture was denied in the hills, and no animals, domestic or wild, now graze the once-abundant pasture.

I had been in the hunting business for six years when I was told by the Forest Service to remove my Petty Mountain corrals at least 100 yards away from the creek. Although they exaggerated their claim that nitrogen from the horse manure would kill every fish in the Columbia River, I agreed with their reasoning. A heavy concentration of domestic animals near streams and rivers does present problems to fish populations so I complied with their wishes. But as I dismantled the poles, I thought of the tons of sewage and industrial waste from Missoula that was dumped in the Clark Fork River every day. Suddenly it seemed that the Forest Service was overly concerned with the pollution from 20 horses who spent half of each day by a stream for three or four weeks each year.

I believed then that behind the edict was harassment from influential hunters in Missoula who often used our logging roads to gain access to hunting areas, and who sometimes took game from our land. When they hunted the roads on the back side of Petty Mountain, which were available for 4-wheel-drive vehicles, it appeared that when they didn't get an elk they laid the blame on my business. Our good neighbor policy with Mother Nature hadn't changed, but our neighbors had. Our land was open to whoever wanted to use it. Some apparently wanted it all.

At the end of the next season I was told to dismantle the mangers and leave them there to rot. I could no longer use the campsite. Reason? The trails into camp were eroding and the entire campsite was overused. As with the corrals, the accusation was unfounded. The small trails leading in and out of camp had been originally carved by game. Their condition hadn't changed since we first used them eight years before. The main trail from the road was of no concern to the Forest Service because it was "maintained by them, graded, and therefore erosion resistant." However, they hadn't touched it for eight years, but it hadn't eroded because, like the small trails, it wasn't overused.

I had made flat walkways at the campsite between the tents, which I refurbished every year, and the land was unchanged. Snow packed all of the trails except for possibly the first week of each season, and they didn't have a chance to erode.

I battled for almost a year with the Forest Service—sitting in on meetings, attending hearings, offering to make new trails, water bar the existing ones—every reasonable condescension I could think of. But they didn't want an agreement; they wanted me off the mountain. I was fighting a power much bigger than myself—and so—camp was permanently moved to the ranch.

Insidiously the changes had crept in. I could see that the day would probably come when I wouldn't be able to hunt commercially at all. It wouldn't happen for a while, but when it did it would be necessary to have already diversified to help sustain the ranch.

Since my dad had lost his herd to bangs disease, it had been an uphill climb to meet even the basic requirements of maintaining the ranch. He was deeply in debt to the farm credit bureau again, and so used to struggling from season to season that he considered it a victory when he was able to pay taxes on the land. I avoided conflict as much as possible by never discussing his financial affairs, but the jolt from the Forest Service made me realize that reality had to be faced or the ranch could someday be lost.

"Keep working hard and some day this will be yours and Pierre's," he said from time to time in his tender moments. Just hard work was not going to be enough. It was time to discuss as rational adults the future of Petty Creek. It wouldn't be easy, but I would try.

23

For days I conceived ways to approach my dad, thinking of a good defense for every possible rebuttal, until I realized that the best approach would be to state what was on my mind and handle the arguments as they came. When we were alone one evening in the kitchen I spoke up. Although I had tried to condition myself for what might happen I still wasn't prepared for the outcome.

"I've been thinking lately about the Forest Service closing Petty Mountain, Dad, and it's started me thinking about other things on the ranch," I said for an opening.

"What do you mean, other things on the ranch?"

"I don't mean anything on the ranch exactly, but things in general. I feel like there are a lot of changes going on out there that we've more or less let pass by us."

"I don't let anything pass by me. I know what's going on."

"Maybe it's just me, then. Losing Petty Mountain made me realize that the day might come when I can't have hunters up here at all."

"So what's the big deal about that?"

"There's nothing big about it. It just made me think that maybe we should start working on an idea here and there to supplement the cattle operation."

"What's wrong with raising cattle?"

"Absolutely nothing. That's what we've got here—a cattle ranch. It's just that it's been rough going for you ever since you lost the herd to bangs, and I thought …

"Maybe you'd better quit thinking. I'll decide if it's rough going or not. Farming's never easy, so you either do it without bellyaching or you get out of it. I like it here and I'm going to stay!"

"I like it here, too. That's the point. I think we have a chance with what we've got here to expand so …

"Expand! Didn't you already expand into a big-shot hunter? Did that put more cows on the range?"

"It helps keep us going."

"Who needs help??? I don't know what you're driving at, but this is my ranch and I'm not going to be told how to run it!"

"I'm not telling you how to run it, Dad. I have a lot at stake here, too. I like to think that after all these years that it's our ranch and together we can improve it."

"Are you telling me I don't know how to run my business? Maybe after all these years it's time for you to leave me alone. Pierre and I can get along fine now."

"I don't think you mean what you're saying."

"The hell I don't! You can hunt here if you want, but in the mean time you'd better take your big ideas somewhere else and see how well you do."

"Dad, you're sinking and it's too much for you to handle. Why don't we …

"We aren't going to do anything. Nobody's going to tell me what to do! If I think I should, I'll sell the place before I'll let anybody tell me what to do, including you. In fact, I probably will sell. Now get out!!!"

"All right. If that's what you think you want, that's what I'll do. I'll cut logs for a while, but I won't desert you."

"So now you think you're going to be a big lumberjack, huh."

"No, Dad, I don't. For a while I'd like to not have to think at all."

I knew that when I shut the door behind me that in a few days he would have calmed before the next storm, but I knew also that it was best to give myself breathing space. I needed time away. Maybe I wouldn't be back, but that would be decided later. I couldn't imagine ever giving up Petty Creek nor could I imagine leaving my dad to struggle on his own if Pierre left. As hard as he was to get along with, the bond between us ran deep. Time would help me put my thoughts in order. Somehow my dad could be reached.

But for the time being I would pick up my chain saw and packsack, and head for the mountains. From time to time for the next several years I would cut my way through sections of western Montana and Idaho, and I would work with every kind of hard-living lumberjack that the woods produce.

24

In December, when I heard about a logging job at Fish Creek, I inquired about it from the falling contractor, and I was hired. As we gathered on the first morning above the logging site for our cutting assignments, I was surprised to see a dignified, sparsely-dressed man of medium height standing quietly aloof from the mingling assortment of well-padded lumberjacks.

"Is that man over there with the white hair an executive from the timber company?" I asked the person standing next to me.

"No, that's Dad English. He's a faller."

"He looks like he belongs behind a desk somewhere, wearing a suit and tie. I can't believe that he works in the woods."

"You'll believe it if you spend any time working with him."

The woods foreman started talking then so my conversation ended.

"Longpre, you and English take area three. Go up the road about a mile. You'll see your section marked with yellow."

I glanced in the direction of the silver-haired man as he looked through the crowd for his partner. I walked over to him, extending my hand.

"I'm Roger Longpre. It looks like we'll be working together."

A pair of intense, steel-blue eyes searched my face while a strong, rough hand grasped mine in a firm handshake. With a soft southern accent and a voice that was so quiet it was almost inaudible, he said,

"I'm glad to know you, Roger. I'm Dad English."

Then he looked shyly in another direction.

"My pickup is right over there, Dad. We can take it to the job if you like."

"Thank you, Roger, that'll be just fine," he said kindly. "I'll get my gear and be right with you."

I was already in my pickup, warming up the engine, when Dad dropped his chain saw and packsack in the back. He jumped in beside me, dressed only in a new pair of Levis, a flannel shirt, and a lightweight nylon jacket. It was 20 degrees above zero and the snow was deep.

"The heater will be red hot in a minute, Dad. You must be frozen," I said.

"No, I'm just right. Thanks."

I looked down at his bare hands that were resting on his knees. They were heavily calloused and as rough as alligator hide.

"I have some extra gloves in my packsack if you forgot yours," I said.

"Thanks, Roger, but I've never had a pair of gloves on in my life. I don't like being bound up any more than I have to."

I looked hard at the lean, sinewy man beside me with his head of thick, white hair, his strong, pointed jaw, high cheek bones, and tan complexion, and I realized that he was probably capable of taking care of himself so I steered the conversation to other topics.

"It sounds like you spent some time in the south," I said.

"I started out in Arkansas."

"That's a long way from Montana. What brought you up here?"

"Bugs."

"You came to Montana for the bugs?"

"No, I left 'em there. You know, the kind that'll bite you on one end and sting you on the other."

His soft, drawn-out statement was spoken so seriously that I broke into laughter. Dad responded with a twinkling smile, and again he looked shyly away.

By then we were at our cutting area. When we had picked up our tools from the pickup and decided on which ends of the strip to start cutting, Dad told me to holler when I was ready to go and he would stop working. He lifted the bar of his ice-cold chain saw onto his unpadded shoulder, held onto the freezing metal handle with his bare hand, and walked quietly away. That man, I thought, is an example of the most retiring display of dynamite I have ever seen.

That night on the way back to his pickup Dad was again reserved and soft-spoken, speaking only when I asked him questions. He told me that he had set up a tent in the snow at Fish Creek because he didn't like driving, and he would make the thirty-mile trip home on weekends. When we reached the job fuel tank where we had met that morning he asked me to stop. I did without questioning him, grimacing to myself when he opened the door. His hands were so chapped from the cold that the cracks were seeping blood. It looked like it would be excruciating to flex them at all.

"I need to oil up my hands," he said as he got out of the truck. "Diesel's the best thing."

He walked to the fuel tank, poured the diesel into a cupped hand, and rubbed them together like he was washing them. When he returned to the pickup he said,

"Amazing what the human body will endure, isn't it."

As our cutting partnership progressed, Dad would gradually lose some of his reserve. I learned to avoid personal questions, letting him unfold information about himself when he chose. For some reason, which I have yet to understand, Dad trusts very few people.

As time went on he talked often about the difficulties of raising his five children through his pack sack logging career. He praised the stamina and staying power of his wife, Lucille, and he told stories of his many outdoor adventures. Whenever we were interrupted by others, though, Dad retreated. He was at home in the woods, not in crowds. But he was the most fascinating loner I had ever met, and I felt honored when I knew that he considered me a friend.

For the next few months Dad and I would work together from time to time, and visit back and forth when we worked separately. I had seen him in the month of February, just after he returned from a job away from home. Three days later my phone rang late at night. I had a feeling when I heard the ring that it was Dad. He had been home just long enough to miss the woods.

I picked up the phone to hear a soft-sounding, "Hey, Rog?" float though the receiver in a slow, Arkansas drawl. Before I could answer, the voice continued,

"Glad you're home cuz I've got something you'll like to hear. They need timber fallers in the North Fork of the Clearwater in Idaho. Ever been in that country, Rog?"

"No, Dad. I never have."

"Well, that's okay 'cause it's your kind of country and you'll do nothing but make money. I said we'd be there Saturday. What do you think?"

"Sounds good, Dad. We'll give it a test."

25

It was late February when Dad and I drove into Orofino, Idaho. Just outside the small mountain town, a boat waited to take us up the North Fork of the Clearwater River. Our destination—Big Island. Our purpose—to clear timber from the soon to be reservoir area of the Dworshak Dam, then under construction on the main Clearwater River at Orofino.

Upon completion, the dam reservoir would slowly back up the North Fork until 53 miles of the rivers' wild shores would transform into a serene mountain lake to supply sections of northern California with electricity. We would fall all the timber, from one half to three miles wide, along that stretch of river, leaving nothing in our wake but fallen logs and underbrush. The reservoir water would raise the logs to its surface to be harvested in the future. We took the job on contract, getting paid to fall by the acre.

Of the nature of the Clearwater country I knew only that it was wild, remote, and the timber was big. Except for the summer months when an old logging road was semi- passable, our job site was accessible only by jet boat or airplane. Work would be available to us for approximately one year.

When Dad and I approached our meeting place to be taken to the job, I saw at the river's edge the shining aluminum boat that would carry us and our gear. Pete, the stocky, sandy-haired woods foreman waited for us at the boat along with our other roommate, Tom Lamb. Dad had worked in the past with Tom, and he said that he was a good working partner.

When we got out of the pickup near the dock, a lanky, dark-haired man in his early forties popped up from the bottom of the boat and almost ran in our direction with a long rubbery stride. His jeans and work shirt looked like they might keep him covered for a while longer, but they had seen a lot of wear since the last washing, and his suspenders were tied on in front with grocery string. His broad smile showed two missing front teeth, one on top and one on the bottom, and his chin hadn't seen a razor for about a week.

"Boy oh boy, it's sure good ta see ya again, Dad," he said as we approached.

"It's good to see you, too, Tom. I'd like you to meet Roger. He'll be camping with us."

"Pleased ta meetcha, Roger. What d'ya think of that there boat? Boy, I jes' can't wait to go zoomin' up the river."

"It looks pretty good, Tom. I…

"You guys got here jes' in time. I got all my gear stacked away and you can put yours anywhere else."

"Thanks, Tom. We'd better be doing just that."

When Dad and I added our saws, tools, and camping equipment to Tom's pile of provisions we covered everything in the boat but the driver's seat. The water line raised a foot on the sides of the boat. I had no qualms, though, about the ability of the craft to make it up the river. With its sturdy, twenty-six-foot aluminum hull and its two-hundred-horse inboard engine with a jet kicker, it was made for the river's wild water. It did look like we had placed too much weight in the back, however, and I mentioned the fact to Pete, who would be piloting us up the river.

"The trouble with you is you know more about horses than you do about boats," Pete told me, half seriously.

I had worked with him in the past and we had gotten along fine so I attributed his statement to the tension that probably accompanied his job as woods crew foreman. I said nothing more as the three of us found our spots on top of the gear.

When Pete revved the engines, the smooth roll of the jets sent streams of boiling water rushing behind us. Then the boat glided slowly up river through calm water. I settled into a pile of duffle to assimilate my new surroundings when I was immediately thrown backwards, rolling head over heels. A pack sack flipped through the air, landing on my head. We had hit the rapids and powered out. The bow flipped up at a 90 degree angle before is slapped back into the water. Then the boat whirled uncontrollably backward until it came to rest in the calm water.

"Everybody okay back there?" Pete asked.

"I guess so," Tom answered as he clutched onto the side of the boat, "but I don't think I like this here boat trip like I thought I would!"

I saw that Dad was all right as he crawled back up from under a tent.

"We're all okay, Pete," I said," but we're not going to stay that way if we don't put some of this stuff up front.

"We don't have time for all that. You and Dad get up on the bow. That'll be enough weight to stabilize us."

I thought about the weighted bow slapping into dips of white water. I was about to protest when I saw Dad crawl quietly forward, averting Jim's gaze, and mine. Dad would avoid conflict at almost any cost, I had learned, and rather than put him in an uncomfortable situation I sat beside him on the bow, leaning as he did against the windshield for a back rest. The boat started again upriver.

"This is probably going to be a cold boat ride, Rog. When it's freezing outside it's not the time to take a swim, but it looks like that's what we'll be doing."

He reached into his inside jacket pocket and drew out a pint of whisky.

"We've got a 32 mile ride ahead of us. Maybe this will help keep us warm," he said, offering me the bottle.

"Thanks, Dad, I hope you're right."

After taking a drink I reached over to hand the bottle back to Dad. Just then the bottom of the boat dipped into swirls of white water. We grabbed the side rails, ducking as waves shot over our heads.

"Don't lose that bottle, Dad," I shouted as the boat shuddered its way through the rough water. "But don't drink it too fast, either. We've got about 31 miles of this ahead."

When we once again glided into smooth water I wiped my face with my sopping jacket sleeve, and settled back again to look at my new country. The canyons' deep gorges had widened, and rolling hills of big cedar, Douglas fir, and tangled underbrush opened up before us. We were traveling through semi-rain forest country that received only a little snow in winter, but enough rainfall the rest of the year to make it a quagmire. Ferns sprouted up through snarled growths of berry vines and alder bushes. Dank, gray canyon walls were painted with moss. When we rode to higher planes, the sky was often hidden by forests of dense cedar. Sunlight streamed through heavy limbs in misty shafts of gold—a primeval ring of virgin land. Dad had been right. It was my kind of country—dense, wild, distant. It was filled with deer—thousands of them that lined the canyon walls and grazed through scattered meadows along the river banks. And the clear, green water was filled with fish. I thought beyond my drenched clothes and chattering teeth, and I looked forward to inhabiting the North Fork.

Four hours after the first freezing waves of water had rolled over us, the boat slowed down as we slipped through the passageway at Big Island where the canyon widens into a long grassy meadow, and the river narrows to intersect it. On the west side of the meadow four frame bunk houses had been built for logging crews. Beside them were two log bunk houses that had been standing for many years. The boat continued past the building until we reached a deserted homesteaders cabin on the east side of the island where Pete pulled ashore. I jumped to dry ground, stamping my feet to start the circulation again. Dad and Tom followed behind me while Pete sat behind the wheel with the engine idling.

"Do you guys want help getting your gear out?" he asked.

"We'd appreciate it, Pete, when we get to the bunk house. Why did you stop here?" I asked.

"The bunk houses are full"

"What about those two old ones? It doesn't look like anybody's staying there."

"I have some more men coming in later. You three can stay in that cabin," he said, pointing to the lonesome shack on our side of the island.

I glanced at Dad as he walked silently to the boat to unload our equipment. In deference to his conciliatory nature, I once again accepted Pete's orders. Tom, who was as happy to be on shore as he was unconcerned about where he was staying, began throwing duffle out of the boat. I joined him, carrying our saws onto dry ground. When the last piece of equipment was unloaded, Pete opened throttle and whisked across the river, leaving us standing in his jet-propelled wake.

"Is there something about us that man doesn't like?" I asked Dad.

"Probably not. He just likes the other crew better. Whoever he likes, it suits me fine to stay here in our own private resort."

"If this is your idea of a resort, Dad, I'd say you've probably spent about thirty years too long in the brush."

"You just don't have imagination, Rog. I'm sorry about that."

He smiled, picked up his saws, and walked up the bank.

When we opened the cabin door to set down our first load, the stench of pack rats hit us so hard that we threw ourselves backward as if we'd been hit with a fire hose. We looked at each other in silence. Even Dad had nothing to say about cleaning it up. I was pleased that the shack was unlivable.

"Well, Dad, it looks like we'll have to make our own resort with tents," I said cheerfully.

"I don't think we'll have to go to all that trouble. Look at that nice little house right back there," he said, pointing to a woodshed in back of the cabin.

"You guys go on ahead and fix up whatever kind of livin' suits you best," Tom said as he set down his gear. "I'm gon'na get my rifle and get us our supper. Seems to me we better worry about our stomachs 'fore we start worryin' about a roof."

He tramped to the river with his long stride, and I followed Dad to the woodshed.

"This really is a fine hotel, Dad," I said. "Just look at this. Walls on each side except for these two sides that are open. As tempting as it looks, I'd prefer a tent to keep the North Fork out at night. This isn't exactly summer yet."

Dad walked quickly out of the woodshed.

"Don't you worry about keeping warm. I've already got that all figured out," he said.

He ran back to the old cabin. In a moment he was out again, staggering across the grass with a soot-covered barrel stove in his arms.

"Here. Let me help you with that," I said as I ran to meet him.

"Thanks, Rog, but I'm doin' just fine."

Dad set down his stove in the middle of the shed and I stood back to admire it.

"That's an efficient looking furnace, Dad," I said. "Its best feature is that it won't even need a chimney with the built in ventilation system this hotel provides."

"I was just thinking about that myself."

We walked to the river then to bring up the rest of our supplies. I built a camp fire with a grill over the flame for cooking. Our clothes were still wet from our boat trip so we stayed close to the fire while I sliced potatoes and onions into a frying pan. Dad filled a coffee pot at the river and set it on the grill. He sat down on a log, leaning close to the fire to warm his hands. In the flickering firelight, his silver-white hair contrasted in brilliance to his soot-covered face and clothes. As he gazed into the flames I knew that he was content. The soft-spoken man of iron found peace in the challenge of wilderness survival and in the company of a person that he could trust.

Our moment of quiet was interrupted when Tom charged back to the hotel with a hind quarter of deer meat on his back.

"I tell you, I could smell them spuds a mile away. Now that I see 'em, I don't think I can wait to get the meat cut up. I'll be back in a minute with some liver."

He dropped the deer quarter in the brush and stomped off to the river. In a minute or two he was back with the rest of our supper.

The bacon grease was sizzling hot when we laid thin slices of fresh liver in the pan. We almost inhaled the meat and potatoes. Too much fresh liver can be hard on the system, but it had been a long time since breakfast so we finished it all.

As soon as Dad's plate was empty he jumped up from his log.

"Before I do anything else, I'm going to get a fire going in the stove so we'll be warm tonight," he said.

"You know it's going to drop way below freezing tonight, Dad. Do you really think your stove is going to keep out all that fresh air?" I asked.

He assured me that his stove would keep us toasty warm, so when our tools and clothes were ready for morning we crawled into our sleeping bags. By then the freezing Clearwater night had crept fearlessly into our un-walled retreat. Tom and I were prepared for cold weather with extra blankets, but Dad had nothing for warmth but a thin sleeping bag.

"Hey, Dad. If you forgot to bring extra blankets I have more than I'll use," I said cautiously so he wouldn't think that I was trying to give him a handout. "

"Thanks, Rog, but I won't need any. If I did, I'd have brought some."

"Okay, have it your way, but don't try to crawl in with me when your teeth start chattering."

Sleep came easily when I slid into my down-filled cocoon until I was awakened by a clanking noise beside me. I sat up so see Dad rekindling a dying fire in the stove. I dived back down in my sleeping bag for protection from the cold, damp night. For the first time that I can remember, I was irritated by the irrational independence of Dad.

"Dammit, Dad. Why don't you take one of those blankets?" I barked.

"Thank you, Rog, but I have a better idea for keeping warm."

Leaving the stove door open for light, Dad picked up an old army cot that he had brought along. He reached up and placed it between two sagging rafters above the stove. He rummaged through a tool box until he found a hammer and nails which he threw, along with his sleeping bag, up on the cot. He lifted himself gracefully onto one of the rafters, crawled on his hands and knees to the cot, and nailed the makeshift bed to the bending beams. He spread out his sleeping bag and slid inside. Except for a rhythmical snoring from Tom, the wood shed was quiet once again—strangely quiet with the addition of a man sleeping directly above a blazing barrel.

"Are you sure you'll be all right, Dad?" I asked.

"You bet. This is the place to sleep for a man that's cold."

When the alarm went off in the morning, I first looked up to see if Dad was still on the rafter. He was, so I gave him a wake up call before I strolled to the river for a splash of cold water on my face. That was the first phase in coping with the day. The second step would follow when I returned to the hotel for a cup of Dad's thick, black coffee.

When the shock from the freezing water popped my eyes wide open, I turned back up the bank. In the gray dawn I noticed an animal of some kind laying at the river's edge, not 50 yards away. It was a deer, green and bloated, that had probably been run into the river a few days before by coyotes. Not a mark was on it except for a slit on its belly. I looked close and saw that the liver was missing. I shivered, remembering our supper the night before.

When I returned to the hotel, Tom was stretching his way out of the sleeping bag.

"Tom, did that liver you brought in last night come from an already dead deer?" I asked.

"Yup."

"From the green one on the river bank?"

"Yeah, why?"

"What was the matter with the liver in the fresh one?"

"Nothin', 'cept it wasn't cool, and if we ate too much it would'a made us sick. What's the matter with you, anyway? You already know that."

"Did you ever think that maybe a green deer might make us sick?"

"Well, did'ja get sick last night?"

"No, I didn't get sick until this morning when I saw that deer on the river bank."

"Then it's a good thing ya' ate it in the dark."

With that Tom laughed so hard that he fell back into his sleeping bag. It was time to drop the subject so I turned to Dad who was busy putting wood on the campfire.

"How did your night go in the ceiling, Dad?" I asked.

"Fine, Rog. I was warm as toast all night."

"Good. If you like, I'll take care of breakfast this morning. Somebody forgot to turn up the heat last night after you went to bed. I'd like to keep moving to keep warm."

"That'll be fine. I'll unpack these regular dishes that I brought up. The plates are bigger than the tin ones we had last night."

Tom recovered from his fit of laughter, pulled on his work pants and ambled toward the river. I chipped ice from two of our big frying pans before I set them on the grill. While they were warming I mixed up a big bowl of pancake batter. When the pans were ready I cracked several eggs into one of them, and poured three big rounds of pancake batter into the other. The white cakes soon turned to bubbles, and the edges curled into a delicate brown.

"Bring the plates over, Dad," I said. "I'm going to flip these cakes now."

Dad carried his ceramic plates from the shed, accompanied by wisps of steam from his mouth.

A peek under the pancakes showed that they were grilled to a golden brown and the eggs had steamed into a firm, sunny side up. I slipped my spatula under the pancakes, scooping them into a pile. With the flourish of a master chef I dropped the steaming morsels onto the plate that Dad held in his outstretched hand. CRRAAACK! The heat broke the freezing plate in two. Dad held half a plate in his hand, watching the pancakes steam at his feet. A moment later he looked up.

"We'll have to get us some stronger dishes," he said.

We finished breakfast on tin plates, and then carried our chain saws and pack sacks to the river bank to be ready for our ride to work. I hadn't taken time the day before to inspect Big Island so I sat down on the canvas bag to look over the country.

On both sides of our island meadow, charred snags towered over heavy stands of alder brush, small cedar, and fir—phantom reminders of ages past. Fire had obviously devastated the original trees, possibly the 1910 burn that had swept through the country from Oregon to Canada. Ferns grew everywhere, thriving under the timber growth in damp, sunless ground. Beyond the fledgling forest was the denseness of the Clearwater's virgin timber. A sodden country, I thought, as I stood up to defend myself from the penetrating dampness. I wasn't used to high humidity. I thought ahead to summer and decided that I had picked the right time to work in the Clearwater.

As we stood on the river bank, the faint sound of jet engines burgeoned into a roar. From around the river bend a silver bullet knifed cleanly through the quiet water of our island channel, then scraped to an abrupt stop at our feet. It was the boat that had brought us in, driven this time by a stout, middle-age Indian.

"Hi, I'm Chief. I have a message for Roger and Tom. Is that you two?" he asked.

"Yes. I'm Roger and this is Tom"

"You're supposed to get a deer every day for the crews. Put it in the river to cool. I'll pick it up the next day and take it to the camps."

"How did we get roped into this?"

"Pete said that you hunt all the time and Tom would rather hunt than eat. Get in now. I'll take you to work."

We had barely seated ourselves in the boat when Chief opened throttle, whisking us three miles down river to the job. We zoomed through quiet, clear water for several minutes until the canyon narrowed into a deep gorge. The boat bounced through slapping waves for a while, and then Chief turned abruptly and glided onto shore.

"This is your contract. I go up and down the river all day so wait here when you're through working and I'll take you back to camp."

When our saws were unloaded he shot ahead again, guiding his boat through the rapids as if it was a sea of glass.

After watching the boat disappear in its wake I turned to appraise the work that lay ahead. Steep canyon slopes climbed impetuously before us. Timber grew in dense patchwork patterns except for sporadic burned over areas where they were only scattered. All over, the ground was covered with ironweed—a plant with fibrous, limber stalks that were six to ten feet tall, with seed pods that hung like brown tassels from their tops. Alder brush, vine maple, and willows contested successfully for space. The inevitable fern carpeted the forest floor. All stalks, two or more inches in diameter, would be cut six inches from the ground. Everything smaller was to be cut waist high.

We leaned hard into our work that day. It was a new experience for me to leave fallen trees without removing the limbs and cutting them into logs. The work went fast. With three of us working side by side between the echoing canyon walls it was as if armies of thunder gods unleashed their power at once. At the end of our work day, countless trees lay in sloping heaps along the river shore.

We climbed down the piles of logs like stalking cats, stepping assiduously from log to log. Chief stopped the boat on shore just as we reached the bottom.

"Don't forget about the deer," he said when he left us off at camp. "The rest of the crews came in today. We can't keep meat in here so we're counting on you for our suppers."

It took one deer a day to feed the Dworshak crews. When Chief dropped us off at camp, he picked up the cooled deer from the day before. He waited while we split the meat into ten-to-fifteen pound pieces then he roared away again to deliver it to the camps up and down the river. Chief ended his day with the meat run while Tom and I hiked into the timber to replenish the supply.

Hunting was easy in the North Fork country, and it became a time to anticipate because when we returned to camp Dad had supper well on its way. And each meal included his specialty, Dutch oven biscuits. As soon as we returned from work Dad prepared for his biscuit making by building a fire in a hole, 15 inches deep. While the fire burned down to red hot coals he made the biscuit dough. He filled a Dutch oven with mounds of the white substance, and placed the lid on top. With his bare hands he removed half the coals, set the Dutch oven in the hole, and put the rest of the coals on top the lid. He knew instinctively how long to leave them there, and when he took them out they were golden brown all the way through and all the way around.

It was in a state of ecstasy that I ate Dad's biscuits every night, so much so that the absence of them was the first thing that popped into my mind when we were told, at the end of three weeks, that we would each have to bring in new crews if the reservoir area was to be cut in time. It had been an enlightening experience camping with Dad and Tom. I had grown so attached to the subtle, forceful ways of Dad that I couldn't imagine life in the brush without him. But if the old saying, "variety is the spice of life" is true, my existence was about to be highly seasoned.

To form a new crew I had contacted three competent fallers that I had worked with in the past—Reuben Sayler who was 30 years old, placid, and amicable, and Al Hunt who was almost 50, wiry, easy going, and retiring. And to add to camp life a vitality that no one else could provide, I called on my power-driven partner from many jobs before, Sparky Moore.

My new contract was further down river, and the closest camping spot was near the end of Big Island at Swamp Creek where the gushing stream tumbled into the Clearwater. When I loaded my equipment in the boat, Chief skimmed us over the water to my new home.

"You'll still get deer every day, won't you?" he asked as I lifted my tent out of the boat. "Tom said he would. We'll need two a day now for all the crews."

"My new partners are hunters, too, so don't worry, Chief. We'll keep everybody's stomach full—yours included."

He grinned and took off with a roar.

I looked down at the supplies spread out at my feet, and decided on the spot that I would first set up the big tent. My new partners would be in that day. I would be ready for them with the luxury of a four-walled residence.

26

After the tent was set up at Swamp Creek I had started splitting firewood when I heard the jet boat engines rumbling up the river. I flipped the axe into the chopping block and walked to the river bank just as Chief raised the boat onto shore. That warm feeling of meeting a long absent friend enveloped me as my old partner, Sparky Moore, jumped onto the bow of the boat before it shuddered to its final stop. He jumped to the ground, rushing up the bank to meet me.

"Spark! You look great!" I said and I meant it. His black hair was slicked back, and he was all decked out in brand new Levis and a red flannel shirt—all 6 feet 5 inches, and 240 pounds of him. His grey eyes flashed with excitement as he broke into a big smile.

"So do you, Roger and so does this country. How's fishing?"

"I haven't had a chance to test it out, Spark. I've been too busy hunting. Maybe now that you're here we can keep the crews supplied with fish."

"I'm going to have a look around. Help the guys unload. I'll be back in a minute."

Sparky disappeared up the creek and I descended to the boat. Al and Reuben had already started to unload. After we exchanged greetings I jumped up front to take out Sparky's fishing gear.

"How did you like your trip from Orofino, Chief?" I asked.

"Boy, that Sparky is a noisy one. He makes more noise than the boat."

"Did you learn a lot about Montana that you didn't know before?"

"I never heard so many things in my life."

"Have you ever heard any Paul Bunyan stories, Chief?"

"Sure I heard Paul Bunyan stories."

"Well, now you can say you've met Paul Bunyan's son."

Chief looked at me, puzzled, as I set the fishing gear on the ground.

We began the climb up the hill on the first of many trips that it would take to deposit Sparky's equipment—his light plant for generating electricity, a big gas stove, piles of new clothes, brand new power saws, enough fishing tackle to outfit at least ten fishermen, and a massive Dutch oven that might possibly hold enough meat to satisfy Sparky's appetite. When we set our loads down inside the tent, Sparky burst in through the flap.

"I'm glad I brought up the fishing gear. I can't believe the looks of the mouth of that creek," he said enthusiastically. "Get that gas stove up here and pump it up. I'll be back in a few minutes with a steelhead for supper."

Al and Reuben watched him leave, shaking their heads unbelievingly.

"Don't take his words lightly," I said. "I'm going to bring up that stove on the next trip."

"I never take Sparky's words lightly," Al answered. "I can't. He says them too loud."

We were settling the final load of supplies into the tent when Sparky reappeared with ten pounds of filleted steelhead.

"Here she is. She's all yours. Be sure and flour it, cook it slow, and don't burn it!"

He mixed a drink from his case of Walkers Deluxe before he retired with his lawn chair to the banks of the river.

"Oh, that sack of socks and gloves is for you, Roger," he said on his way to the river. "You've been up here long enough that you're probably running out of both."

It had been almost six months since I had last worked with Sparky, and I still wasn't used to the stillness that permeated the woods in his absence. Chain saws, skidding jammers, cats, and logging trucks were all sources of ringing melody compared to the unique discord that Sparky contributed to a logging operation. His usual job in the woods was to run the skidding jammer, the big machine that skids and decks the cut logs. It's a complicated piece of equipment so it's prone to break downs and foul-ups. Sparky had his own philosophy for coping with the irritation of running the jammer.

"There's only one way to skid logs, and that's to stay mad all the time," he once said when I questioned him about the effectiveness of spending his day screaming at the machine. "The louder I holler, the better the jammer pays attention to what's going on. It understands fits better than monkey wrenches so that's how I have to handle it."

With the least bit of resistance from the jammer, Sparky would jump up from his seat, throw the levers ahead, and shout,

"What the hell's going on down there??"

"I don't know!" (That in a whining, irritated voice)

"Can't anybody do anything right????"

"What kind of a no good outfit is this???"

"I QUIT!"

Sparky quit at least 15 times a day, and by doing so he decked probably more logs than any skidder in the woods. While he screamed at the jammer, the noise of the machine was in his ears so he didn't realize that the rest of the work crews grew silent to listen to the fits. No one minded them, in fact they came to stand as a symbol of job security. Whenever Sparky screamed we knew that production standards were being met and the whole logging operation was humming along.

"Brush fits" is the term that was coined for Sparky's woodland rages, and the phrase was extended to include a general display of temper by anyone.

But Sparky came to the North Fork to fall timber instead of operating the jammer. Spring was in the air when the new crew arrived, and new energy came with the season. Sparky was in his element when he sent those Idaho giants crashing to the ground, and the relatively uncomplicated atmosphere of falling timber was not conducive to a need for rages. So the absence of brush fits in the Clearwater was sometimes disquieting. It was as if something was missing from the accepted order of things.

But then about a month after we started working together, Sparky and I clashed over a very sensitive aspect of his nature, and things returned to normal.

Sparky was tall, big boned, hard, and lean, and it took more pounds of food each day to keep him that way than I have ever seen another human being consume. As much as he liked to eat, he disliked cooking just as much. Al had never cooked in his life, so I took over as chef with Reuben as my assistant.

Feeding Sparky wasn't a difficult job. He was satisfied as long as the quantities were enormous. I soon learned that I could plan for the average man's appetite and multiply it by three to satisfy Sparky. Each night, Al, Reuben, and I together ate half a hind quarter of deer meat, and Sparky ate the other half by himself. Since six potatoes satisfied the three of us, I cooked another six for Sparky. A dozen biscuits were served at almost every supper, two for each of the three us, and six for Sparky.

Reuben and I put effort into our cooking. Every night we browned the meat before steaming it in the Dutch oven with herbs, onions, and garlic. We roasted corn-on-the-cob in hot coals or seasoned large quantities of canned vegetables. I followed Dad's formula for brown and flaky Dutch-oven biscuits, and Sparky complimented our results at every meal. He was satisfied with his camp cook—until the night that I went wild with a can of oregano.

It was at the end of Sparky's second week in camp that the weather turned warm. A bush plane landed on Big Island on weekends to take us to town, and it was that weekend that we decided that we needed some diversion from living in the brush. Besides enjoying our time in Orofino, it would be a treat to bring back to camp a few days supply of fresh vegetables, milk, bread, and all the perishables that we couldn't usually keep in camp. We would also need meat for our Monday night supper because we couldn't leave deer meat or fish to spoil over the weekend.

It was on the plane ride, about five minutes after Sparky had left the security of his food source, that he hit upon an idea for his homecoming meal.

"I've got Monday's super all figured out!" he shouted at us over the roaring engines of our Cherokee, six-passenger plane.

"Terrific, Spark!" Reuben yelled back. "I've been worried about it ever since we left."

"You're going to have a treat like you've never had in camp."

No one showed further interest so I screamed, "What's it going to be???"

"Corned beef! I can almost taste it now!"

The rest of the weekend was devoted mainly to discussions of Sparky's corned beef dinner. While we visited the dam construction site, lounged in the luxury of our motel room, ate in the cafes, and caught up on the local news in the bars, Sparky inevitably turned the conversation to his plans for our corned beef supper. By Sunday afternoon he had decided that we would all go to the store together to pick out the best cuts of corned beef.

"Sparky, I trust your judgment. I know I'll love every bite," Rueben insisted.

But Sparky insisted louder, and we left as a foursome for the grocery store. When we finished shopping we carried out the regular groceries that we would use in camp, plus twenty pounds of corned beef. To accompany it we had sacks filled with cabbage, carrots, celery, onions, green peppers, pepper corns, whole cloves, and bay leaves. When we left for camp there was barely room in the little plane for ourselves and Sparky's Monday night supper.

Sparky's excitement over his meal was not such unusual behavior for someone who works and lives in the outdoors. Food is important because it's necessary to eat in large quantities, and it's one of the few luxuries to enjoy in camp. But the usual emphasis on food was exaggerated by Sparky because of his natural enthusiasm for everything he did. It was unfortunate for us that week end that his only undertaking was the purchase of corned beef.

By the time we finished work on Monday the responsibility for Sparky's supper was weighing heavily on my shoulders. He turned off his chain saw several times through the day to talk about it. I felt that letting him down would be like telling a child there wasn't a Santa Claus. I had never cooked a piece of corned beef so I wasn't sure that I could meet his standards.

I had soaked the meat the night before, and when we returned to camp after work I changed the water before putting the big pot on the stove to simmer. While I was busy with that phase of the meal, Sparky fixed me a drink from his supply of Walker's Deluxe. He said that the drink was for the benefit of the corned beef. He wanted to be sure that I was relaxed and happy when I added the rest of the ingredients.

The chopped vegetables and seasonings were added when the water came to a boil, and as the spicy aroma of pepper corns and cloves filled the tent, Sparky kept busy serving rounds of Walker's Deluxe. Before long, even Al and Reuben were caught up in the corned beef mania.

"You know something?" Al was about to contribute to our meal preparation for the first time. "I've been thinking,' and it's been botherin' me. Something's missing from the corned beef. I just realised that it needs tomatoes," he said in his inebriated state.

"Good idea," Reuben added. "Why didn't I think of that?"

"Sounds fine, Al," I said. "What do you think, Sparky?"

"That's just what it needs. Good thinking, Al."

"If we put in tomatoes, we'll need a little oregano," I added.

"Oregano! Thash it. A little, tiny bit of oregano" Al agreed.

Sparky and Reuben joined in the discussion, and it was unanimously agreed upon by four hungry, tired, whiskey-filled loggers that a pinch of oregano would add the final perfect touch to the feast.

As I stirred cans of tomatoes into the vegetables, I reached into the box of spices for the oregano. When I pried off the lid I turned the can sideways over the pot, tapped it lightly, and watched half of the container's contents spill into the water. I tasted the broth and winced. The oregano was so overpowering that it took my breath away. No one saw it happen. My sense of logic at that moment told me that if I walked away from the pot and let it simmer for a while, the strong flavor would boil out.

"If the oregano's going to do the job, we'll have to let it simmer a while," I said authoritatively to the group.

By the time I announced that the corned beef was ready, no one except Sparky cared much if they ate or not. He left Al and Reuben to their deep discussion in the corner of the tent as he dashed to the stove. He served himself approximately five pounds of meat for his first helping, along with as many vegetables as his plate would hold. He carried the pile carefully outside and sat down on a log. I watched him while he thrust his fork into the tender meat, and raised it to his mouth. The fork disappeared from sight ... and then we had our old fit-throwing Sparky back.

"WHAT in the HELL did you do to my corned beef???"

He jumped up, stomping back and forth with his plate in his hand.

"Can't you do ANYTHING RIGHT???"

"What kind of jack pine savages are you????"

"I don't know!" (That, in a whining, despairing voice.)

"You can't depend on anybody any more."

"I QUIT!!!"

"I'm sorry, Spark. I didn't mean to ruin your corned beef," I sputtered. "The lid fell off the can. I couldn't help it."

"Well, if you were supposed to put it in with a scoop shovel, they'd sell it in hundred pound sacks instead of two ounce cans."

Al and Reuben continued their discussion in the corner of the tent, oblivious to the uprising outside.

Sparky did have reason to complain. The next morning I noticed that Al spent much of his time on the job sitting on a log. I hollered at him across the canyon to see if anything was wrong, but he didn't answer me. Later, when we ate lunch, he said,

"When you hollered at me I couldn't answer. I had such bad heartburn I thought I was having a heart attack."

I asked him if he had heartburn often and he said, "No, it was that overdose of oregano boiling in my stomach."

"I'm sorry about that, Al. At least you're good natured about it, and I appreciate that."

So the Clearwater spring was filled with sunshine, budding wild flowers, songs of returning birds, and ... Sparky Moore. The tent walls rippled with Sparky stories every night—stories of the biggest fish ever caught, the biggest elk ever packed out of the mountains by a man, the fastest horse ever ridden, the longest hike ever taken in a snowstorm, all accomplished by Sparky himself. But the hours that we spent listening to Sparky spin his yarns were made tolerable, in fact interesting, because they were true. Our modern-day Paul Bunyan grew up in backwoods poverty with a life that was packed with adventure. He isn't only big, tough, and short-fused. His fits, his sense of humor, and his need to excel were wisely laced into his personality to keep a balance between the rugged existence in which he was raised and his underlying sensitive nature.

When you knew Sparky well, you knew when his susceptible side was camouflaged by excessive behavior. We saw a classic example of that during a memorable event in the North Fork.

27

In early summer we were able to drive the roads of the North Fork, and it was then that I learned to fully appreciate the country. Its woods and rivers made me feel at home, as any timbered country would, but it was the life style of its people that made it special.

Since the turn of the century, the life blood of the North Fork people had originated from the Potlatch Mill in Lewiston, Idaho. The town was built around the big lumber mill, and the whole North Fork population survived on it. Homesteaders' cabins lined the thick-timbered banks of the Clearwater, homes that squatters had built from the time that the mill began. The people either worked at the mill or harvested timber that the mill received. At night they came home to their little farms on the river where they tended to their milk cow and chickens, their gardens and their fishing. When they needed meat they got a deer in their back yard, and when they wanted whiskey they cooked up a batch on their woodshed stills. The peaceful, unadorned life of the North Fork people had remained almost static since the beginning of their existence in the country. Their needs were met by the resources that their surroundings gave them.

I developed a fondness for the little town of Orofino that was tucked in the heart of the Clearwater country. Its few stores carried basic provisions for homespun ways of living, small cafes displayed paintings of Clearwater cabins and houseboats, and friendly people stopped in town for a chat with the strangers who worked on the dam.

But it was also in early summer that the serenity of the country transformed into a cauldron of activity when people gathered from every corner to participate in the annual Clearwater log drive. At high water, a years' accumulation of decked logs was rolled into the river to ride the tumbling current to the Potlatch Mill, and the North Fork population had reason to celebrate. Loggers watched their year's labor roll down the river to produce work for their neighbors. For the mill workers, the sight meant a payday every week for the coming year as the mill ponds filled with timber. For all of them, the sight brought to mind the bond between them. They were partners who depended on their country for their livelihood and their way of life.

For twenty-eight days a rolling bed of timber filled the river from bank to bank, heaving and crashing through a forty-mile-an-hour current. As in the days of my granddad, men bounced from log to log, guiding them on a straight course through swirling rapids and deep, narrow gorges, pushing apart potential log jams with long pipe poles. When their work day ended they stepped across the lots to their river home—ten rubber rafts tied together sideways to support three bunk houses, a cook house, and a D-4 cat for breaking up log jams. For the duration of the drive, the men never left the river.

On the first weekend of the drive, the four of us from Swamp Creek sat down on a log in front of the tent to watch the rumbling spectacle.

"How would you like to be a North Fork native today?" Sparky asked after watching the spectacle in silence for a long time.

"Even less than I like the idea that I contributed to this event," I answered.

"We're watching an era end. Well, I'll say one thing. This one's sure going out with a bang."

Sparky was referring to the fact that the logs were riding down the Clearwater River for the last time. The days of log drives were over, not only to the Potlatch Mill but for the whole United States. The Clearwater drive was the only one left in the country, and when the diversion tunnel for the Dworshak Dam was plugged, the whole river would transform into a lake, 52 miles long with 400 miles of shoreline in and out of all the draws and valleys. When the drive ended, the Potlatch Mill would receive its timber from diesel-driven trucks.

The people that lived along the river had deserted their homes. The lake would swallow them up in a few weeks. Most of them moved to Orofino—town dwellers now to satisfy the need for more electricity.

"What gets me, Sparky, is the fact that the people don't resent us," I said. "Have you ever been around a friendlier bunch?"

"Do you resent the road hunters that crawl over Petty Creek?"

"I wish they weren't there."

"But you don't run them out."

"No. They have a right to the country, too. And a lot of them are nice people—in fact some of them half-way move in. But I still wish things wouldn't have changed to open up the country."

"Did you ever think that the Indians wished you weren't there?"

"All the time."

"That's the way Chief must feel about the people who settled here. You can't keep the world from changing."

"There's a difference, Spark. We don't always like the invasion of outsiders, but we try to be good neighbors. These North Fork people have given up their homes so others can have electricity from their river. And what do those from the city who use it think when they drive through Orofino? They think it's a crime that these seedy North Forkers eat deer meat. While they're cooking their T-bone steaks on electricity that's generated by the Clearwater River they'll talk about conserving wildlife, but eating a steer won't count because it wasn't raised in the woods."

"I know. Have you thought about what's going to happen to a lot of these deer this winter? They'll be chased by coyotes through the woods like they always have been, but that reservoir is going to freeze, only not very hard, and then it'll be covered with snow. The deer won't know anything about the new man-made lake. They'll run onto the ice and fall through, and either drown or stay trapped until they're eaten by coyotes or until they freeze to death."

"I hadn't thought about it, but you're right. It isn't a very pretty picture, is it. But the conservationist who uses the electricity will never know a thing about it."

"You know, Spark, I was twenty-five years old before we got electricity on Petty Creek, and I still get a thrill out of turning on a light switch. The point is, I'm not denying anyone, including myself, the benefits of progress. I just get tired of the one-way attitude that seems to be taking over the country. Like I said, we've tried to be good neighbors. But there's a lot of people out there who spend their time building fences to keep the neighbors out."

"I know. It's a fast–changing world for those of us who aren't equipped to handle it. I don't let myself think about it too much. The old world keeps on spinning and there's nothing we can do about it."

We lapsed into the silence of our own thoughts then while the timber thundered by in front of us. Then a chopping noise above our heads caught our attention.

"Speaking of changes," Sparky shouted as the noise grew louder, "look what's coming into the North Fork now."

"I think somebody made a mistake," Al hollered back while a big red and white helicopter skimmed across the trees, dropping straight down in front of us on Big Island. Its noisy props churned the sand into dusty whirlwinds before it lifted straight up, dipped across the river, and set itself down again, right by our tent. We ducked from the force of the wind until the whirling blades gradually came to a stop. A helicopter didn't land next to our tent every day, and we all just sat there, glued to our log and tongue tied, while two men climbed down from the machine and walked toward us.

"Do any of you know anything about this log drive?" one of them asked.

Sparky came to life.

"I can tell you about the log drive. Where are you from?"

"I'm a reporter from CBS television" he said, introducing himself and his camera man. "We've been assigned to cover the log drive for national news."

Sparky's eyes danced with flames of fire.

"Oh! Well, I was raised 30 miles from here, and I've been on a lot of log drives myself. My name is Sparky Moore. What do you need to know?"

"We'd like a little history of this country, when the log drives started, what the dam means to the people around here—anything that you can tell us. Who are these men?"

"These are my partners, Al, Reuben, and Roger. We're falling timber for the dam reservoir."

The three of us nodded silently, letting the reporter know that we weren't interested in participating in the interview. He looked at us briefly before he turned back to Sparky.

"Okay, Sparky. Can you give me a brief history of this country about the time it was first settled?"

"It was about the turn of the century," Sparky began while he reached into his shirt pocket for his Prince Albert tobacco.

"Hold it right there! We'll be back in a minute to set up!" the reporter shouted as he walked quickly to his equipment.

"I'm going to find myself a drier log to sit on," Al said. "I don't think I can stand to watch this."

"Stay here, Al. You'll never have entertainment again like this in the North Fork," I told him.

Al remained seated, shaking his head, muttering, "Oh, that Sparky," while the reporters returned from the helicopter with their camera equipment. When they were set up and ready to film, the reporter said,

"Okay, Sparky. We're ready now. Roll your cigarette and start again."

Sparky was informed on his subject, and he presented a sensitive portrayal of North Fork history, beginning with Indian life before the white man settled the country and continuing to the present. While he talked, the reporter intermittently said, "Roll another cigarette. I like that."

For at least an hour Sparky regaled the reporter, answering questions and bringing up new topics to include in the interview. It was obvious that he was having the time of his life. But at the same time, as he explained how the building of the dam changed the lives of the people, he became too emotionally involved in the subject to keep the interview on a conversational level. I could tell that he was afraid that the fun was going to end because he suddenly stopped talking, his eyes sparkled, and he took a deep breath. I braced myself while Al continued to shake his head and mutter to himself.

"Hold on, Al. I have a feeling he's just getting going," I said.

"Getting back to the log drive itself," Sparky said to the reporter, "you have to realize that this is the modern age and the log drivers aren't made of the same stuff as they were thirty years ago when I started in the business. We didn't have cats to help us break up the log jams. The whole show was up to us. I was just a kid when I rode the rapids on my first drive with the toughest men in the business—the Swedes and Norwegians. When four of us came out of the rapids together into a stretch of quiet water, we found a 300 foot log jam in the middle of it. Several men were already crawling over the tangled pile of logs, trying everything they knew to break it loose.

"When my log drifted toward the pile, I crouched so I'd be ready to jump up to help 'em. Remember now, this was my first drive and I was as green as grass. Just as my log smacked into the pile, I jumped. When my feet touched the nearest log they slipped off the slimy side, and before I knew what happened an undercurrent had sucked me down under the jam.

"I started swimming down river under the logs. Whenever I found a hole, I raised up for air, and then I plunged down again and swam with every ounce of strength I had. Five minutes later I surfaced at the head of the jam. I raised myself up on the nearest log and crawled to the top of the pile. One of the Swedes was standing on the edge of the logs looking down the river for me. I ran up behind him and grabbed his cant hook. Before he even knew what happened, I ran up to the main log and hit it dead center with the hook. Wham! The whole pile broke loose. It sounded like the sky was filled with thunder. While everybody scrambled to a log to get their footing, we were back in the white water, ripping down river to the mill."

When the helicopter lifted off, Sparky shuffled in the direction of our log. His head was cast down and a self-conscious grin turned the corners of his mouth. The three of us sat mutely on our log, staring at him as he approached. We hadn't recovered yet from the interview.

"Well, it was first-class b.s. anyway, wasn't it?" he said as he walked into the tent.

"Yeah, Sparky, it sure was that," Al muttered as he stood up and walked away.

I stayed on the log for a while after everyone left, thinking about Sparky's and my conversation before the helicopter landed. I ended up falling into Al's head shaking response. Sometimes it was the only way to react to Sparky.

He had said there would always be changes but the world would keep on spinning. He was right. It wouldn't get us down as long as there were people around like him to help keep it all in perspective.

28

It's not worth it, I thought, as the train of machines writhed their way, inch by inch, down the steep descent. It wasn't worth another all-night trip through the mountains to bring in an unnecessary plaything. But there was nothing to do about it then but ride the engine through the still, black tomb, and hope for the best.

We were in the situation because it occurred to me just before the log drive began that we would enjoy the use of a small boat in camp. We felt like we were punching a time clock when we waited for Chief to pick us up in the morning, then again in the afternoon, to transport us back to camp, and we weren't used to such a lack of independence. If we brought in a boat, the rapids between camp and our contract weren't so swift that we couldn't navigate them, and there were quiet spots along the way that we could fish during our leisure hours.

So the idea was a good one-with only one flaw. The only road into the North Fork was still impassible from snow in the high spots, and a small boat would never make it through the rapids on the trip to Big Island. Then we heard that the company's fuel trailer was going to be filled.

Along with the bunk houses, Big Island was home for a 10,000 gallon steel tank that supplied fuel for the cats, the jet boat, and our chain saws. When the trailer needed filling, a cat pulled it over the road in any kind of weather to the fueling station at Headquarters, Idaho. Since that same machine could pull much more than just a fuel trailer, I decided to bring in my pickup to drive when the road would be usable again. I told Dad about my plan the next morning on our way to work, and he thought that he might bring in his little trailer to live in for the summer. So the decisions were made and our Big Island caravan was born.

That Friday after work, Dad and I climbed aboard the bush plane on Big Island for our trip back to civilization. Throughout his life Dad had thrilled at topping the tallest trees, but when the little Cessna sailed above the timber he sat rigid, in total silence, staring straight ahead. Even so, I didn't lack companionship because I had the company of Boyd Dieble, our talkative pilot, who enjoyed hearing about our exploits in the timber. Always on the lookout for wildlife, I scanned the ground as we flew along, and I was doing so when Boyd asked me if we were bothered by bears in camp.

"Not too bad at this time of year," I hollered to him above the engine's roar, and at that moment I saw a big black bear lumbering through a meadow below us.

"Look, there's one now!" I said.

"Let's have a closer look," Boyd shouted as he dove straight down.

My stomach flew up to the tail of the plane while Dad turned white, clutching my arm When we were just a few feet from the meadow, Boyd pulled us up like we were taking off into space, then he banked at a 45-degree angle. Dad turned green.

"That's a big one," Boyd yelled as he leveled the plane and began to climb.

Some time later, when we were flying forward again at a respectable altitude, Dad let go of my arm. He looked at me sideways and said, slowly and emphatically, "Don't-you- EVER-show-him-a-bear-again."

Dad recuperated from his plane ride over the weekend, and we met early Monday morning at Headquarters. Pete, the woods foreman, had fueled the tank, and he was ready to take it back to the job. Al had come with Pete in case he needed a hand along the way. Dad was ready with his pickup and house trailer, and I had my boat attached to my pickup. And with that we put our caravan together.

First in line was the big D-8 cat. Behind it we attached the 25-foot-long, 8-foot high fuel tank. Next in line was my pickup followed by the boat and its trailer. Behind the boat trailer we hooked a 4-wheel drive pickup that belonged to the construction company. Following that was Dad's pickup, and last in line was his little house trailer. No string of Gypsies ever looked so prosperous.

When everything was secure, the big cat revved its engines and we were off, crawling up the snow-covered mountain road like a prehistoric angle worm. Pete drove the cat, and the rest of us rode in separate pickups. An eighteen-mile trip lay ahead, ten miles up the mountain before the descent into camp. The road was covered with five feet of snow but with its wide tracks to keep it on top, the cat purred along, pulling the creaking caravan behind. As I relaxed in my pickup with a cup of coffee the cat suddenly slowed way down, close to the summit. I stuck my head out the window to see what the problem was, but the caravan picked up speed again as the big engine pulled us to the top. Then suddenly we jerked forward three or four times before creaking to a stop. The cat sunk, miring under the snow in an oozing bed of mud.

Dad had a power saw in his pickup so he plowed through the soft snow to find road-building material. He fell eight-inch trees which he cut into four-foot lengths to carry to the cat. Pete put the cat in gear as we laid out the logs, one at a time, in front of the spinning tracks, hoping that they would suck enough of them under to make traction.

ZIP! The first log disappeared. We threw down another. ZZZIP! It was gone. Twelve logs later we knew that the tracks would continue to chew up the wood as the cat sunk deeper in the mud. Pete and I left the summit to hike to Big Island to bring back the company dozer.

It was almost dark when we returned to the stranded cat. Since no one had thought to bring a flashlight, Pete quickly maneuvered the dozer into position while there was still enough light to see. When we hooked it onto the cat, the dozer gears ground into a forward position, and the caravan lurched ahead, this time with all of us riding on the dozer. The snow had firmed with the setting sun, and I knew that the dozer wouldn't fall through the crust. It was a relief to be on the way again until I thought about exactly where we were.

We had been so intent on returning to the island that none of us thought about the danger of getting there. We were on the descent of a narrow mountain road with probably a quarter-mile drop beside us. It was black dark then, and all that we had to keep us in the middle of the road was Pete's judgment. The beaver dams that I had crossed while I hunted were child's play compared to this middle-of-the-night trek. There would be no recovery if the dozer and its entourage tumbled over the mountain.

I looked around the dark, wondering what made Pete think that he could get us safely to Big Island. The road and any guidelines such as trees or brush were obliterated by a cocoon of solid black. I crawled across the dozer to suggest to Pete that we spend the night in our pickups. Then I saw a small circle of light flickering up ahead.

The light came close, suspended in the air, bobbing up and down as it moved forward. When Pete stopped the engine, an old, grizzled voice called out.

"See here, what are you doing up here at this time of night? Where's your light? Do you want to get killed?"

An old hermit who carried a lantern had left his cabin to investigate the noise on his previously deserted road. When we explained our mission, he handed the lantern to Al.

"You boys take this light. You need it worse than I do. You can bring it back in the summer when its daylight."

Al walked the old man back to his cabin. When he returned, I saw in the light the dozer track—twelve inches from the edge of a long way to the bottom.

"I'll be the headlight. Let's go," Al said as he climbed onto the blade.

We all took our positions on the dozer as the noisy hulk clamored ahead. Al balanced on the blade like a beacon in the night, swinging the lantern from side to side all the way to Big Island.

When we reached camp one of the construction foremen ran up to meet us.

"Where have you been?" he asked with anxiety in his voice. "We saw the dozer missing after work, and we thought something happened. We were about to organize a search party."

"You didn't need to worry," I said. "We were as safe as if we were in God's pocket. All that it takes to travel through the woods after dark is a little imagination."

29

After four months in the North Fork country, Al, Reuben, and Sparky decided that they had had enough of our isolated existence, and they left for home. It was tempting for me, too, but since Dad would be staying we would partner again, and that gave me the incentive to continue on until hunting season. It wasn't only the thought of working again with Dad, but the fact that I had grown attached to the North Fork that helped me make the decision. We had already been given a taste of a Clearwater summer so I knew that it would be a challenge to camp in its jungle-like conditions. But I would probably never pass that way again, and I wanted to experience the country in its extremes.

The strip of timber that was assigned to Dad and me was too far inland to bring in his trailer so we set up our tent on a river sand bar which was the only source of water in the area. Even in early summer the sand was steamy hot, and the insects that thrived in it were vicious. But the rocky little spit was the only piece of brush-free land along the river.

To take advantage of the coolest part of the day, we started work at daylight. By 10:00 a.m. we were drenched with sweat. As the temperature climbed during the morning, bald-face hornets and mosquitoes circled through the timber, stinging and biting while we worked. Sawdust clung to our skin, trickling into our eyes when beads of sweat ran down our foreheads. Working slow or stopping to rest didn't help. The humidity was too high to dry us out.

When temperatures passed 100 degrees in the afternoon, we returned to the sand bar to wade neck deep in tepid water. We tried to cool down with lukewarm drinks that we kept in the soupy creek, but it didn't work. As hot and tired as we were, pounds of flesh melted away with the heat. At the end of the day the thought of food was nauseating. At night sand fleas hopped in our bedding, biting like little stinging bees. When we left the tent to seek relief, mosquitoes bit and no-see-ems filled our noses. Insect repellant attracted more of them.

After a night of fitful sleep, our eyes were swollen shut. We would pry open one of them, then stumble to the river to make a mud patch for the other eye. We held the mud in place with one hand while using the other one to cook breakfast, aided by a 20 percent vision in the half-open eye. We were lucky to have breakfast at all. Bears pilfered through our tent during the day, eating everything that wasn't anchored down.

It was near the end of the contract, on the day that Dad received the full brunt of a Clearwater summer, that I decided to give up and let Mother Nature win the round. I had finished falling a tree on a steep hillside when Dad called me from his work area not far away. When I reached a red fir snag where he was standing, he pointed to its top.

"Look up there, Rog. Do you think we should leave that one for morning when the bees aren't so busy?"

I looked up to see a swarm of bald-face hornets circling around the tree.

"I sure do, Dad. We're having enough trouble with the ones we aren't even bothering."

We let the snag stand while we continued to clear the landscape for the rest of the day.

It was just turning daylight the next morning when we reached the top of the hill. Below us, the dry, bee-filled trunk stood alone, towering above the tangled heaps of fallen timber.

"It looks like they're still asleep," Dad whispered. "I've had more experience with bugs than you have, Rog, so I'll cut it. I don't want you to get too close to that thing."

Before I could reply, Dad flew down the hill with his saw wide open, hopping over logs and brush. Within seconds the rotting snag fell to the ground, breaking up in hundreds of flying pieces as it crashed to the bottom of the canyon. Dad turned off his saw, sat down by the stump, and lit a cigarette. I decided to stay where I was. I was a little doubtful about the results of his bee extermination.

With a tree for a back rest, I had just sat down to enjoy the last cool moments of the morning when I heard a deep-throated scream from the other side of the hill. I jumped to my feet to see Dad struggling up the mountain with a swarm of bald-face hornets right behind him. There was nothing I could do to help him so I ran around the side of the hill, out of sight, and called to let him know where I was.

Soon I heard his foot steps and then he was at my side. He looked like a giant strawberry from the mass of red welts that covered almost every inch of exposed skin.

"They must've gotten shaken loose from their nest on the way down and they came back to look for it," he said quietly. "We better start working now, Rog. We're late already and it's going to be a hot one."

"You can't work today, Dad," I called as he walked away, but he didn't turn around to answer.

One hornet sting is painful, five or ten would be excruciating, any more than that would flatten the average person, but Dad worked through the day with at least 100 of them covering his body. When we returned to camp he stripped off his clothes and sat down at the edge of the river. The hornets had stung him through his shirt and pants. His entire body was flaming red and swollen.

"Do you know what I remind myself of?" he asked as he patted himself with hand-fuls of mud, "a fly-infested elk that's wallowing in the mud."

"You remind me of somebody that's been poisoned to death."

"The stings won't hurt me. I've built up an immunity. This sand feels awfully good, though. I'm going to have to take a bath like this more often."

When we woke up the next morning Dad pried open his eyes in the usual manner except that his hands were crusted and swollen. When we finished eating breakfast he picked up his pack sack and climbed into the timber to begin another work day. For him, a hundred hornet stings was nothing more than a hazard of the occupation. For me, it was a good excuse to store the Clearwater in my memory and return to Petty Creek to get ready for the season ahead.

"I'll let you know where I'm working this winter, Rog," Dad said when I was ready to leave. "I'm going to look for a job that's closer to home. When hunting season's over maybe we can partner again."

"I'll think about it, but I believe I'll spend the winter on the ranch. I'll be in touch, though. If you don't make it up during hunting season, I'll see you when it's over. Tap it light, Dad. I don't want to see you played out before your time."

30

When my pickup climbed the mountain road away from Big Island I knew it was time for me to leave the North Fork experience behind. I had been back to the ranch to give them a hand several times during the summer, and every time I turned up Petty Creek Canyon that solid rock wall jutted skyward like a welcome sign. I had said nothing more to my dad about future plans, and he seemed happy to see me each time I returned.

But time alone, away from day-to-day ranch pressures, had given me freedom to think objectively about its problems. Also, from my association with a people who had been forced to give up their homes, I was made more keenly aware of the value of our country.

Change had come to Petty Creek; it was inevitable. So now I would use the changes to our advantage by expanding our operation into other areas. So many plans ran through my head I somehow felt that my dad's advancing age and lessening physical capabilities would contribute to his acceptance of ideas that could bring the ranch into prosperity.

It was so logical to diversify, to use the crop land more efficiently, to capitalize on changing trends. For a long time I had wanted to utilize the existing stock and hunting facilities for a summer boys' camp. As far as capital outlay was concerned, I needed only to dredge a swimming hole to expand our recreation business into a lucrative, satisfying area.

Quality rodeo stock was in demand. Development in those lines could be easily incorporated into the basic cow-calf operation. Existing timber could be harvested without destroying the aesthetic value of the land. Young trees could be thinned and sold in the growing fence-post market that land developers had created. Unlimited potential for controlled growth lay right at our doorstep. I felt that I had a life time ahead to bring Petty Creek into the present and put it on its feet.

It felt so good to return home with a bright outlook for the future, I decided, as I turned up the canyon road, to let tomorrow take care of itself while I spent the present moments thinking about recovering my lost pounds. The thought of plunging into my mother's refrigerator seemed like the best first step in any successful venture, and the feeling was intensified when I stopped at the yard gate.

As I drove through the canyon I had enjoyed the spectacle of scattered choke cherry branches drooping low like Christmas trees from the weight of countless baubles of red. I knew that some of the fruit had been harvested when the sweet smell of steaming jelly surrounded me as I stepped down from the pickup. Before I opened the screen door, I saw my mother standing at the stove, stirring through the steam in her canning kettle. Wisps of dark hair clung to her dampened cheeks. When I pulled open the door she turned away to look at my dad who sat at the kitchen table, staring into a cup of coffee.

"Hey, I know that I still have a little of the Clearwater on me, but do I have to take a bath before I'm welcomed?" I said as I entered the kitchen.

My mother stirred harder, scattering wisps of steam around the stove, and my dad stared deeper into his cup. I hung my hat on the peg and sat down at the table.

"Something has obviously happened that I'm not going to like to hear. Did somebody die?"

My dad shifted positions in his chair, speaking without looking up.

"I sold the ranch. The new people will be moving in the bunk house in a couple of weeks. We can stay here until we get a new house built. I kept 80 acres for us at the mouth of the canyon. You'll have to find another place to hunt from. Uh … I guess that's all there is to say."

"I see. Well, if that's what you wanted I'm glad it worked out for you. It's a good thing I came back early. It looks like I have more to do than I thought."

I picked up my hat and reeled out the door.

"Would you like something to eat?" my mother called behind me.

"Thanks, Mom, but I'm not hungry right now. I'll be back later."

I wouldn't let myself think as I drove back down the canyon road. I hadn't been home for three weeks, so I didn't know when the transaction took place, but if it had been as long ago as the day before the news would have spread through Alberton. The best place to hear any news was at the local tavern so I stopped my pickup in front of Cockey's Bar.

The small, dimly-lit barroom was deserted when I entered except for a stranger, an old man who sat at the end of the counter with both hands wrapped around a half-empty glass. Cockey Smith, the young, likeable owner of the place, was leaning on the shiny bar surface. He was obviously lost in thought. Only the top of his head faced the room as he studiously polished an empty glass. I was glad that he wasn't busy at the moment. He was an understanding friend and a good listener, which may have resulted in part from his stuttering problem. He would have heard the news and he would be willing to let me talk it out.

"You look like someone who doesn't have a lot to keep him busy this afternoon,

Cockey," I said as I sat down at the bar.

He looked up abruptly. "W-W-Well, I sure do welcome you, Roger. I was just think-ing about you. W- What'll it be? A beer?"

"No, partner. I think you'd better make it whisky."

"H-h-how long are you home for this time?" he asked as he poured the drink.

"It looks like not as long as I thought."

He set the glass in front of me, leaning on the bar again.

"Oh, y-y-you got the news then."

"I'm afraid so. I came down to get the details from you. I don't want to dramatize the situation, but I was too shocked to stay and discuss it with my dad. That probably wouldn't have been a good idea, anyway."

"Y-You don't need to explain a thing. I felt the same way myself. P-P-Petty Creek without a Longpre on it just doesn't make sense. I c-can't believe he did it."

"He's scared, Cockey. He told me a while back when he wasn't in a good mood.

that he'd sell if he had to, but I thought he'd forget about it when he cooled down. He's been in financial trouble so long that he can't believe that anyone can put the ranch back on its feet. You know how he is."

"I-I'm afraid so. Everybody k-knows that it would have gone under a long time without you, if that's any consolation."

"Thanks, but it doesn't matter now, does it. Well, what's done is done, and we can't dwell on the past. I've been learning that lately. But I don't like to think about my dad's future, either. You know he won't let himself and my mother enjoy a retirement with the money. He's going to be off and running like a blossoming tycoon. Only God knows where he'll run."

"Y-y-you've got a point there. I guess there's nothing anybody can do for him in the way of advice, is there."

"There sure isn't. I have a feeling that only his lawyers are going to end up with bulging wallets."

"Y-you always say that we have to make our own mistakes. I-I guess that means even when we're old."

"Yes, Cockey, you're right. It's his life to live whatever way he chooses. Now, tell me about the new owners of Petty Creek."

The ranch had been sold to a large timber corporation. They planned to log it and run a few cattle. Later they would turn it into a resort for their executives. The hay meadow would be made into a golf course at one end and a landing strip at the other. They would tear down the buildings, except for the barn and the house, which would be left as museum pieces.

"I-I guess they want the folks to feel like they're roughing it in Montana when they see the old barn and the log house," Cockey said.

The price that the corporation paid was a little over half of what the land was worth, and my dad included in the sale every piece of equipment from the thrashing machine to my kettles in the cook house.

As Cockey continued with the details of the sale, I kept thinking about the loss of a big, deep fryer from the cook house. It was installed when the cook house was built, and I thought at the time that we probably had the only hunting camp in the state with a deep fryer. It was institution size, and from it would come one of my favorite dishes—deep fried sea food. For me it was a symbol of the ultimate in accommodations for our hunters, and I had been very proud of it. It was strange, though, that I dwelled on it at that moment. Thirty-four years of my life had been swept out from under me, and I mourned for a cooking utensil.

When Cockey finished telling me about the ranch, we talked about other matters for a while, then I thanked him for the information and picked up my hat to leave.

"D-do you think you'll be heading back to the Clearwater?" he asked.

"No, Cockey, not right now anyway. I'm booked up for the season. I'll have to get busy and find a new place to hunt from."

That fall I leased a house with ten acres at the mouth of the canyon. It was big enough to accommodate the hunters, so we drove from there in pickups each morning to the West Fork mangers. The ranch caretaker had given me permission to use them for the season. We hunted beyond the ranch property on Forest Service land.

When hunters asked about making reservations for the following year, I told them I would contact them later. I didn't have time to make definite plans, but I thought I would look into buying an already existing hunting business or find a piece of land near a wilderness area to build one of my own. Either way, I would make provisions for a summer boys' camp. That would be a beginning. My plans would evolve from there.

When the dust settled from the seasons' activity, the big house at the mouth of the canyon was suddenly too quiet for comfort. With two feet of snow on the ground it was not the time to look for recreation areas, so I decided to go back to the Clearwater. The lake hadn't swallowed all of the river country yet, and timber would still be falling at the far end of the canyon. My hunting equipment was stored in the basement of the house, and I had only the horses to bring down from the mangers. I would take care of them the next day, but until then I needed company to fill the evening hours. I got in my pickup and turned it toward town to see who might have stopped in at Cockeys.

With hunters to take care of I hadn't seen Cockey since the day that he told me about the ranch. He caught my eye after I had been in the bar for a few minutes, but he barely had time to nod a greeting. It was a busy night at Cockeys. Several of my friends were there plus a lot of people from town that I had known all my life. It was the ritualistic gathering of end-of-the-season story tellers. They would stay until every elk that had been taken from the mountains, plus a few that hadn't, were hunted in memory several more times. I always thought that if the yearly stories of action and drama were true, Alberton, Montana would have the greatest collection of hunters on earth, and there wouldn't be an elk left in western Montana to hunt. It was Cockey's busiest time of the year, and for me it was always enjoyable to sit back for awhile at the end of the season, listen to yarns develop and grow, and make up a few of my own..

When I entered the bar a group of townspeople motioned for me to sit down at their table. From their smiles and welcomes, it looked as if they had been enjoying themselves for quite a while.

"Another pitcher! Roger's here!" one of them stood up and shouted.

I sat down to join in the conversation while Cockey hurried around the tables with trays of drinks in his hands. When he set down a pitcher and a glass in front of me, one of the more saturated members of the group waved his glass in the air.

"To Rosher—the greatesh outfitter on Petty Creek," he called.

I waved my glass back and said, "You're right. When you're the only one there you've go to be the greatest."

Then a sudden shift in mood rippled through the crowd as if we were reminded that somebody died, and I guess a part of me had. Petty Creek was no longer mine. There hadn't been time through the season for that idea to really penetrate my thoughts. Exaggerated condolences for my loss swept around the table, and I could see that the happy mood of the crowd was diminishing into gloom. I changed the subject to questions about hunting, and soon they were happy again, outdoing each other with stories of hunting heroics. But I had cast myself into solitary thought, and it was a strain to join in the fun. I thought that more beer might ease the tension, so I ordered several rounds for the table. After I had drunk my fill, my mood deteriorated further, so I made my excuses and left.

I had just reached the door when I heard someone call to me from a corner of the noisy room. I turned around to see a friend of mine press through the crowd in my direction. (I will call him Tom because I do not want to implicate him in the events that followed.)

"Why are you leaving so soon? We've been waiting for you to join us at the other table," he said.

"Thanks, Tom, but I have a bunch of hungry horses at the mangers. I'm going to drive up to feed them."

"Can you use some help?"

"Sure."

"Then let's go."

When we got into the pickup, Tom said, "It stinks, Roger. That's what it does. Let's rob a bank and buy it back."

"That's not a bad idea. I hadn't thought of it."

The night had turned to freezing cold, and I shivered as we drove out of town. After we crossed the river, a bright, full moon cast abstract shadows through the canyon's snowy depths. In its icy, shaded stillness, it looked as if the least disturbance into its precarious order would shatter the high, brittle walls.

"It's hard to explain the effect this canyon has on me, Tom. In all these years it's never lost its ability to remind me how dependant we are on the power of Mother Nature. It's a beauty, isn't it. I sure haven't been around the world, but I think that if I saw it all this would still be my favorite spot."

"I've never heard you get sentimental like this."

"I was always told that wasn't the thing to do. I guess it's the alcohol. I drank more than I should have, and I'm feeling a little top heavy. That plus the fact that I'm tired. It always takes a few days to unwind at the end of the season."

"You've got a lot to unwind about this year."

"I suppose so, Tom, but it's not the end of the world. There are lots of places in this state to hunt. I'll find a good one. Maybe it's time to move on."

"I'd go along with that if you were moving of your own accord. But leaving this paradise to a corporation? That's sacrilege!"

As we wound our way up the canyon, Tom's words sunk into my thoughts with melodramatic effect. I was no longer in a melancholy mood. I was fighting mad at the giant corporation that robbed me of my home.

"You know what's the worst part of the whole deal? I said as my irritation grew. "That caretaker's sleeping in my bunk house and cooking in the deep fryer that I put in when I built the cook house. I was so proud of that big deep fryer. You have no idea what fabulous meals have come out of it—shrimp, lobster tails, chicken, onion rings. The cooks really spread it on, and we loved it."

By that time we had reached the 100-ton hay shed that I had built at the north end of the meadow. It stood out boldly in the moonlight along with several cows that huddled together beside it.

"Do you see that hay shed, Tom? I built that, too. And those cows standing there? I can give you the history of every one of them. The mother of the third one from the right died from pneumonia a month before she was ready to calve. I took the calf out of her and fed it in the kitchen with a bottle. That one standing over there by itself had the worst prolapse last spring that I've ever seen. I worked on her all through the night. It was daylight before I got her sewed up. I wonder if the caretaker knows about those things."

"Probably not."

"So you know what the corporation paid for all this, including the cows and my deep fryer?"

"Yes, I heard. It's not enough. And even it was, as far as I'm concerned you can't put a price on this country. It should never have been let out of your family."

"It wasn't supposed to, Tom. At least that's what I was told all these years. I can't buy it back, and I don't think I'll ask them for my deep fryer, but I have an idea for taking part of it with me, at least as far as to my friends in the Clearwater."

"Oh?"

"Those young steers over there are new to the ranch. The corporation bought them last summer. They look just right for eating, don't you think?"

"Hey, wait a minute. I suggested robbing a bank, not cattle rustling. That's practically a hanging crime in this state."

"But I won't get caught. We're too far around the corner for the caretaker to hear the shot, and I can dress a steer or a deer in three minutes flat without getting blood above my wrists. Someone taught me that once."

Before Tom could reply I grabbed my rifle from the gun rack and bolted to the fence. With two cracks from the gun, two steers were down in the meadow. I jumped back in the truck, spun it around, skimming over the icy road toward town.

"We can't lift those by ourselves. We'll get help in town," I said.

"Now you've done it. We're going straight to jail."

Tom crouched in the corner of the pickup, pulling his jacket over his head. He didn't say another word until we stopped at the bar.

"If you don't mind, I'll just slip in quietly a little later," he said "Maybe nobody will know I've joined your outlaw gang."

"It's your choice, but you're missing out on a lot of fun."

Self-indulgent bitterness, unexpressed anger, self pity. Who knows what demons the alcohol released that night. I will make no excuses for my actions nor offer any explanations because I can't understand them myself. I know only that I was carried through the night by an hysterical sense of retribution that increased as time wore on.

When I returned to the bar I routed two young, strong boys from their stools, and we thundered back up the creek together. The meadow was quiet. The caretaker hadn't heard the shots. I turned off the headlights, slipped the pickup through the gate at the far end of the field, and crossed the meadow to the steers. They were dressed, halved and loaded almost as quickly, I thought, as they had dropped. I didn't dress them in Clay Holman style, though. In my frenzy I covered myself with blood and hair.

As we zoomed back down the road to town, a new plan formed in my mind for disposal of the animals.

"What do you think boys," I asked. "Do you think that the people of Alberton might like to try a little of this meat?"

"Sure. Why not?"

When I screeched the pickup to a halt in front of Cockeys, I told the young men to unload the steers and my axe on the sidewalk. When I walked inside I saw that the crowd had thinned, but those who were left had kept the noise level at deafening heights. I approached the table where I had been sitting and leaned over one of the patrons. He looked up at me, startled, and then the whole table suddenly turned stone quiet. Like an outgoing wave, the noise receded throughout the bar while every head turned in my direction. I had forgotten how I looked so their actions puzzled me. I leaned closer to the man and whispered,

"Pass the word around to whoever you can trust. I have two of the corporation's steers outside to auction off."

Then I quickly turned around and slid back out the door.

The steers were laid out on the sidewalk with my axe beside them. I had just leaned over to pick up the axe when Tom burst through the door, stumbling over the steers.

"What are you doing?" he screamed. "Are you completely crazy???"

"Probably. Most geniuses are, and I've masterminded an ingenious plan tonight. Let's watch that corporation try to operate now!"

"Do you really think that losing two steers is going to make a difference to them?"

"You bet I do."

"Well, it isn't."

He broke into an inebriated grin. "But I like the idea anyway. Here, let me give you a hand."

Tom held the steer halves while I quartered them with the axe. By the time we finished, about a dozen people from the bar had gathered in a circle around us. I stood up with the bloody axe in my hand, waving it in the air for emphasis.

"To show how much they appreciate us letting them intrude upon our country, the new owners of Petty Creek have given us these young, tender steers," I said to the crowd. "So that all of Cockey's customers may continue to enjoy themselves tonight, we're going to auction them off and the proceeds will go into a pot for drinks for the house. We'll start the bid for this first front quarter at two dollars. Do I hear a bid of two?"

After a long hesitation a feeble "Here" was heard from a stranger who stood beside me with his hands on his hips, shaking his head as he watched.

"Do I hear ten?"

A hand was raised by a friend of mine who was also a member of the town council. He stood stiffly in the doorway of the bar as if his distance from the group dismissed him from participation in the proceedings.

"Sold to the gentleman in the cowboy hat for ten dollars! You see how easy it is, folks, to own all this delicious meat and contribute to a good cause at the same time. Let's all join in now. Seven more of you lucky people are going to leave tonight with the most inexpensive prime beef you'll ever have a chance to buy. Now, who'll give me two-fifty for this second front quarter?"

My speech must have made an impact on the sodden crowed because they suddenly came alive.

"Three!!!" yelled a tipsy bystander.

"You can't give him three yet," a voice from the crowd shouted defiantly. "He only wants two-fifty!"

"Two-fifty then. What kind of an outfit is this?"

"Who'll give me seven?"

"You can't go to seven. You didn't do three yet," the voice hollered.

"Yes he can! Seven!!!" hollered the mayor's wife.

"Sold to Mrs. Mayor for seven dollars!"

It was in such a manner that the travesty against the institution of auctioneering continued. Tom, who had by then lost all inhibitions concerning the ethics of my actions, ran through the crowd collecting money in his hat from successful bidders. He never had the right change so everyone just threw in whatever bills they had.

"That's it, folks!" Tom announced when the last quarter was sold. "You can pick up your meat now. Follow me into the bar. The drinks are on you!"

He paraded back through the barroom with an uproariously happy meat-laden crowd behind him. With a flourish, he spilled the contents of his hat on the counter.

"A pitcher for every table, Cockey, until the money's gone!" he said.

"O-o-o-kay, but I don't know w-w-what I'll tell the sheriff when he arrests me as an accomplice."

"Don't worry about him. If he objects, we'll just give him a quarter of beef and he'll never say a word."

Tom and I broke into fits of uncontrolled laughter.

"Didn't I tell you it could be done, Tom?" I sputtered in between convulsions. "See how happy we've made the town of Alberton tonight??? Do you know why they're so happy? They're happy because they got to join in on something big. And if they're happy, think how happy I am. Do you know what we did tonight, Tom?" We let 'em have it with both barrels. WE JUST TURNED OUT THE CORPORATION'S LIGHTS!!!"

31

The sound of saws and hammers rang again at Petty Creek. The West Fork, the hay meadow, Printers Creek, and hidden flats along the canyon road are matted with houses—everything from ragged cabins to the finest in vacation lodging. As ten to fifty-acre lots are sold, buildings continue to sprout. The barn and house still stand, the corrals are tumbling, and the bunk and cook houses are faded red. Like my plans for Petty Creek, the corporation's intentions were altered by a change in administrative policy. They didn't build a golf course or a landing strip. They logged it and they developed the land with houses. But contrary to my ideas on auction night, they did not go under.

I woke up the next morning after the beef auction with a splitting headache and an understanding of the seriousness of my actions. But before I made any decisions about rectifying the situation, I still had hungry horses to feed that had been neglected the night before.

Outside, the morning air was biting cold. I let the heater warm the pickup before I got in for another trip up the canyon road. My throbbing head blocked serious thoughts for my immediate future until, on the way back from the corrals, a red light flashed behind me. I stopped the truck and waited for a Missoula County Sheriff Deputy to approach. The headache vanished as I prepared for the worst.

"May I see your driver's license?" he asked politely before placing me under arrest for cattle rustling.

He took me to his car, questioned me about my whereabouts at time of the steer shooting, and then let me go. Had I really been under arrest, he would have taken me to jail. He was hoping for a confession, but I didn't give it to him. When he released me, he assured me that he would be talking to me in the future. I realized then that only a lawyer could defend me.

The attorney that I chose was known as one of the best criminal lawyers in the state.

But when charges were formally made against me, even he couldn't persuade the new owners of Petty Creek to drop them. He told them that I would either replace their two steers or pay market value for them. They said that because of their membership in the Cattlemen's Association they were obligated to press charges.

It was county election time, and for a while I was big news in the state of Montana. It had been a long time since a cattle rustler had been caught, but the sheriff's office felt that they had this one under control, and they assured the public that the culprit would soon be behind bars. Had I not had a good lawyer it would probably have worked out that way. However, at the end of lengthy proceedings I was given seven years' probation, and my outfitter's license was revoked. Why, I wondered, had I caused it to happen.

Was it meant that with the loss of Petty Creek I should be wrested from my final link with a way of life that was over? I was uneasy as a young child, knowing that we had dispossessed the Indians of their traditions. I had watched with sorrow the changes that gradually smothered our own way of life. Certainly I had expressed my feelings of losing the ranch in the wrong way. But had I done so because I tried too hard to claim for my own what was never really mine?

I always knew that the boss lady was the owner of Petty Creek. Maybe my relationship with her would have diminished if I had stayed. It takes a mind for business to run a ranch today. Successful farming is a venture into the science of animal husbandry and economics, and with it, piles of paperwork are required. To expand on Petty Creek into other areas that I had envisioned would require permits, inspections, waiting for government decisions before taking the next step. I grew up at a time when it was easier to live as a part of the land. Now, like Clay, "I don't belong to their ways."

I had grown tired of trying to cope with my dad's refusal to turn Petty Creek into a viable means of making a living. He was what he was, and trying to make him into anything else would never have worked. At the time I was bitter. I had put a lot of years under his control, believing him when he told me that I couldn't make it without him. But I know now that he had his own set of problems to deal with, and although he was my dad, that didn't give me the right to change him. It was sad for all of us that he wouldn't listen to the many friends and relatives who tried to convince him of practical matters concerning the ranch, but it isn't the saddest of tales in a world that has been much less kind to others than to me.

So I leave with a grateful heart to start a new life. Part of me will always be in the mountains of Petty Creek, and I'll miss it. But Mother Nature made places all over where mountains rise high and timber grows tall, and without a claim on any corner of her land I'll find the space to enjoy her again.

I know now that there's a time and a place for everything. I was given my place just in time, and I'm a lucky man.

I almost missed it.

Roger erecting a tent pole in the early days of outfitting.

Packing out the last elk of the season.

Roger headed for camp with Happy and the pack string.

Contemplating conditions for the days' hunt.

Roger & Jack showing their out-of-state visitors how it's done in the West.
The rider in back is Janice, who would one day gain first position on the horse.

A group of Texans ready to leave for camp.

*Hunters in the cook tent at the end of a hunt,
too tired to smile Mr. & Mrs. Rigaby are seated at left.*

Art Scheffer at work.

About the Author

When Roger Longpre left Petty Creek, Montana, he eventually settled in southern Idaho where he lives with his wife, Janice, at the edge of a mountain village.

Janice joined him near the end of the Petty Creek experience, but their life together continued in the same tradition of rugged adventure that has characterized all of Roger's existence.

The addition of years and a series of injuries have finally softened Roger's resilience, but he continues to live his past adventure through his stories that are sought today by both young and old. His story was written because those who rode with him believe that his unique contribution to western history should be shared beyond his borders.

His horses are few in numbers now, but he is still passionate about them, and even more so about passing on his legacy to a little girl named Montana, who calls him Grandpa.

CPSIA information can be obtained at www.ICGtesting.com
Printed in the USA
LVOW110949040613

336877LV00004B/63/A

9 781425 105532
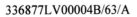